"Al fin, finally! *Trespassers on Our Own l...*
1967 Tierra Amarilla Courthouse raid a... .. ..
that have plagued northern New Mexico for generations. Never-before have
the events leading up to the raid, the raid itself, the escape of some of the par-
ticipants later that evening and the turbulent political history of the era been
presented in one narrative. *Trespasser's* has finally identified why and how the
United States intentionally relieved a number of Spanish and Mexican land
grants of millions of acres of treaty protected lands and the fact that the federal government continues to this day to refuse to admit it unlawfully took the
land or to compensate the heirs for the taking."

—Lawrence E. Sánchez, President,
Town of Tomé Land Grant
Adelino, New Mexico

"*Trespassers on Our Own Land* is an oral history of the Juan P. Valdez family
and a snapshot of the maltreatment forced upon our Pueblo Indian, Spanish and Mexican people by the United States government. In *Trespassers*,
Mike Scarborough has presented a comprehensive history of the adversar-
ial relationship our ancestors had with the United States government
between the signing of the Treaty of Guadalupe Hidalgo in 1848 and 1912.
Trespasser's brought back memories of my childhood in Coyote and Capulín
and a renewed understanding of the difficulties my ancestors endured while
struggling to survive on the San Joaquín del Río de Chama land grant. I recommend this book as a must read for anyone interested in an in-depth and
comprehensive oral history and study of New Mexico's land grants."

—Leonard Martínez, President, San Joaquín del Río
de Chama Land Grant Association
Cañon de Chama, New Mexico

"*Trespassers* . . . is compelling and authentic; occasionally, it is hilarious;
sometimes it is poignant. . . . It is fitting that a book that brings this man's
experiences to life is set in the broader context of the history of land grants-
mercedes. These *mercedes* mattered so much to Juan Valdez that he risked his
life to bring attention to the enormous injustice [the grantees and their
heirs] had suffered at the hands of the U.S. government. In these pages we
begin to understand why."

— From the Foreword by Prof. LM García y
Griego History and Chicano Studies,
University of New Mexico
Albuquerque, New Mexico

TRESPASSERS ON OUR OWN LAND

mike Scarborough

TRESPASSERS ON OUR OWN LAND

STRUCTURED AS AN ORAL HISTORY OF THE JUAN P. VALDEZ FAMILY AND OF THE LAND GRANTS OF NORTHERN NEW MEXICO

MIKE SCARBOROUGH

FORWARD BY LM GARCÍA Y GRIEGO

First published by Dog Ear Publishing
4010 W. 86th Street, Ste H
Indianapolis, IN 46268
www.dogearpublishing.net

ISBN: 978-145750-584-3

This book is printed on acid-free paper.

Printed in the United States of America

To the Heirs of the Pueblo Indian, Spanish, and Mexican
Land Grants Who's Ancestors Suffered the Loss of
Millions of Acres When the United States
Unlawfully Took it Without An Offer
of Compensation or Apology.

FOREWORD

Juan Valdez is a wiry man in his seventies who reminds me of my uncles. As a small boy he worked on the family farm. As he got older, the work got harder and it seemed endless. This childhood shaped his character in significant ways. As an adult, Juan Valdez is eminently practical. Like my uncles, he also is forthright in speech and has uncommonly good sense. Valdez goes about his life in an unhurried, but steady pace. And in some respects, Juan is quite conservative. This is certainly not the profile one might expect of a man who led an armed raid on the Tierra Amarilla Courthouse on June 5, 1967, and who successfully guided a band of fugitives through miles of wilderness in the midst of the most intense manhunt in New Mexico in recent memory.

It is no accident that this man's name is Juan Valdez. He is a descendant of Juan Bautista Valdez, who with ten families founded the land grant—*merced* of that name in 1807—during Thomas Jefferson's second term as president and just four years after the U.S. had extended its boundaries west with the Louisiana Purchase. At the founding of the *merced de* Juan Bautista Valdez, New Mexico was the furthest northern outpost of New Spain. Several generations of Valdez descendants lived on that land grant until the twentieth century; some still remain. But in the early 1930s, Juan's father Amarante, then a young man, left the *merced* because the diminished common lands could no longer support everyone who lived there. Amarante Valdez moved thirty miles north to join relatives in the village of Canjilón, where he later married and began a family. There his son Juan was born in the late 1930s, outside the *merced* that bears his name.

Amarante Valdez's experiences in Canjilón strongly shaped his young son's growing awareness that they were living a great social injustice. Canjilón is a village of a few hundred souls that lies on a short elevated plain overlooking an elongated green valley dotted with ponds and crossed by a stream. It is surrounded by the Carson National Forest. There is no private or even common forested land. While Juan was still a boy it pained him to see his father's spirit diminished as Forest Rangers denied him the grazing permits he needed to support his family. In the 1940s and 1950s Amarante taught Juan how to trespass on what were former common lands, to graze animals surreptitiously, to hunt, fish, and cut wood. Not surprisingly, in the 1960s Juan Valdez was attracted to the Alianza Federal de Mercedes, led by a fiery preacher, Reies López Tijerina. He soon became a member of the inner circle. About his experiences in the Alianza and the attempted citizen's arrest of the district attorney in Tierra Amarilla that went awry, I will not write anything here. Apart from brief interviews that Juan gave to reporters of the *Río Grande Sun* many years ago, he tells his complete story here for the first time.

The New Mexican *mercedes* that Juan talks about in this compelling narrative are referred to as "land grants" in English. Though serviceable, the translation is imperfect. It has led many persons to equate Spanish/Mexican land grants of the Southwest with the grants of land that Congress gave private individuals in other states, such as Michigan and Missouri in the years before the war with Mexico. Like the private grants of land made by Congress before 1848, the *mercedes* were eventually patented, and in the case of New Mexico, two distinct processes were followed between 1854 and 1904. However, unlike those private grants of land, the *mercedes* of the Southwest had previously been granted by Spanish or Mexican authorities. Under the terms of the Treaty of Guadalupe Hidalgo they should have been recognized by the U.S. government exactly as Mexico would have done under its laws of 1848. This did not happen. Some land grants that should have been recognized were not recognized at all. The vast majority of those that *were* recognized were greatly diminished in size. Eventually the U.S. government adopted the rule that *no* common lands were to be awarded to community land grants; i.e., that the Spanish/Mexican *mercedes* should be reduced to their individual allotments and stripped of the common lands that for generations Spanish/Mexican settlers had used for subsistence.

During the colonial and early Mexican periods, one of the central goals of the Spanish and Mexican authorities in assigning new community land grants in New Mexico was to protect existing communities from attack, especially by Comanches and Apaches. For the settlers of newly established *mercedes*, life was hazardous. The people willing to assume these challenges were, in the main, not the Spanish elite of the major towns, but the lower class *mestizos* (biracial children of Spanish and Indian parents) and *genízaros* (Indians who were no longer attached to a tribe and who lived among the Spanish in a second-class status). These *mestizos* and *genízaros* hungered for land of their own and were aware that they would face periodic attacks by nomadic Indians, absorb casualties, and lose crops and animals. Not surprisingly, only a fraction of the initial settlers of these land grants remained for more than a few years and some *mercedes* were abandoned because they were subjected to frequent attack. The descendants of those who stayed were hardy individuals who survived because they came to know their land well. These survivors, and their descendants, became deeply attached to their land. Until the mid twentieth century most of the Spanish/Mexican descendants on these land grants could not read or write, but in their oral traditions, they had acquired a name for every significant landmark, every hill and valley, every turn of the river or stream.

Though much older and more proximate to the Spanish towns on the Río Grande, the Indian Pueblos also were subject to frequent attack by nomadic Indians. To defend their communities Pueblo warriors were drafted as "auxiliaries" in the defense of Pueblo/Spanish towns and villages, and for the punitive expeditions that set out in pursuit of Comanches and Apaches. These "auxiliaries" often constituted more than half of the defense force led by the Spanish. Their participation reflected both the enormous security challenges that all land grants faced and the close if conditional cooperation that existed during the eighteenth century between Pueblo and Spanish communities.

As in the case of Spanish/Mexican land grants, Pueblo communities held common lands set aside for the use of villagers. Some land in the village also was held in private allotments by individual families. Thus, the federal reservations we now see in New Mexico, from Isleta Pueblo in the central part of the state to Taos Pueblo in the north, were once community land grants. Like their Spanish/Mexican counterparts, they were adjudicated by the United States government as land grant-*mercedes* under the Treaty of Guadalupe Hidalgo.

There also were important differences. During the 1850s and 1860s, Indian agents were assigned to advocate for the timely adjudication of Pueblo land grants, and they were among the first to be recognized under U.S. law. The common lands of Pueblo villages were generally smaller in size than their Spanish/Mexican counterparts, but their access to surface water more reliable. The Pueblos had been established centuries before the arrival of the Spanish and most were founded along the Río Grande.

Unlike the Navajos and Apaches, the Pueblo Indians did not sign a peace treaty with the United States. The Pueblos thus still rely upon the Treaty of Guadalupe Hidalgo (among other legal sources) to protect their property rights. Contrary to what one may expect, and in sharp contrast with the experience of Spanish/Mexican land grants, the Pueblos have had some success in obtaining access to former common lands under the Treaty of Guadalupe Hidalgo.

Many sources have pointed out that, as distinct as the Indian Pueblos and the Spanish/Mexican communities are in their history, identities and customs, they have some important characteristics in common, including a strong attachment to their land. Cultural similarities were reinforced by trade and interaction, through intermarriage, the absorption of *genízaros* by Spanish/Mexican communities, and the incorporation by these communities of Indians expelled from the Pueblos. Moreover, there were experiences that overlapped in unexpected ways. Abiquiú, now a Spanish/Mexican community land grant, once was considered an *genízaro* Pueblo Indian grant that eventually opted out of federal tribal status. Pojoaque (P'osuwaege) was a *merced* populated by *mestizos* that reverted to Pueblo Indian status.

Other important differences emerged later. Under the terms of the Treaty of Guadalupe Hidalgo, the former Mexican citizens who remained were recognized as U.S. citizens. While Pueblo Indians initially retained their status as Mexican citizens under the terms of the Treaty, advocates who believed that political participation would ultimately be injurious to Pueblos fought for their disenfranchisement in politics. The Pueblos lost

U.S. citizenship and did not regain it until the twentieth century. Unlike the Spanish/Mexican land grants, the lands of Indian Pueblos, including individual allotments, were not considered private property by the United States and thus were held in trust by the Bureau of Indian Affairs. And, while the Indian Pueblos also suffered substantial losses of land during years that forest reserves were established, some had those lands returned. The story of how the area of Blue Lake was returned to Taos Pueblo is discussed in these pages.

Trespassers puts special emphasis on three community land grants: San Joaquín del Río de Chama, La Petaca, and Juan Bautista Valdez. La Petaca and Juan Bautista Valdez have been classified by some authors as individual grants, though they have functioned for decades as community land grants. La Petaca was originally surveyed in 1878 at over 186,000 acres; when it was confirmed and patented, it received 1,392 acres in a small valley surrounded by the forestland that it had lost. A similar story can be told about the San Joaquín del Río de Chama, which was surveyed at over 470,000 acres in 1878 and reduced to 1,422 acres in 1901. Renamed Cañón de Chama, it was stripped of its extensive forestland and only the individual allotments along the Chama River remained. A final blow to this land grant came years later when much of its former common lands were designated as wilderness land by Congress, a status that implies lands untouched by human settlement to be protected from the traffic of modern civilization. That supposedly untouched wilderness includes a cemetery that was established by land grant heirs many years ago. At the time *Trespassers* is being published, the San Joaquín del Río de Chama Land Grant Association is working to have the cemetery and those lands returned.

After the Alianza became defunct in the 1970s, the *mercedes* went their separate ways. Some continued their individual battles with little success. The statewide struggle for land recovery revived in the 1990s when former Lt. Governor Roberto Mondragón, an heir to the Anton Chico land grant, and several other land grant heirs, started the Land Grant Forum. The Forum stimulated connections among heirs from many land grants, including those that had survived with intact boards of trustees and others whose boards had disappeared. In the late 1990s the Forum succeeded in generating congressional action leading to a bill passed by the U.S. House of

Representatives that would have established a commission to correct and complete the adjudication process. The bill died in the Senate. Instead, U.S. Senators Pete Domenici and Jeff Bingaman and Congressman Tom Udall secured an appropriation for the U.S. General Accounting Office (GAO; later renamed the Government Accountability Office) to prepare a historical and legal study that would determine whether the United States government had fulfilled its obligations under the Treaty of Guadalupe Hidalgo in New Mexico.

It took time, but the GAO deeply disappointed the land grant movement. The GAO decided to not address the question of whether the U.S. had fulfilled its obligations as a matter of international law. It found that the adjudication process established by Congress, notwithstanding inconsistent standards, met the constitutional requirements of due process. Land grant activists who had pinned hopes on the possibility that this study would show the rightness of their cause were dismayed when the GAO concluded that the confirmation process complied with all U.S. domestic legal requirements. Even so, it is noteworthy that the GAO *did* recognize inconsistencies in the legal standards that were applied, and hardships in the consequences. It also identified as options for congressional action that the U.S. could return some common lands or compensate land grant heirs for their loss. In this manner the GAO recognized inequities in the results but no injustice in the legal process.

Some years before the GAO report, Juan Valdez had approached Mike Scarborough to put his life story to writing. Scarborough had been a friend of his for years. He had grown up in Española, knew many of the land grant activists, had practiced law in northern New Mexico most of his life, and was familiar with much of the local history. They talked about Juan's family history, but they also discussed the history of the land grants in the region. After the GAO report was published they discussed that as well. Both Mike and Juan viewed the 2004 GAO report as a whitewash of land grant issues. Scarborough researched the Court of Private Land Claims process and the Forest Reserve Act of the 1890s and early 1900s, and the establishment of numerous federal forest reserves under President Theodore Roosevelt. In this book he argues that the forest reserves grew at the expense of land grants, both Spanish/Mexican and Pueblo Indian.

Scarborough also identified many of the shortcomings and omissions of the GAO report. As mentioned earlier, he focused special attention on those land grants associated with Juan Valdez's life: Juan Bautista Valdez, San Joaquín del Río de Chama, and La Petaca. He also examined the different treatment of two other land grants: Piedra Lumbre and Polvadera.

The result is this remarkable book. It tells the story of Juan Valdez's life and family history, just as he told it to his grandchildren and later to the author. It also tells another story: the conversion of *merced* common lands by the U.S. government for the purpose of establishing forest reserves and national forests. The story is narrated through a series of conversations between Juan and a teen-aged grandson. The narrative is compelling and authentic; occasionally, it is hilarious; sometimes it is poignant. These pages remind me that often people who face harsh adversity not only manage to survive, they sometimes develop a unique sense of humor.

It is fitting that a book that brings this man's experiences to life is set in the broader context of the history of land grants-*mercedes*. These *mercedes* mattered so much to Juan Valdez that he risked his life to bring attention to the enormous injustice they had suffered at the hands of the U.S. government. In these pages we begin to understand why.

LM García y Griego
Associate Professor of History and Chicano Studies
Director, University of New Mexico Land Grant Studies Program
Cañón de Carnué
June 2011

PREFACE

On June 5, 1967 Reies López Tijerina and members of his Alianza Federal de Mercedes, an alliance he had formed several years earlier, entered the Río Arriba County Courthouse in Tierra Amarilla, New Mexico. Their mission was to attempt a citizen's arrest of Alfonso Sanchez.

Thirty-five years later Juan Valdez, the first member of the Alianza to enter the Courthouse that day asked me if I would help him write his family history. I agreed and thus began an odyssey through 150 years of personal and political history I would never have imagined.

Our objective from the outset has been to increase public awareness of a century and a half of governmental mistreatment suffered by a countless number of families whose "sole transgression" was that they had been born to ancestors who had refused to abandon the land grants they had received from Spain and Mexico decades before the United States became obsessed with Manifest Destiny and the northern half of Mexico.

Shortly after I began my research I realized that a book limited exclusively to Juan's family history could be viewed as just another account of the past as seen from one family's perspective. Moreover, I wanted the story to highlight the broader issues which had faced rural New Mexican communities for centuries. I decided that in order to provide a completed portrait of the past it was necessary that we present the federal government's political reaction to its realization that the Spanish and Mexican citizens, whose families had settled the Southwest centuries earlier, had no interest in "returning" to Mexico—to a country totally foreign to them in every respect.

More specifically, we needed to describe three historical events which occurred subsequent to the 1848 signing of the Treaty of Guadalupe

Hidalgo and which would control the future of New Mexico for generations to come.

The first event occurred on March 3, 1891 with the passage of the Forest Reserve Act and the establishment of the Court of Private Land Claims. Next was the Court of Private Land Claim's admitted "recovery" of 30,000,000 acres of land from the grants and its "return" to the public domain.

Last, but certainly not the least in importance was President Theodore Roosevelt's conversion of millions of acres of "public lands" into forest reserves—over 1,000,000 acres of which had lawfully belonged within Pueblo Indian, Spanish and Mexican land grants in New Mexico long before the United States "acquired" its illegitimate interest in them. We refer to the United States interest as illegitimate simply because the taking of the land was contrary to the intent of the Treaty of Guadalupe Hidalgo, contrary to international law and contrary to the equal protection, due process and property protections afforded by the United States Constitution.

Juan's story is one that challenges the belief, prevalent at the time, that the federal government would never intentionally take private properties from their lawful owners without offering to pay a fair price for it.

After Juan and I had discussed the evidence we were to use and the fact that I wanted to incorporate it with his family history, I decided that structuring the narrative as a series of conversations between Juan and a grandson was the best way to present the information. I used Juan's voice and the editorial "we" to explain information of political and historical significance rather than interrupt the dialog and awkwardly interject the information into the narrative. Once I had decided to present the story as an oral history my next concern was to try my best to limit the evidence to primary and secondary sources—to avoid reliance on rank hearsay and ill-founded statements of opinion.

I would, to every extent possible, place my reliance on actual statements by identified government officials which were unquestionably contrary to the government's interest, because—of all the evidence available—such statements, more often than not, would reflect the true intent of the speaker and generally be irrefutable. For example—in order to establish President

Benjamin Harrison's 1889 state of mind regarding New Mexico's Pueblo Indian, Spanish and Mexican land grants and grantees, I would focus on Harrison's State of the Union addresses to establish his profound prejudice against the grants and the settlers living on them.

In order to establish Secretary of Interior John Noble's state of mind regarding who he believed President Grover Cleveland should appoint to replace him I would use his response to the specific question.

I also felt a need to present Juan and his grandson's conversations in a format that would not only be informative but hold the reader's interest as well. My resolution was to stagger the conversations. The first conversation and every other one thereafter would concern the Valdez' family history. Following each personal family conversation there would be a discussion of timely political events of historical significance. The conversations were altered in that manner throughout the book.

As written, the book offers several ways to approach it. One can read it as we read most books—from cover to cover. On the other hand one can read only the odd numbered chapters for the family history or the even numbered chapters for the political history.

Supporting citations and attributions were placed as end notes so as not to interrupt the narrative and are identified by text and page number rather than by superscript for ease in following the narrative.

It is Juan's hope, as well as mine, that those who read the book will recognize the devastating effect 150 years of intentional maltreatment by presidents, cabinet secretaries, members of Congress, and justices of the Court of Private Land Claims and United States Supreme Court had on the Pueblo Indian, Spanish and Mexican grants, grantees and their heirs.

I cannot close without thanking a number of people who have participated in making this book possible.

First and most important, I wish to thank Anita, my wife, for her patience and understanding of what I was attempting to do and for her terrific suggestions all of which made the project much easier to complete. Equally important, was Anita's miraculous ability to survive five long years (1,825 days and nights) of my jabbering about "the book, the book, the book—the facts, the facts, the facts."

I want to thank Juan and Rose valdez and their family. Had Juan's health (and his family's patience) not survived to see this project to its conclusion, Juan's recollections of his family history would have been lost forever.

I wish to offer a special "Thank You" to Dr. LM Garcia y Griego, Director of the Southwest Hispanic Research Center and associate professor of history at the University of New Mexico; Leonard T. Martínez, President of the San Joaquín del Río Chama Land Grant; and Lawrence E. Sánchez, President of the Town of Tomé Land Grant, for their careful and painstaking critique of the manuscript and their numerous helpful suggestions.

Finally, I wish to extend my appreciation to Dr. Henry J. Casso, Elmer Maestas, Dr. Robert Hemmerick y Valencia and Dr. Rose Diaz for their encouragement.

The good counsel of all of those mentioned has resulted in *Trespassers on Our Own Land* being a much better representation of the consequences of this dark period in Southwestern history than it would have been had they not offered their sound advice.

I am solely responsible for the content of this book.

M. S.

Table of Contents

Illustrations (Following page 145)

-1-
In The Beginning

I gotta tell you, Grandpa, I thought this day would never come. After Mom told me you were in the hospital again—that you'd had another heart attack, I was scared that after all the times we'd talked about our past you might die without ever getting around to telling our family history.

When I told my teacher you were back in the hospital, he said our chance to learn our history might be lost forever if I don't get off my butt and record what you have to say about when you were growing up—and what you learned about when your parents and grandparents were growing up.

When I was there in the hospital, after the second attack, I was thinking about the same things your teacher was—that we might never get the chance to talk about our story. Thank goodness God gave us another chance. This could be our last chance, Hijo—if we don't stick with it.

Can we start by talking about the shootout at the courthouse?

No. We'll talk about that later. We need to start by talking about what happened to our family during the 150 years before we went to the court-house. You need to know why we went there before I say what happened when we got there. It wouldn't make any sense to start our story in 1967 and tell it backwards.

We need to start in the beginning—talk about our ancestors and what happened during their lives. Go back even before Juan Bautista Valdez, my great, great; great-grandfather, who was given land by Spain in 1807. Let's do it this way—I'll start with your great-grandfather, my father. We'll talk about his life and when I was growing up; then we'll talk about the land grants. We'll go back and forth, talk about our family; then talk about what's been going with the government over the last 150 years and how it affected

1

our people. Go back and forth—one time we'll talk about our family, the next about the government.

My teacher told me to remind you to tell everything—even what you've told me before. He said if you leave out what you've already told me, the ones that hear our story in the future won't know about the part we already talked about.

Good idea. I'll do it like he says—but I need to start before my father moved to Canjilón.

In 1932 when my father, Amarante, was twenty-five, he and his brother, Elizardo, and the rest of our family, and the other families living in Cañones, started to understand that since the government had taken almost all of their land, about ninety-eight percent of it, there was never going to be enough land for all of them to feed their animals and raise the crops they needed for their families. I need to start our family story in 1807 when Juan Bautista and his wife, my third great-grandmother, María de las Nieves Martín-Serrano and their children and grandchildren moved to Cañones to live on the grant. (Fig.1).

Juan Bautista was already fifty-eight years old by the time Spain gave him the land. Our family had lived there at Cañones throughout Mexican independence, the invasion of New Mexico by the United States and the Civil War—lived on the grant for over 85 years by the time the government took 145,000 acres of the grant and left all the people in the four settlements with less than 1,500 acres. By taking all that land, the United States government was leaving 350 people who had lived on the grant for generations to try to survive on less than five acres a person.

My father and his brother agreed in 1932 that one of them had to move—that they couldn't both survive on what little land they had left. My father agreed to move. But before he did he went to the National Forest Office in Coyote and asked if he could transfer his cow and sheep permits to some other forest since they were refusing to give him any permits. He said to me after I got a little older that they had told him that if he'd move to the Carson National Forest he might be able to get permits. Since his sister, Edulia, and her husband were already living here in Canjilón he moved in with them until he could save enough money to buy some land and build a house. (Fig.1).

A few years later he bought this land—where we are today—here in Can-jilón and after he and my mother got married they built our house. You know the house, Hijo, but like you said, I gotta say where it is for the ones who hear this later. It's the house back there to the north side of the pasture. Like you said, I need to tell this like I haven't told you anything before—like you're hearing it for the first time. (Figs.11, 18).

In those days when people would build a house, they were lucky if they had enough material to build two rooms. They started by building two rooms like most people did. I remember my father telling me that when families would start having a lot of children they would add more rooms and as our family got bigger my father did, he added two more rooms. I think I was about ten when he added them.

After my father bought the land and while they were building the house he went to the Forest Service Office here in Canjilón and tried to get some permits. He told them what the people at the Coyote had said. They gave him temporary permits for that year, 1937, but they never would give him permits after that. Since he could only afford 160 acres and it wasn't enough to feed our cows and sheep and grow the crops we needed, all he could do was plant the crops. The only way we could manage was to sneak our cows on the forest in the morning and bring them back at night.

The house we were just talking about is where I was born. My older sister was born there—and then after me there were five more—three girls and two more boys, all born in that house. It was crowded. But it was a good house.

I'd like to see you live like we had to, Hijo. We didn't have running water or a bathroom—just a well and an outhouse. We didn't have electricity or gas, just a wood stove for cooking, heating water and keeping warm. My folks and I brought in propane heaters years ago but when we found out how much the propane cost we went back to burning wood. When I was your age there weren't any telephones in Canjilón—no cell phones—no radios. We didn't have cars or trucks. Just horses and a wagon and smoke signals to talk to our neighbors.

Come on, grandpa!

Just making sure you're paying attention.

Life's a lot different now. If you want to go somewhere you just grab your Mom's keys from the kitchen wall, get in her car and take off. Right away you have a couple hundred horses working for you. I know gas is expensive today but it's not nearly as much trouble as having to find feed for the horses. When you don't have enough pasture it's hard. And our wagon didn't start with a key, Hijo, if we needed the wagon we had to catch the horses and hitch 'em to it.

We didn't have chain saws to cut the trees—or tractors. If we wanted to plant a garden we had to use a horse and a Fresno to level the ground; then a plow to turn the dirt over. We couldn't just run down to the store and buy groceries. We didn't have milk to drink and to make cheese, unless we milked the cows. If my mother needed something she'd tell me to go to Wal-Mart and get it.

Wal-Mart?

Yeah—Wal-Mart. Not really, but it's close to what we called it. There was a man who had a little store in his living room and his name was Waldo. Back then we called it Waldo's. If we needed sugar—cooking powder—my mom would tell me: "Juanito, you need to go for some things." Most of the time she wouldn't have money so she'd send me with some beans or corn meal to trade for what she needed.

Are you kidding about having to trade for things?

No. I'm just trying to show you how lucky you are. You're so used to having stuff you don't even appreciate it. We didn't have the things you have. No toys. No fancy tennis shoes—and we didn't wear pants lying on our butts that looked like they were made for shot legged, four hundred pounders—like your friend wears. By the way, did you ever stop to think what would happen if some bully was chasing him and he'd have to keep reaching down—pulling his pants up? Why he'd get his butt kicked before he'd ever have a chance to get away. You kids. I don't know how parents put up with their children.

Anyway, back to when I was a boy.

I bet I know what you're going to say. You had to walk to school every day, five miles, up hill—in the snow—right?

I didn't have to walk five miles either way. And I didn't have to walk up hill. I guess you were listening to that thing you plug in your ear the other day when I was saying that I only went to the third grade because my father took me out so I could help with the cows and sheep—and the garden. I had to plant, water, hoe weeds, bring in the crops—take the cows to the forest, check on the sheep. There was no way my father could do it all. Since I was the oldest boy, the only boy in the beginning, I was the one that had to stay home and help.

Sorry, Grandpa, I shouldn't have said that. Can we talk about what you used to do for fun?

I had to work—and if I was lucky I only had to work from when the sun came up until it went down. Sometimes in the winter I even had to work in the dark.

That doesn't sound exciting.

Look at it this way, Hijo, if you ever had to get up before the sun came up—and there was a foot of snow on the ground—and the wind was blowing twenty miles an hour, and you had to go outside to get wood—and all you had was an ax—you'd have been excited when you finally finished chopping the wood and was heading for the house. You'd have been excited—if, after you finished milking, you could go inside, back up to the stove and get warm.

I used to get excited when I'd hoed the weeds to the end of the last row in the garden; planted the last seed; finished irrigating, realizing I could go to the house and have something to eat. And I'm talking about when I was only ten or eleven years old.

Sometimes even work can be exciting. Especially when you finish a chore and you're proud of what you did. Of course, nowadays, you kids—you don't have to help just so the family can eat. There's no way for you to know how exciting it was to finish your chores.

Come on, Grandpa, there must have been things to do other than work. What's your favorite memory of having fun?

I don't know. Maybe it was when my mother would take us to see the drunk chickens on Saturday afternoons.

Drunk Chickens?

Yeah. If my brothers and sisters and I had worked real hard all week, done all our chores she might let us watch the drunk chickens on the way to our grandmother's house.

Can you tell me about the drunk chickens?

I'll tell you later, but first we need to have a little talk about money.

You know how, when you need money, you go to your mom and say, "Gimme ten dollars—my girlfriends mom's going to Española, she's gonna leave us off at the movies." How you never ask—you just say, gimme me, gimme me, gimme me?

If I had talked to my father the way you talk to your mother—he'd have given me something—but it wouldn't have been ten dollars—I'll guarantee you that. He'd have thought I'd lost my mind—and would've kept thinking it, too—while he was slapping my butt with a switch for disrespecting him. Of course, nowadays, if a parent spanks their poor little, helpless children— the kids take out their phones and complain to the cops that their parents are treating 'em bad and the parents wind up in trouble. All I can say about that is that the government should hand out free paddles to parents instead of threatening 'em when they're trying to teach their children respect.

And all you can think about, Hijo, is going to the movies. Why, when I was growing up there weren't any movies—none of the fancy things you have today.

You mean like CD players? iPods?

Whatever you call them. When I was little we were lucky if we had a neighbor that had a radio. Sometimes our mother would let us go down the road to our neighbor's and listen to the radio. But most of the time we couldn't hear anything because of all the static. We didn't get our first radio until after the War.

I started to ask you which war, if you were talking about the Civil war, Grandpa. But I knew better than to do that. Anyway, what do you remember listening to Grandpa?

I was talking about the Second World War. My favorite program was the Friday night fights—the Gillette Friday Night Fights. My father, and your great-uncle Tony—we loved to listen to the fights. I remember we'd be listening to a fight, a championship fight if we were lucky, and the announcer would say something like, "he just got hit with a terrific right,—he's down,—he's hurt." Then we'd here everyone yelling, and the referee counting—"seven,—eight," and then nothing. Nothing but static. The static would go on for two or three minutes and when it would go away we would hear the announcer saying, "there you have it ladies and gentlemen—what an ending—that fight's gonna go down in history as one of the greatest championship fights ever. Now don't forget to tune in next week for another great—Gillette—Friday Night Fight." It would usually be a day or two before we'd ran into someone that could tell us who'd won.

I need to get back to what I was saying about money. About you saying, "gimme, gimme, gimme." I don't think I ever saw ten dollars at one time before I was eleven or twelve years old. We didn't use money. We grew all our own food and what we didn't eat, we'd trade. The only times we had money was in the spring when we'd sell the wool and in the fall when we'd sell our calves and lambs. Let me give you an example of how we were able to get by. Up in the canyon, at Donald Martínez' cabin—the one ole Man Bateman homesteaded. They survived by growing potatoes. They grew them about a mile north of the cabin near the Canjilón Creek. In the fall they'd dig up all the potatoes and haul them to some root-cellars they had by the cabin. They'd leave them there all winter, putting 'em together by size. In the spring they'd bring them to Canjilón by the wagon full and trade with us and the other people for dried beans, dried corn, flour, corn meal, lard, candles, soap—whatever we'd been able to keep and what we'd made through the winter.

They lived there all winter? Did they ever come to Canjilón? What'd they do for Christmas?

Good questions, Hijo. I can see you're starting to pay attention. That's good. I can see already that after I explain about when I was growing up you'll have a better idea how tough times were for the homesteaders compared to the way we live today.

It's nine miles from here to the Bateman cabin. In a normal year there could be as much as five or six feet of snow on the ground at their cabin at any one time. The only way they had to get out of there was if someone stopped by and gave 'em a ride on a snowmobile.

There you go again!

Just comparing how they lived to how easy we have it today.

I'll start over. The only way they could get there and back in the winter was on homemade skis. The one I remember seeing coming by here was Albert Bateman. By the time he was passing here his father had died and he was running the ranch. Once in a while I'd see him bringing a couple of his children with him but most of the time he was alone. Every week or so I'd see him coming for supplies. I started to say he was coming to pick up a copy of the TV guide just to give you another idea how easy we have it these days.

Now that's really corny, Grandpa.

You know what, somehow I just can't see you covering eighteen miles in one day—on homemade skis.

Or you either, Grandpa.

One time I asked him what they did for Thanksgiving and Christmas and he said they'd usually go to El Rito. They'd carry the children that were too young to ski. They'd stay three or four days before heading back. Try to imagine a family skiing ten or fifteen miles up and down the mountains to El Rito and back carrying little kids.

Why didn't my great-grandpa get a homestead—like Bateman did?

After what had happened to our grant and with the Forest Service treating him like they did, he didn't trust the government enough to apply for a homestead. It was safer buying land from someone who had already homesteaded the land.

Most of our people were afraid to apply for a homestead. They figured if they did apply the government would let them live on it for five or ten years and then, after they'd built a home and put in a garden, built root cellars and corrals, it would say there'd been a mistake and take it away—like what happened to the grants. Just think, our ancestors lived on those grants for more than 80 years believing they owned them only to have the government come in and take 'em away.

I remember my father talking about some of the people in Cañones—and here in Canjilón, who applied for homesteads. He'd say that the government people would even help fill out the papers and after the people would go to their land—and after they'd fix it all up, lived on it, the government would tell them there'd been a mistake in the paperwork and kick 'em off the property.

The only reason our people had the General Land Office, the GLO, prepare the papers in the first place was because they couldn't read or write. And what was even worse—the people would live there for years before they'd go for their patent only to find that the government was going to take the land away.

That's terrible.

There was another reason why they wouldn't want to apply for a homestead, but we'll talk about that later.

It seems like, from what you're saying, the work never ended. Did you have a favorite season or did it seem like the whole year was nothing but work, work, work?

I always liked the end of summer. After we'd taken in all the crops my father would hitch up our wagon, fill it with beans, corn, carrots, radishes, peas, onions, squash—flour, cornmeal, jerky—whatever we had to trade and take off for Cañones. It'd take him a day or two to get there and back and when we'd see him coming down the road we'd run out to meet him. We knew anytime he'd been to Cañones the wagon was going to be full of things we loved. Especially watermelons. Do I remember those watermelons. Talk about something good.

Why didn't you grow your own?

It's too cold here—the altitude's too high—the growing season's too short.

I said a minute ago that I liked the end of summer. But fall was also a sad time.

In the fall we had to harvest what we'd been growing all summer. We'd pull all the root crops, turnips, beets, onions, carrots, and put them in the shade to dry. We'd cut the wheat and corn and stand them up to dry. Later we'd shuck most of the corn and after it had dried we'd take it, along with the wheat, to the mill to grind.

You've got to be kidding—there was a mill here in Canjilón?

Sure was, on the north side of the road leading out to the Chama Highway, near La Mesita. You've seen it a hundred times, just didn't realize what it was. It's that pile of rocks by the creek on the right side going toward the highway. We'd take the corn and wheat and if it had been a good year we'd wind up with enough flour and corn meal to last all winter.

After we'd finished with the flour and cornmeal we'd put the root crops in the cellars and take the dried beans out of their pods.

As hard as it was living back then you need to know something that I'm proud of, something that was important. We never went hungry, Hijo. We didn't eat a lot of meat because we had to sell our calves and lambs in the fall but—we never, never went hungry.

When you did butcher how would you keep the meat from rotting?

I think you're going to find that interesting. When we'd run out of ice in the cellar, usually by the end of June, if we still had meat we'd lower it in the well. We'd tie the rope so that the meat would stay just above the water—where it was cool and it'd keep that way for a while. Most of the time though we'd make jerky out of it when it'd start looking like it might spoil.

What did you do to keep the milk cold? The same thing you did with the meat?

We'd lower the bucket of milk in the well like we did with the meat, but we'd lower it into the water, almost to the top to keep it cool. I can still remember when we got our first refrigerator. It ran off of propane and sure made a difference.

When are you going to get around to telling me about the drunk chickens?

Later. You need to learn patience. Before I tell you I want to explain the reasons why, like I said earlier—why fall was also a sad time.

It was sad because everything was changing. The days were getting shorter, colder, and we knew that before long it would be snowing. The air in the morning would let us know the hardest time of the year was just over the mountain.

One of the saddest things I remember in those years were the poor people who would come to our house after we had taken in most of our crops. They were people that didn't have any land—didn't have any way to grow crops or raise cows and sheep—people who didn't have anything to trade for food. There were no jobs around here in those days, and in some of the families the men had left to Colorado and Utah to look for work. Most of the time they wouldn't even come home for the winter and their families usually didn't have anything to trade for what they needed.

They'd come to our house and ask if they could go through our garden and look for any vegetables we had missed. They'd ask permission for their children to crawl down the rows and pick up beans that had dropped off the plants and look for carrots, beets, anything we might have missed. The little children would get down on their little hands and knees like if they were picking piñon from under the trees, and crawl along looking for anything they might find to eat. It was terrible. We would watch them for a while and before long I could see my father was starting to feel so bad that he'd call the parents to the cellar and give them some of what we had stored. Most of the time he'd wind up giving them some jerky, too, if we had some. One time I even saw him give a woman who had four little children following along behind her a little lamb. It used to make us feel terrible to see those little five and six year old hungry children crawling down the rows.

We were poor too, I guess, but we didn't feel poor. The women with the little children—that would ask permission to crawl through the garden, now those people—they were poor.

-2-
The Adams-Onis Treaty
And The Mexican-American War

Before you start something else, Grandpa, can you tell me about the drunk chickens—about what happened during the shootout?

Not yet. I told you I was going to alternate what I was going to be saying; talk about our family and then about our history. Next time, when we are talking about our family, I'll tell you about the chickens.

Then can you start by saying what happened during the shootout?

Stop calling it a shootout.

Sorry.

I need to ask you a couple of questions before I go on. Do you know when, what you're calling a shootout happened?

Sure, June 1967.

And of course you know where it happened?

Yes—the courthouse in Tierra Amarilla.

Why'd we go to the courthouse that day?

I don't know—that's why I keep asking.

It's important to know why we went. But before I get around to telling you, you need to know the history of what had happened in the years leading up to that day—to the "raid," as the newspaper and TV people like to call it. Before I get around to telling you what happened I want to make sure you know why it happened. It's every bit as important, more important actually, for you to know why we went there, than it is to know what happened when we got there. You need to understand why so many people in Río Arriba County—in New Mexico—in the 1960's, and before, were so

12

upset about how the government had been treating our ancestors and their grants.

If I don't take the time to explain what happened leading up to us going to the courthouse, what I'll have to say won't make any more sense than what's been written about it over the last forty-three years. Other than what Reies, his daughter, Rosita, our cousin, Moisés and I—and a few others have said in the Río Grande Sun over the years—and what Larry Calloway has reported—very little has been said about what really happened that day. When I finally get around to telling you what happened—and why it happened, you'll be one of the first to hear the whole story.

I know you want me to say right now what happened but you need to wait—you need to hear the history—the background.

Right now I want to talk about how the government was treating our ancestors compared to how it was treating the other people back in those days; explain the difference in how the government treated different groups here in New Mexico; how it treated our people compared to how it treated the people in other States and Territories. How Anglos were treated different from Indians—and different from our people; how the Indians were treated different from the Spanish and Mexican people. I need to show how people in California were treated compared with people in New Mexico; how people in the Oregon Territory were treated compared with the way our ancestors, who were supposed to be protected by the Treaty of Guadalupe Hidalgo, were treated.

There were times when our people were treated fair and other times when they weren't. Sometimes the government acted like it had a conscience and at other times it didn't. Most of the time it didn't.

Before I forget, at some point I'll be talking about when I was a member of the Alianza; about when I had to go to court and all that. I need to talk about how Geronimo Barunda, we used to call him " Indio," how he tried to take the blame from me by testifying that he was the one that shot Nick Saiz—how he wound up in prison for lying. And I'm going to have to talk about bad things that I did during my life. I can't expect people to believe what I say unless I tell my whole story. I'm going to be telling about the bad times as well as the good times, otherwise, we'll be wasting our time. If I don't tell it like it happened it won't be our history.

There's something else I need to point out before we go on. Some of what I'll be saying will be embarrassing to me and to our family but whether it's embarrassing or not it's important to tell it like it happened. If someone listening to this years from now doesn't agree with what I'm saying, with what I remember it's not going to be because I didn't tell it the way I remember it happening. I don't want someone years from now thinking what I'm saying's is a bunch of bullshit. You need to take that part out, Hijo, I shouldn't have said it like that. Can you change it?

Sure. After we finish I'll go through and fix it and take out the part where we're talking about taking it out, too. But why not just leave it in, it's the way you talk?

Come on, Hijo, I don't like to use those kinds of words in front of my grandchildren. What if after we finish this, one of your children or grandchildren, or one of their cousins, takes this to school and the teacher lets the other children listen to it. Anyway, we need to move on. Just make sure you take the bad words out.

From everything I've learned over the years and from what Mike has told me about, the problems our ancestors suffered from began long before they were born. What was happening around the time Juan Bautista Valdez and the other grantees received the Cañones grant in 1807, and what happened during the Mexican War—it all had a lot to do with the way our people have been treated. We believe the fact that Mexico refused to sell the northern half of its country to the United States caused our ancestors a lot of suffering over the last 150 years.

Now don't get me wrong, I'm glad I was born here and proud that some of our ancestors were originally from Spain, but I just can't understand why our Indian, Spanish and Mexican people were treated so different than the Anglos that came here from the east.

That's enough about that. I need to start with the 1800's.

In about 1845 after the United States had bought Texas, President Polk offered to buy the northern half of Mexico. Mexico refused to sell and after a little shootout between the two countries on the north side of the Río Grande—across the river from Matamoros, President Polk went to Congress for a declaration of war. He told Congress that Mexico had attacked the United States and killed some of our troops. He also said that if he didn't get a declaration of war the security of the United States would be in danger.

Before I go on, I need to say that in addition to the notes Mike has given me to use, most of what I will be saying about our political history I've learned from him and my other friends who have studied our history. I don't want you to think that just because I'm telling you about something that happened in the 1800's that I knew about it in June, 1967, when we went to the courthouse. I watch the History channel now and then but I don't think it was even around back then. Most of what I'll be telling you is from what Mike and my other friends have told me over the past twenty years.

One of the problems with what President Polk was telling Congress was that the news he had from Texas was two or three weeks old when he was telling it because in those days it took that long for news to get across the county.

What President Polk didn't know at the time, because it took so long for the news to get to Washington, was that there had been a major battle near Matamoros and that the Americans had defeated the Mexican troops who, after the battle, crossed the river and headed south. In that one battle over a 1000 Mexican soldiers were killed and the United States lost less than fifty.

There wasn't really any question after that battle that the poorly equipped Mexican's were no match for the Americans. Maybe, if Polk had known what had actually happened he wouldn't have been so quick to declare war. Or maybe it wouldn't have made a difference since his real reason for a war wasn't that some U. S. soldiers had been ambushed and killed—or that Mexico was even a threat—it was that he and the rest of the government wanted the northern half of Mexico.

At the time Polk succeeded in convincing the Senate to give him a declaration of war the Río Grande wasn't even the border between Mexico and the United States. The real border was the Nueces River which ran from West Texas south-east to the gulf near Corpus Christi—the entire south valley between the Nueces and the Río Grande rivers was actually in dispute.

The real reason as I just mentioned, Hijo, was that the politicians in Washington and across the country believed the United States was entitled to all the land between the Atlantic and the Pacific—believed it was God's will that the land belong to the United States.

But at the time Polk wanted to attack Mexico not everyone in Washington was in favor of the war. One important person who was not in favor of the war was Abraham Lincoln. In one of his speeches he compared President Polk's wanting to start a war with Mexico to a farmer who, when asked if he was greedy, said he wasn't. Lincoln said that all the farmer wanted was the land he owned—and whatever land was next to it.

Even after Congress approved the war and gave President Polk millions of dollars to pay for it the war didn't begin for months.

After Congress gave President Polk the declaration of war but before he ordered the troops to cross the Río Grande he sent Colonel Stephen Watts Kearny and a few hundred troops to capture New Mexico and California.

As it turned out Kearny was able to capture New Mexico without firing a shot because the Governor of New Mexico at the time, Manuel Armijo, supposedly accepted $50,000 to leave New Mexico as Kearny was approaching from the east.

Now that I've brought up the name of Governor Armijo, there's something you're going to be learning, Hijo—not all the bad people in our history were gringos.

Kearny was already in control of New Mexico and about to gain control of California by the time Polk ordered the American troops to cross the Río Grande toward Monterey. The way my friends and I see it the war in Mexico wasn't even necessary to the capture the land Mexico was forced to give up when it signed the Treaty.

During the war President Polk went back to Congress for additional money and increased his offer for the land, but again Mexico refused.

There's something I forgot to say. We need to back up about thirty years and talk about something that happened even before the war with Mexico, talk about how the United States wound up claiming Mexico started the war.

The United States and Spain signed a treaty, the Adams-Onís Treaty, in 1819, settling the border between the two countries at the Sabine River along the border between where Texas and Louisiana are today. The treaty stated that the United States would own the land east of the Sabine and Spain would own the land to the west—from the Sabine to the Pacific Ocean. After the treaty was signed the United States knew it didn't have any claim to the land west of the Sabine River but that didn't slow it down in scheming how to get some of it.

In 1821, two years after the Adams-Onís Treaty was signed, Mexico won its independence from Spain and took Spain's place under the terms of the Adams-Onís Treaty.

For the next twenty or so years Mexico continued a practice begun by Spain of allowing land to be granted to the Anglos who were moving from the United States into what is today East Texas, so long as they swore their allegiance to Mexican law and agreed to become Catholics.

After about 35,000 Anglos had settled west of the Sabine River they formed what they called the Republic of Texas which at the time was bordered on the east by the Sabine River and on the west by the Nueces. At about the same time the new Republic of Texas and Mexico began to have disputes that resulted in battles and unease over ownership of the area south and west of the Nueces River.

In 1845 the United States totally ignored the existence of the Adams-Onís Treaty and offered the Anglos who had established the Republic of Texas $10,000,000 to join the Union even though the offer was in clear violation of the Adams-Onís Treaty and would be adding an additional slave state to the Union. After buying Texas and granting it statehood the United States began to use Texas as an excuse to continue its move south and west of the Nueces River and beyond.

Shortly after Texas became a state, President Polk ordered troops to move south from Corpus Christi toward the Río Grande in an attempt to force Mexico into declaring war or doing something, anything, that would give the United States an excuse to start a war.

American troops under orders from President Polk marched to the Río Grande and Mexico still refused to fight. So in order to force a fight the United States built a fort across the river from Matamoros. Mexico, seeing the United States building a fort on the north side of the Río Grande began building its own fort on the south side of the river. The standoff lasted for weeks but in the end Polk ordered his American troops to cross the river.

Mexico's army was made up of poor peasants most of whom had no equipment or weapons and no clue how to fight. They were only in the army because they had been gathered from the countryside by Mexican generals passing through towns and ranchos on the way north. As an army they never had a chance.

I need to read something that President Ulysses S. Grant had to say in his memoir some years later—after he'd been president. During the war Grant had served as an officer in Mexico under General Taylor and knew from personal experience what he was talking about. Here's some of what he had to say about the annexation of Texas:

Generally the officers of the army were indifferent whether the annexation was consummated or not; but not so all of them. For myself, I was bitterly opposed to the measure, and to this day regard the war, which resulted, as one of the most unjust ever waged by a stronger against a weaker nation. It was an instance of a Republic following the bad example of European monarchies, in not considering justice in their desire to acquire additional territory.

The occupation, separation and annexation were, from the inception of the movement to its final consummation, a conspiracy to acquire territory out of which slave states might be formed for the American Union.

Even if the annexation [of Texas] could be justified, the manner in which the subsequent war was forced upon Mexico cannot. The fact is, annexationists wanted more territory than they could possibly lay any claim to, as part of the new acquisition. Texas, as an independent State, never had exercised jurisdiction over the territory between the Nueces River and the Río Grande. Mexico had never recognized the independence of Texas, and maintained that, even if independent, the State had no claim south of the Nueces.

In taking military possession of Texas after annexation, the army of occupation, under General Taylor, was directed to occupy the disputed territory. The army did not stop at the Nueces and offer to negotiate for a settlement of the boundary question, but went beyond, apparently in order to force Mexico to initiate war.

After the war Mexico was forced into a treaty that was to the liking of the United States. The reason I say it was to the United States liking, is because Mexico was under the threat of a continued war and the possibility of losing even more of its territory if it did not agree to the terms of the Treaty, paragraph ten of which had been stricken by the U. S. Senate.

Mexico had to know that the United States wasn't going to live up to the terms of the treaty after the way it had ignored the Adams-Onís Treaty. But having just been brutally beaten and facing continuing threats of further war—and hints that if it refused to sign the treaty the way it had been approved by the Senate—the United States might, as it was threatening to do, take Mexico's five remaining northern States; Mexico had no choice in the matter, it was forced to sign the treaty.

There's something about the actual signing of the Treaty of Guadalupe Hidalgo that I want to talk about. When the representatives of both countries sat down to sign the treaty one of Mexico's diplomats, as he was signing the treaty, turned to Nicholas Trist, who was signing for the United States and said that he, Trist, must be as happy about signing the treaty as the Mexicans were sad in having to sign it. Trist was quoted later as having said, in a letter to his wife, that he was more devastated in signing the treaty than the Mexicans were, considering how Mexico had been forced into signing it.

What happened after Mexico signed the Treaty?

After the treaty was signed the U.S. gave Mexico $15,000,000 dollars to pay for the damages caused by the war and several million more to pay off debts Mexico owed to some Americans.

Even though Congress had initially given Polk millions to fight the war and to pay some of Mexico's personal debts by the time the war was over the war had cost the United States over $100,000,000. But, Hijo, when you consider that the United States got half of Mexico—would up with New Mexico, Arizona, California, Nevada, Utah, and parts of Colorado, Wyoming and Texas—it didn't really turn out to be that expensive.

Here's something to think about. Ninety percent of our soldiers that died during the war—ninety percent—died from disease. Only ten percent died fighting. Hundreds died without ever firing a shot—or even being shot at—without even crossing the Río Grande.

One more point before we move on. Remember when we were reading about President Ulysses S. Grant having fought in Mexico under General Taylor and about what he had said about the war? About how opposed he was to it, calling it as unjust as any war ever waged by a stronger nation against a weaker nation?

Yes.

In addition to considering how Grant felt about the war we believe it's important for our family to know what President Taylor was thinking about during his presidency: What he had to say in his first and only State of the Union address about California and New Mexico:

> No civil government having been provided by Congress or California, the people of that Territory, impelled by the necessities of their political condition, recently met in convention for the purpose of forming a constitution and State government, which the latest advices give me reason to suppose has been accomplished; and it is believed they will shortly apply for the admission of California into the Union as a sovereign State. Should such be the case, and should their constitution be conformable to the requisitions of the Constitution of the United States, I recommend their application to the favorable consideration of Congress. The people of New Mexico will also, it is believed, at no very distant period present themselves for admission into the Union. Preparatory to the admission of California and New Mexico the people of each will have instituted for themselves a republican form of government, laying its foundation in such principles and organizing its powers in such form as to them shall seem most likely to affect their safety and happiness. By awaiting their action, all causes of uneasiness may be avoided and confidence and kind feeling preserved. With a view of maintaining the harmony and tranquility so dear to all, we should abstain from the introduction of those exciting topics of a sectional character, which have hitherto produced painful apprehensions in the public mind; and I repeat the solemn warning of the first and most illustrious of my predecessors against furnishing any ground for characterizing parties.

I also recommend that commissions be organized by Congress to examine and decide upon the validity of the present subsisting land titles in California and New Mexico, and that provision be made for the establishment of offices of surveyor-general in New Mexico, California and Oregon and for the surveying and bringing into market the public lands in those Territories.

When Taylor said he was repeating the solemn warning of the first and most illustrious of his predecessors against furnishing any ground for characterizing parties he was referring to George Washington's farewell address. Here's what Washington had to say, Hijo:

In contemplating the causes which may disturb our Union, it occurs as a matter of serious concern that any ground should have been furnished for characterizing parties by geographical discriminations, Northern and Southern, Atlantic and Western; whence designing men may endeavor to excite a belief that there is a real difference of local interests and views. One of the expedients of party to acquire influence within particular districts is to misrepresent the opinions and aims of other districts. You cannot shield yourselves too much against the jealousies and heart burnings which spring from these misrepresentations; they tend to render alien to each other those who ought to be bound together by fraternal affection. The inhabitants of our Western country have lately had a useful lesson ... they have seen, in the negotiation by the Executive, and in the unanimous ratification by the Senate, of the treaty with Spain, and in the universal satisfaction at that event, throughout the United States, a decisive proof how unfounded were the suspicions propagated among them of a policy in the General Government and in the Atlantic States unfriendly to their interests in regard to the Mississippi; they have been witnesses to the formation of two treaties, that with Great Britain, and that with Spain, which secure to them everything they could desire, in respect to our foreign relations, towards confirming their prosperity.

Zachary Taylor and George Washington knew how important it was to treat people from different areas the same; Northern and Southern; Atlantic and Western. If President Taylor had lived, Hijo, New Mexico probably would have become a state at the same time California did.

Are you starting to see why studying New Mexico history is as important as talking about our family history?

I never realized there was going to be so much information. But I'm starting to understand why you say we really can't begin to know what caused our people to be treated the way they were without studying the political history.

-3-
Two Sheep Herders,
Grandpa—For Twenty Sheep?

I guess it's time to tell you about the drunk chickens—since dragging it out seems to be driving you a little crazy.

On Saturdays and Sundays after our chores were done, my mother would call us all together and say that since we'd been good all week and had done all our chores she was going to take us to see the chickens. Darn, Hijo—it just slipped my mind what I was going to say about them—I can't remember what it was.

Grandpa!

Oh, yeah, now I remember. Our mother liked to visit her mother on Saturdays and since she lived near where the chickens were our mother would take us as far as the still and let us watch the chickens while she was visiting our grandmother.

Still?

Yeah, the machine that was used to make *mula*.

Mula?

Whiskey—moonshine—Taos lightening. The people in Canjilón called it *mula*.

Anyway—every time they would finish making a batch of mula they'd empty the barrels—throw what was left of the corn on the ground so they could start another batch. There were always a bunch of chickens around where the corn was thrown and as soon as it hit the ground they'd run to eat it. Pretty soon they'd start flapping their wings— falling sideways—and then trying to get up. We'd sit there all afternoon watching 'em, laughing, having a good time. Our mother knew we'd worked hard all week—hoping she'd take us to see the chickens and that if she let us watch the chickens we'd probably work real hard the next week hoping we could go back to watch them.

That's funny, I wish I could have seen them.

Maybe someday we can get some whiskey an—but not now. We need to keep going.

What else did you do for fun?

Just the usual things children who don't have any toys do—play with marbles; have rock throwing contests; roll barrel rings and old tires down the road, chew tar from the road if we could find some. I bet you never played marbles the way we did, Hijo. Do you remember ever playing a game of marbles where you had to yell "medio" when your marble got stuck in a circle?

No.

When we would play marbles the first thing we'd do would be to draw a big circle on the ground. One of us would stand with a stick in the place where we wanted the circle to be and turn around drawing the circle; before we'd actually start the game we'd take turns throwing our favorite marbles at a line to see who could get the closest and be the first to shoot. After we'd figured who was going to be first we'd each drop five marbles in the circle. Then we'd take turns shooting at the marbles in the ring. When you knocked a marble out of the circle you got to keep it as long as your marble wound up outside the circle. If your marble stayed inside the circle someone would yell "medio" and you'd lose your turn—and your favorite marble.

I'm glad you finally told me about the drunk chickens, Grandpa. You sure had me going. I really like it when you talk about our past. That's the interesting part to me. But my teacher's more interested in the political history part. I let him hear what you've said from the last time we were together and he asked if he could have a copy when we're finished and I told him I'd have to ask you.

I don't think I want him to have a copy. Remember, Hijo, we're only doing this for our family.

So now that you're going to be telling more about our family can we start with the shootout?

I thought I made it clear that I wasn't going to talk about what happened until after I've filled you in on why we went there. You're just going to have to wait—and if you call it a shootout one more time—I'm going to make it the last thing we talk about. Listen to what I'm saying. We only went there to arrest Alfonso Sanchez. We didn't go there to shoot anyone.

It just sounds more exciting if I—never mind. Sorry!

When we were talking before about my childhood I said that my father took me out of school when I was in the third grade so I could help him with the work.

But, Grandpa, you already said that—Oops—hold on, I need to change the tape. Okay, start again!

When we were talking about my childhood I said my father had to take me out of school so I could help him with the work. But that wasn't exactly the way it happened. For a few years after he took me out of school the school police, I guess that's what they were called—would come by our house and threaten my father. They would tell him that if he didn't put me back in school they were going to take him off to jail. So, whenever they would come to our house he'd tell them he was going to put me back and he'd have me go for a week or two. But the next time he needed me to help he'd take me out again. That went on until I was eleven or twelve and after that I never saw them again.

When I'd go back to school the teacher would always put me back in third grade even though I was getting way too old. If they'd kept it up for a few more years I would have been closer to the teacher's age than the kids. When I'd show up the kids would start laughing. Especially when the teacher would tell me to read. It didn't take long for her to realize that having me read wasn't a good idea and it didn't take the kids long to know that I didn't like them laughing at me. A couple trips to the playground and they had it figured out.

Didn't it make you feel bad that you had to work while the other kids were getting to go to school?

Not really. I was actually the lucky one. The kids that got to go to school were the ones that were unlucky. Don't get me wrong, they were lucky to get to go to school while I had to stay home and work, but the reason they were able to go to school was because their parents were poorer than we were. They usually didn't have any land to farm and their fathers had to go to Colorado or Utah to herd sheep or work in the mines. The ones whose fathers were herding sheep or working in the mines only got to see their fathers every year or so and their mothers had to raise them by themselves. That's what made it possible for them to go to school.

Since my father had some land and didn't have to go away to work I was able to grow up with him at home. It would have been better to grow up with my parents and go to school too, but that wasn't possible. I was lucky to grow up with my father being home, but unlucky because I couldn't go to school.

When I was still real young one of our horses fell on my father's leg and for a long time after that he had trouble walking so he would send me to the mountains with food for our sheepherders. I was so small that after my father would put the saddle on the horse I'd have to walk him into the ditch so I could get on. That's the only way I could get in the saddle. I couldn't reach the stirrups unless I took him into the ditch.

There you go, Grandpa—trying to get me to believe that you were poor—but wanting me to believe you could afford to have sheepherders.

We had two sheepherders. And they had to eat. So sometimes if I didn't take food to them they would show up at the house. And they never came down together—they were trained that one always had to stay with the sheep while the other came to eat.

You told me you only had a few sheep. Now you're saying you had two sheep-herders. I don't get it—wait—wait—what were their names?

We used to call them "Pastore 1" and "Pastore 2."

Now I know you're not telling the truth. There wouldn't be any sheepherders whose names were "Pastore 1" and "Pastore 2." What're you going to say next that they were brothers? I'm not believing you.

That's what we called them—and come to think about it—they were brothers.

I thought you said when we first started that you were only going to say the truth? How long are you going to keep this up before you admit it's not true, Grandpa?

It is true. They would come to eat and if they didn't show up I would have to take food to them. Let me give you an example about when they would come to eat. One day I was sitting on the porch and when I looked up "Pastore 2" was coming toward the house from out there near the corral and I yelled to my mother that "dos" was coming to eat. Whenever I used to tell her that one of them was coming she'd go to the stove and get the leftovers and put them on the porch. As soon as he got close enough he jumped on the porch and start eating.

Grandpa!

When he got through he jumped off the porch and went over to where it was real sunny, leaned forward with his legs as far out in front as he could get them, raised his butt up in the air, stretched back as far as he could and plopped his butt on the ground. Then he put his chin on his legs and went to sleep.

You're still not willing to say it's not true, Grandpa?

Wait. I'm not through. When my mother would catch him sleeping she'd throw a bucket of dishwater at him and yell, *"Vete, huevón—curre con las borregas."*

He'd jump up, shake back and forth to get rid of all the dust, gave her a *mal ojo* and take off for the hills as fast as his four legs would carry him.

Eeeeeeee—Grandpa! You should have been a comedian. You sure had me going. It's starting to sound like your life really wasn't all that bad.

Let me say some more about what I had to do in those years and then you decide if I had it made.

But, Grandpa, the way it seems to me all you had to do was plant in the spring, irrigate and hoe weeds in the summer—gather the crops in the fall, and help with the animals. It sounds like you had a lot of time to goof off.

I guess I forgot to tell you about the Fresno, the scrapper, the plow, the disc, the spring tooth harrow and the mower—having to walk behind a team of horses from daylight to dark, day after day.

Since you already told me that you didn't have a tractor, I guess you're going to say you trained the Pastores to help pull all that equipment around the fields.

If I had talked to my father like that, Hijo—never mind—forget it. We had a team of horses to do the pulling. When we weren't leveling, plowing, grading, cutting or mowing hay we were helping our neighbors since we were the only ones around that were lucky enough to have a team and all the equipment. By the way, I didn't tell you what a Fresno was. I guess you already know—right?

I don't know what a Fresno is, Grandpa. I don't think I'd ever heard that word until you just said it. Wait, wait, wait. I know—I know. It's a town in California.

You know what, Hijo—you're starting to be a real—burro. A Fresno is a big, heavy scoop pulled by a team of mules or horses and used to level fields and build roads. After you scoop up a load of dirt and pull it to the place where you want it, you dump it by pushing the handle on the back of the scoop forward so it'll flip upside down and dump the dirt; then you jerk it around and turn it right side up and go back where you were getting the dirt and do it all over again. You do it over and over until you've moved all the dirt you need. Fresno's have been around for years. They were even used to build railroads in the 1800's.

Sounds like that's one of the pieces of equipment that was replaced by a backhoe.
Sure was.

So, all those rusty pieces of equipment behind the barn, with the funny looking iron wheels—were what you used when you were growing up?
Exactly—and in the fall we'd lend our team and the mower to our neighbors and they'd take them to the pastures in the forest to cut the dead grass and bring it back as food for their animals during the winter.

What would happen if the Forest Service caught someone cutting the hay and bringing it down?
They'd make them pay for it. And if they didn't have the money to pay, the government would take it away from them.

The dead grass from the forest? The government would make the people pay for dead grass—or take it away if the people couldn't pay for it?
Sure would.

Did they ever catch you cutting hay in the forest?
I don't remember ever going to the mountains to cut hay. But if we had had to, we would have cut it and brought it down at night. That may sound like stealing, Hijo. But even if it would have been it couldn't have been as bad as the government taking the land and leaving the people with no way to feed their animals without having to sneak into the forest for dead grass—and having to pay for it if they got caught.

Did the Forest Service people give you and my great-Grandpa a lot of trouble?
We were always in trouble with them. The Forest bosses were all Anglos from somewhere else, usually from the South. They were always after us for running our cows and sheep on the forest without permits. They kept telling us we couldn't have permits and couldn't use the forest, but we had

to survive—we had to feed our cows and sheep. The way I saw it—and the way my father saw it for sure, was that Spain had given our ancestors the right to use the forest and then eighty or ninety years later along comes the government and takes it away. We had to trespass on the land that our ancestors had the right to use—just to survive.

I think I'm starting to get an idea how bad it was, Grandpa. Sorry I wasn't more serious when we started talking about our history.

Well, we've come to the time to start talking about the 60's—talking about the San Joaquín del Río de Chama Grant. The grant Reies Tijerina used as an example of what the government had done. The Government ignored its name and called it the Cañón de Chama even though that was only the name of the settlement. I'll be calling it San Joaquín del Río de Chama or just the San Joaquín when we talk about it. It was on the San Joaquín that we had a standoff with the Forest Service at the Echo Amphitheater in October, 1966. It was the grant that caused us to go to the courthouse the next year. (Fig. 14)

Is the San Joaquín the main grant that our family belonged to?

Some of our family lived on it but, actually, as descendents of Juan Bautista Valdez most of our family lived on the grant named for him. Canjilón was in the original San Joaquín until the government came along and changed the boundaries. So, when you hear me saying we're trespassing on our own land, Hijo, that's why I'm saying it—because where we are now was part of the San Joaquín.

One day when I was, I don't know, maybe eleven, I was working in the garden with my father when we heard a lot of noise coming from the road. When I looked up—there were our cattle with some Forest Service men on horseback pushing them out of the forest. My father went over and opened the gate so they could run them into our place.

When the Ranger saw him opening the gate he yelled out for my father to close the gate that he was going to impound our cows. Medardo Trujillo, a cousin of mine that was working for the Forest Service, yelled back to the Ranger that he was going to run them into our place and he spun his horse around and chased them through the opening. When Medardo got back to the Ranger Station they fired him for running our cows into our place. At least that's the way I remember it.

Was that the only time they tried to impound your cattle?

No! They were impounding our cows, and other peoples cows, all the time. But our friends, like Tobias Leyba, that hated the Forest Service and the way it was always treating us—whenever someone had their cows and sheep impounded—Tobías, and the others, would go to the corral at night and turn them loose.

We need to read a couple letters my father saved from all the ones he got from the Forest Service. And while we're reading them I want you to keep in mind that we never had money except in the spring and the fall. The rest of the year we survived by trading.

The first letter says:

Permits- C&H -Carson, Valdez, Amarante.

Dear Sir.

Reference is made to your 1937 application to graze livestock on the Canjilón Allotment and our letter of recent date advising you that your application was disapproved.

At a meeting of the Canjilón Livestock Association on March 13 it was explained to the members that the Canjilón Allotment is now overstocked and that consequently it would no longer be possible to approve increases over present preference numbers or issue new permits. The Advisory Board of the Association, however, requests that we give consideration to the difficulty of disposing of stock at the present time with the view to granting temporary permits for this year only, to all new applicants in order to give them an opportunity to dispose of their stock or provide range for them elsewhere.

We have given serious consideration to this request and have decided to approve all new applications on a temporary basis. You have no preference for use of the range and it will not be possible to grant you a permit after this year.

All stock permitted under temporary permit must be removed from the range by October 31, 1937. This should give you sufficient time in which to make other arrangements for your stock.

When we took our cows off the forest that year—on October 31, 1937—that was the last time we had a permit. During my whole life we never had a permit to put our cows, sheep and horses on the forest.

Before we read the next letter keep in mind that the one I just read was written less than fifty years after the government ran our people off over 600,000 acres of their land, leaving them with less than 3,000 acres. I'm going to have you read this one. It's kinda long—so take your time.

Dear Mr. Valdez,

Ranger Alan Lamb of Canjilón, New Mexico, has submitted a report to us showing that you had 9 head of cattle grazing on the Canjilón Allotment of the Canjilón Ranger District on July 1, 1954. His report states that Mrs. Valdez admitted that those cattle were on the National Forest on July 1st.

Since these cattle were not authorized to graze on National Forest land, we have no choice but to charge you the commercial rate for the period they were on National Forest Land. Private pastures in the vicinity of Canjilón are being leased for $3.00 per cow month or 10 cents per cow day. This has been established as the commercial rate in the vicinity of Canjilón.

Your cattle were on National Forest land one day for a total of 9 cow days. Using the commercial rate of 10 cents per cow day, the charge for this use is 90 cents. A statement for this amount is enclosed and it will be appreciated if you will forward the payment immediately. We hope that you will be able to take care of your stock in the future without putting them on the National Forest.

It is our understanding that your cattle have grazed without permit on the National Forest several times in the past. You have also stated that your cattle would be on National Forest land at times because you did not have enough private pasture for them.

Failure to keep your cattle off the National Forest can result in our rounding them up and impounding them. If this is done, you will be charged the costs of rounding the cattle up and feeding them, before they could be released to you. Please do not force us to invoke this procedure.

Grandpa, you said the Forest Service would round up your cattle and run them out of the forest. Did they ever get your sheep?

They would have—if it wasn't for our pastores.

There you go again.

No, I'm serious. We had the meanest pastores in Canjilón. We trained them to be mean. The people that worked for the Forest Service knew better than to get close to our sheep. Their dogs wouldn't even go near our sheep when the pastores were there—even their horses knew better.

I have another question?

Okay, but before long I need to say some more about the grants that belonged to our ancestors—the ones my father had been telling me about since I was a little boy.

If you only had about ten cows and ten or twenty sheep and you had to sell the calves and lambs in the fall to get money, how'd you ever have meat to eat?

Well, that's another story about trespassing. When I was thirteen, maybe fourteen I used to get an old rifle that my father kept in the shed and go to the hills and kill rabbits, turkeys—deer. Whatever I found that we could eat.

My father was afraid for me to do it. But the way I saw it he'd been telling me about how the Spanish government had giving our people the right to use the parts of the grants that were left after everyone had taken the little pieces of land where they had built their houses. He had told me how Spain had given our ancestors the right to use the common land for whatever they needed. I was only doing what our people had been allowed to do for centuries before the government took it all away. What would the people in the cities do, Hijo, if the government locked the doors to the grocery stores? They wouldn't just sit there and starve. They'd do whatever it took to survive—to feed their families. That's all I was doing—making sure we had some meat to eat.

-4-
Ignoring The Treaty Of Guadalupe Hidalgo

When you began our story you said you'd talk about things that had happened before you were born. Now that you've mentioned the war with Mexico, I'm confused. How did the war affect our ancestors lives and what did you mean when you said that our future was already being decided long before we were even born?

The first thing that comes to my mind, Hijo, is the way the politicians were referring to our ancestors after the war. The way the politicians and army officers were saying our people were dumb—were lazy.

Almost everything I've heard seems like the United States never had any intention to live up to the Treaty of Guadalupe Hidalgo—and that Mexico, with all its problems, couldn't do anything about it.

What was the government doing that made you believe the United States wasn't living up to the Treaty?

Well, first,—Congress passed a law allowing California land grants to be settled one way and four years later it passed a different law to settle the land grant claims in the rest of the territories—other than Texas, in a different way. The grants in all the territories should have been decided by the same law. By the law used for California. All the territories should have been treated the same. New Mexico and the territories, other than California, had to have their grants decided by a surveyor general. I've heard that when two countries have a treaty, it's an agreement, and it's not fair to use the treaty one way for one group of people and another way for another group; its not fair to have one part of the land covered by the treaty settled with one set of laws and other parts of the land settled with a different set of laws.

Another problem was that Texas, which had been a state since 1845, was allowed to use an entirely different method to settle its grants. In other words, if the United States had lived by what the Treaty said, all the grants in California, Texas and New Mexico—all the Pueblo Indian, Spanish and Mexican grants would have been settled using the same law. The law used in New Mexico made the grantees prove their titles rather than have the government review the titles like happened in California.

The California grants and the Pueblo Indian grants here in New Mexico were settled in less than twenty years with the only exceptions being that some of the appeals took longer. The California system wound up with the grantees keeping about seventy-five percent of their land. By the time the government got around to settling our grants, forty-some years later, our people wound up with less than twenty-five percent of their original land.

Under the system that was used in Texas, where the grants were settled by the state, the acreage confirmed was even higher than in California—the grantees were originally allowed to keep close to ninety percent of their land.

The twenty-five percent figure I used for New Mexico isn't really accurate either because it includes some huge grants that shouldn't have been included. The Maxwell, Luis María Baca, Sangre de Cristo, Pablo Montoya and Preston Beck, Jr. Grants, just to name a few, were supposed to be limited in their size—but they weren't. Congress approved the Maxwell Grant at over 1,700,000 acres and the Sangre de Cristo with over 990,000 acres. If the Mexican law had been followed they would have been limited to 97,500 acres each. The Pablo Montoya and the Preston Beck were supposed to be limited to 48,800 acres but the Montoya was allowed to keep 655,000 acres and the Beck wound up with almost 320,000.

And that's not all, Hijo, Congress gave the Jose María Baca heirs script, piece of paper allowing them to pick out five 98,000 acre grants, almost 500,000 acres. And they were allowed to pick the land they wanted so long as it was in New Mexico, Colorado and Arizona. They used the script to select one grant in Colorado, two in Arizona and two in New Mexico. The first grant they chose was the Baca Location Number One—the one that used to be called the Valle Grande, that's close to Los Alamos. (Figs. 4, 14)

The United States recently bought it for over $100,000,000 claiming it was being purchased to protect the area. We don't believe that was the real reason the government bought it. We think it was bought because it's in an area that is one of the best, if not the best, geo-thermal areas in the United States. We think that's probably the real reason the government bought it.

If you subtract the 4,000,000 acres covering the Maxwell, Sangre de Cristo, Montoya, Beck and Baca grants, and the other big grants, like the 500,000 acres from the Tierra Amarilla, our people wound up with less than twenty percent of the land they'd been granted over thirty before the United States took over the entire area.

An interesting thing about all this is that Texas, even though it had fought with Mexico over the territory, wound up treating the Spanish and Mexican heirs better than the California Commission and the surveyor general in New Mexico treated their grants.

By using different laws to settle the grants the government was not only ignoring the treaty it was ignoring international law and the equal protection and due process protections of the United States Constitution.

And to make it even worse for our ancestors, Congress passed a law in 1891 requiring New Mexico and Arizona grants and the ones in several other territories, other than California and Texas to be controlled by a court—the Court of Private Land Claims. Congress set up the CPLC so that the government could take even more land from our grants than the surveyors general had been taking.

You said that most of the California and Pueblo Indian land grant claims in New Mexico were settled within a few years but that the grants belonging to our people weren't decided until over forty years later, why weren't ours decided at the same time?

I think the best way to explain it is that the politicians in Washington were upset that our people hadn't left after the war—had refused to go to Mexico. It seems like the government had figured that by making life hard on our people they'd leave and the government would wind up with the millions of acres that were left behind. So, after our people refused to leave the government had to come up with another plan to take the millions of acres that belonged in our grants.

To give you an idea of just how far the government was willing to go to take land from our people and the Pueblos, we need to read something about Matthew Reynolds, who President Harrison had named U.S.

Attorney for New Mexico and who was required to work with justices of the Court of Private Land Claims. Listen to what's been said about him:

> Reynolds has been characterized as a man dedicated to the defeat of as many [land grant] claims as possible. If he could not defeat them, he strove to reduce the acreage confirmed as much as possible.

I need to stop for a moment and explain something. What I just read comes from an article which was referring to an annual report Reynolds had sent to the United States Attorney General in Washington D.C. in 1894. While I read the next few sentences I want you to imagine how Reynolds, a U.S. Attorney, could have had the guts to say what he did in an official report he was sending to the United States Attorney General. You want to know why I think he didn't mind saying what he did? From what the article was saying it's clear that he and the rest of the politicians in Washington didn't care who knew how they felt about our ancestors—or about the Pueblo Indians. The article goes on to say:

> In his 1894 Report to the Attorney General summing up the activities of his office, Reynolds boasted: "In New Mexico and Arizona the total area claimed in suits disposed of ... was 4,784,651 acres; amount confirmed, 779,611 acres; amount rejected and not confirmed 4,005,040 acres. The result is very gratifying to me ... you will notice that in most of the grants where judgments were obtained, the areas have been much reduced ... the amount of land saved ..."

We need to stop again—for a minute. Try to imagine before I start reading again what he might be going to say. What do you think a United States Attorney assigned to represent the United States before five Court of Private Land Claims judges who'd been appointed by the same President, in a case involving a treaty—would say next?

There's no way for me to guess, as young as I am, what he was going to say. But one thing I know for sure is that you wouldn't be asking me to guess if he was going to say what we believe he should be saying.

I'm proud of you Hijo. That's good—real good. Here's what he said:

> The amount of land saved in this way alone during the term of court just past will more than compensate the Government for the cost of this court and the salaries of its officials during the entire time for which it was created.

It's pretty clear, from what he was saying and considering who he was saying it to—that the real reason the court was established was to take as much of our ancestors land as it could.

Now it's time to let you in on why Reynolds and the CPLC did what they did in this particular case. Reynolds went on to say:

> The celebrated Cochití cases, four in number, were all tried, two defeated entirely and the other two so reduced in area as to make a complete victory for the Government, and this has relieved the public excitement growing out of fear that confirmations might be made so as to include the recently developed mining district covered by these claims.

We can't afford to forget that last part—where he's explaining that the Cochití cases were a "complete victory" for the government and had "relieved the public excitement." It's clear that the court intentionally decided the cases the way it did to make sure the mining district was protected. The public excitement he's talking about, Hijo, wasn't coming from our people, the grantees and their families, it was coming from the people the government was concerned about—the people in the Anglo mining communities.

We'll be talking about this some more in the months ahead but for right now I need to make it clear where the mining district he's talking about, the Cochiti Mining District, was located. It was around Bland, a ghost town today but in those days it was an important mining area and it was important to us for a reason that had nothing to do with mining. Remember that. We'll be talking about Bland some more later. (Fig.1).

Now I want to talk about a 2004 report published by the Government Accountability Office—the office that does investigations for Congress. Before 2005 it was called the Government Accounting Office. In 2000 New

Mexico Senators Pete Domenici and Jeff Bingaman announced that they and Congressman Tom Udall were requesting the GAO investigate whether the United States had complied with the terms of the Treaty of Guadalupe Hidalgo when the New Mexico land grants were being settled.

After the Senators announced that they were requesting an investigation there was a lot of excitement among the people whose families had been involved in land grants issues for generations—a lot of excitement that maybe there were finally going to be some official government answers about how our grants had been treated after the signing of the Treaty of Guadalupe Hidalgo.

After the report was published in June 2004 it didn't take long for our people to realize that important issues concerning violations of the Treaty; concerning violations of international law and denial of due process and equal protection; concerning property having been taken by the government without the owners having been compensated for it; concerning property having been taken from minors, married women and incompetent owners without guardians having been appointed and court orders entered allowing it to be taken; and concerning racial hatred against the grantees and their heirs—had all been ignored—intentionally ducked by the GAO.

We had hoped that there was finally going to be a fair investigation; that the report wasn't going to be just one more example of publicity seeking politicians bullshitting the public.

Should I take that out, Grandpa?

No, I heard someone else say it, I can't remember who, but I'm just quoting what I heard. Its not me talking. Leave it in. I might as well tell you something right now, you're going to find out anyway as you get older. Politicians only have three goals in life—to get elected; to get reelected; and to act like they care about the people who keep electing them. When Domenici and Bingaman announced that they were requesting an investigative report on the Treaty, and that Congressman, Udall was joining them, like I said before, we were excited. We believed we were finally going to get some answers. Ha!

We couldn't wait for the Final Report to come out. When it did it was just one more cover up of what the government had done and hadn't done. Once more we'd been suckered into putting our faith in believing the government was finally going to tell the truth—admit that the Treaty of Guadalupe Hidalgo had been intentionally violated.

If we had just stopped to think about it, we would have realized that the GAO couldn't have told the truth if it had wanted to. It would have had to admit what we've known for a century and a half—for 150 years: that the government intentionally converted millions of acres of Pueblo Indian, Spanish and Mexican land grants into public land. I'd come right out and say the government stole the land but we'd just have to take it out, so—why say it?

But you just said it, Grandpa. I'll go ahead and take it out.

Okay! That's probably the right thing to do, we don't want to get caught calling a liar a liar and a thief a thief if we can help it.

While the GAO was preparing its report it not only ignored our ancestors constitutional rights of due process and equal protection and international law, it ignored the fact, that we talked about earlier, that Congress passed different laws for California, Texas and New Mexico. And it refused to do any comparisons. It refused to compare how the people in other parts of the country, in the Oregon Territory for example, had been treated compared to how our ancestors were treated. And then, in the end, it had the nerve to say that the government had a duty to protect Indian grantees and their grants but didn't have a duty to protect our ancestors grants.

Before anyone starts to call us un-deserving, whining, son of ah-ah-never mind. Hopefully, they'll listen to what we have to say before they start calling us names.

You have anyone in particular you're leading up to?

Let me give you an example while we're still talking about the GAO Report. There's a man that works at the Forest Service by the name of Robert Cordts. He works at the Regional office in Albuquerque, at least he was working there when he wrote a so-called "Briefing Paper" dated June 15, 2004—eleven days after the GAO had advised Senators Domenici and Bingaman and Congressman Udall that the Final Report was being released. Just think, Hijo, it only took this Cordts fellow eleven days after the release of the GAO Report to prepare a Forest Service "Briefing Paper" praising the GAO and the report. Read the part that's highlighted in brown.

The Region's view on the recently issued Report is that it is a highly credible independent source confirming the legal foundation of the subject National Forests; and, therefore the USDA—Forest Service as the agency with jurisdiction and proper authority as stewards for administering these National Forest Lands.

I'd love to talk to that Cordts fellow, who had the title, Regional Lands Claims Specialist, at the time he wrote his "Briefing Paper." I'd like to point out to him how absolutely worthless the GAO Report really is. But I'm sure it would be a waste of time because, from what he wrote we can tell that he isn't the type of person who would let any facts get in the way of his opinions. Especially after he said that the report had confirmed the legal foundation of the subject [Carson, Cebolla and Santa Fe] National Forests.

After Mike and I talked about Cordts "Briefing Paper," I asked him what he thought about it. He started by saying that he had loaded the GAO report on his computer and searched some of the terms in Cordts' "Briefing Paper." He said he looked for : "Santa Fe National Forest," "Carson National Forest," "legal foundation of the subject National Forest," "stewards for administering these National Forest Lands," words Cordts had used in his so-called "Briefing Paper." Mike said that every search he made using those words ended with the message, "Reader has finished searching the document. No matches were found."

Just think, Cordts was telling his supervisors and the employees of the Albuquerque Region that the GAO was "a highly credible independent source" that had confirmed "the legal foundation of the … subject National Forests." None of what he was claiming the report was saying, Hijo, was even mentioned in the report. There doesn't appear to be a single word of truth in what Cordts was claiming. The report didn't even mentioned the Forest Service.

Here's a letter we found that was written three days after the GAO released its report that might have had something to do with Cordts writing what he did. It's from Senators Domenici and Bingaman to "Dear Wayne":

> You should be receiving shortly from the General Accounting Office (GAO) its final report entitled Treaty of Guadalupe Hidalgo:

Findings and Possible Options Regarding Longstanding Community Land Grant Claims in New Mexico (GAO-04-59) …

> This report has been some four years in the making, and it is a comprehensive investigation into the Treaty and its implementation in New Mexico. The report is based on an extensive legal analysis, archival research, and interviews with land grant heirs, historians, and scholars, and numerous comments from the public. The report contains a lot of new information, and we too are just beginning to study and reflect on it …

Before I forget—I was told that the man that letter was addressed to, Wayne Thornton, passed away recently and I don't want anyone thinking I was trying to disrespect him by reading the letter. I only mentioned his name because the letter was written to him.

Mike and I can't believe that Senators Domenici and Bingaman would send a letter to the Forest Service, three days after the GAO had published its report, saying: "This report … is a comprehensive investigation into the Treaty and its implementation in New Mexico," knowing when they were writing it that what they were claiming couldn't have been further from the truth. Long before they sent that letter, Hijo, the two of them had secretly agreed with the GAO that it didn't even have to investigate the Treaty or its implementation.

Did Mike or any of your other friends find any "Dear Grantee" or "Dear Heirs to the Grants" letters from Senators Domenici or Bingaman, explaining to the people who had been affected by the land grant history that the GAO "had completed its comprehensive investigation into the Treaty and its implementation?"

No, but we did try unsuccessfully to find out whether Domenici or Bingaman had bothered to question Cordts factually incorrect conclusions.

Mike did run across another interesting letter though. It was written by Harv Forsgren, who was the Southwest Regional Forester from 2002 until 2007. He had written Congressman Udall on July 8, 2004, a little over a month after the GAO Report came out. Other than moving his paragraphs around his letter was an almost word for word copy of the Cordts "Briefing Paper."

Here is the first paragraph of his letter to Congressman Udall:

Thank you for your June 7, 2004 update on the recent final report by the General Accounting Office (GAO) entitled *Treaty of Guadalupe Hidalgo: Findings and Possible Options Regarding Long-standing Community Land Grant Claims in New Mexico* (GAO-04-59; June 2004) and providing an opportunity for us to share our thoughts.

I've compared the two letters, Grandpa, and like you said they are almost exactly alike in what they say. I showed them to my teacher and he said that it was ridiculous for a Regional Forester to have fallen for what Cordts had said, but what was even worse was that he sent it to Congressman Udall who was one of the requesters and who, if he had bothered to read Forsgren's letter, should have known immediately that it had a fake conclusion. What part of the country did the Southwest Region cover at the time Forsgren wrote the letter, Grandpa?

He was in charge of the National Forests in Arizona, New Mexico and the panhandles of Texas and Oklahoma, Hijo.

What happened here, Hijo, probably happens all the time with the government: a politicrat takes it upon himself to make up information and then sends it out as an official analysis to supervisors and members of Congress who don't even bother to read their mail and who then rely on the information to make their future decisions.

Was there anything else in that letter that would explain why the Forest Service was so interested in the GAO Report, since it hadn't even bothered to mention the Forest Service?

Unfortunately. In Cordts "Briefing Paper he said:

Options that would involve the transfer of federal lands would only tend to continue to promote the belief that lands were unduly lost by land grant communities at the behest of the federal government, and it is difficult to see that there would be a reasonable and agreeable process to provide an equitable solution to address all perceptions of inequity by land grant heirs.

Which appears to have been interpreted by Forester Forsgren as:

> Options that would transfer federal lands could also put at risk
> the title and interest of the U.S. beyond those lands at issue in the
> GAO report, in addition to having a detrimental impact on effective
> and efficient management of remaining National Forest Lands.

There you have it. Never mind that millions of the very acres these letters are talking about had been unlawfully converted from land grants to the
public lands. The Forest Service, in these letters, was lobbying Congress to
protect "its land " from the heirs of the original grantees who had lost the
land to begin with. Apparently, since we could find no follow-up letters
from Senators Domenici and Bingaman and Congressman Udall, they
were all in agreement with what the Forest Service was saying in Cordts
"Briefing Paper" and Forsgren's letter.

*Were any "Dear Grantee" or "Dear Heirs to the Grants" letters from Senators
Domenici or Bingaman or Congressman Udall explaining the GAO Report to any
of our grant people ever found, Grandpa?*

Not that we know of. As if what the Forest Service was thinking after
the report came out isn't bad enough, we need to discuss who the GAO
report stated it was dealing with. Just who our people were—are.

The report, in referring to the Spanish and Mexican grantees and their
heirs didn't bother to refer to them as Spanish and Mexican grantees and
heirs—it apparently found it easier to refer to them, us, as "non-Indians."

Where do you see that, Grandpa?

At page 156.

Don't get me wrong, I'm not saying anything against the Indian
grantees—I'm glad they've been as successful as they have. But for the GAO
to refer to our ancestors, the Spanish and Mexican grantees and their heirs
as "non-Indians" shows that the government believed the Pueblo Indian
grantees were supposed to be treated different from the Spanish and Mexican grantees and that it didn't have to concern itself with our ancestors
when it was writing the report.

While we're talking about this, a question comes to my mind, Hijo.
What would the reaction be if a GAO report said that during the last
100 years the government had acted appropriately by awarding the

Anglo settlers over $130,000,000 million dollars and 1,700,000 acres of land while refusing to award any money or land to the non-Anglo settlers? In the six years since the report came out we haven't heard one word from any member of Congress criticizing the GAO for classifying the people protected by the Treaty as Indian and non-Indian. Apparently Congress is comfortable with the GAO classifying Spanish and Mexican people, our people, as non-Indians—at least until the next election when once again they'll try to show an interested in how all us non-Indians will be voting.

But really—what can we say? In the beginning the government planned to kill all the Indians and wound up killing most of them. Then it allowed Blacks to be brought here as slaves, and later, at the end of the Civil War, General Sherman said each freed slave could receive forty acres and a mule and the government actually patented over 400,000 acres to freed slaves—only to take it all back when the white plantation owners started complaining. And then after all of that the government came west and took over 30,000,000 acres of Guadalupe Hidalgo Treaty protected Indian and non-Indian grants without offering a penny of compensation for any of it.

At least Sherman's Special Field Order 15 offered freed Black slaves forty acres and a mule. Forty-five years later, after thousands of our men had joined the New Mexico Volunteers and fought for the Union the government turned right around and took our forty acres—and starved our mules.

Now that I've mentioned the New Mexico Volunteers it's as good a time as any to discuss the Civil War.

At the beginning of the war, Texas (that just happened to have been paid $10,000,000 to become a state) joined the confederacy, captured Fort Bliss, and headed north hoping to capture Fort Union and continue on to the Pacific.

The government in Santa Fe realizing a confederate army from Texas was heading north became concerned. Governor Henry Connelly believing the Union troops assigned to New Mexico might not be able to defeat the Texans called for volunteers and over 5,000 of our ancestors voluntarily joined the Union Army.

Even though our Spanish, Mexican and Pueblo Indian volunteers were supplied with out-dated weapons and worn out clothing and equipment they were still willing to and did fight for the Union. Their first battle was near Ft. Craig, south of Socorro.

While at Ft. Craig and under the command of Kit Carson, they were ordered to march north on the west side of the Río Grande to support the regular troops that had already crossed the river and were fighting at Valverde. Since our volunteers were inexperienced, Colonel Carson held them back to watch the fight for a while before joining the experienced Regular army troops. Late in the day after Carson and his troops had joined in the battle and while it was appearing that the Union troops were holding their own, Colonel Canby, the Union commander, ordered Carson to retreat across the river and return to Ft. Craig.

Listen to what someone said later about how Colonel Canby had ordered the retreat.

> Kit Carson and his volunteers couldn't believe Canby's order. From the point of view on the Union far right the battle was faring well. In fact, they felt they were on the verge of victory. Capt. Rafael Chacon, fighting with Carson, wrote that he could not understand the signals of retreat. "We had penetrated the enemy zone and considered that our charge had won the battle."

After the battle at Valverde the Texans moved north toward Albuquerque hoping to increase their supplies and find more horses and mules as they had lost most of their supplies and animals at Valverde.

Canby sent word to Albuquerque to destroy or hide all the supplies so the Texans couldn't get them.

After Albuquerque, General Henry Sibley, feeling quite confident, marched his Texans to Santa Fe without having to fire a shot.

Colorado Volunteers, who numbered more than a thousand, and who had earlier been told the Texans were moving north from El Paso marched from Denver to Fort Union in less than two weeks arriving about the same time General Sibley was setting up camp in Santa Fe. The Colorado Volunteers moved west out of Fort Union and met the Texans at Apache Canyon on March 26.

Two days later the Texans and the Colorado Volunteers fought again at Glorieta Pass. They fought all day and at sundown the battle was pretty even with each side losing less than 50 dead and 100 wounded. Although neither side knew it at the time the Civil War in New Mexico was as good as over.

Before dawn and without the troops from either side knowing it Colorado Major John Chivington, guided by Lt. Colonel Manuel Chávez of the New Mexico Volunteers, took between 400 and 500 troops across the top of Glorieta Mesa to try and get behind the Texans. Around noon Chávez spotted the rebel's supply train surrounded by several hundred horses and mules.

In the next few hours Chávez, Chivington, and the troops destroyed the wagons and supplies and killed the horses and mules, ending any chance the Texans had to fight again.

If Lt. Col. Chávez and Major Chivington had not found and destroyed the Confederate camp the Texans might have captured Fort Union and gone on to the Pacific. Wiping out the Texan's camp ended the Civil War in New Mexico.

Grandpa, I don't know that much about military rank but when I told my teacher what you were going to be talking about he said I must have gotten it backwards—he said Major Chivington should have been guiding Lt. Colonel Chávez, not the other way around—and that there was no way Chivington could have been the guide since he was from Colorado and would have had no way of knowing where he was or where he needed to go.

You're teacher has it right. Chávez never got credit for what he did.

I was told that after the battle at Apache Canyon a Texas officer said that even though they'd felt like they'd won the battle—when they got back to where they'd left their supplies and saw what had happened—saw that everything they'd left behind had been destroyed and all the animals had been killed—they realized that even though they might have won the battle—it was clear they'd lost the war.

As you might expect, Hijo, the volunteers never got credit for fighting for the Union. I guess those who'd normally hand out credit considered it wasn't necessary to give credit to a bunch of Indians and non-Indians. But what happened after Apache Canyon was really no different than what happened after the battle at Valverde. After Valverde Colonel Sibley sent word to Washington saying the loss was because the "Mexicans" had cut and run when the battle was actually lost because he'd ordered the troops to retreat at a time when it looked like they were winning.

The battle at Apache Canyon may have ended the Civil War in New Mexico, but it didn't end the military service of hundreds of our men who stayed in the army and were ordered to protect the wagon trains coming across the Santa Fe Trail—wagon trains carrying the speculators, lawyers and politicians who once they got here turned right around and stole millions of acres of our grants.

You said the other day that 5,000 of the soldiers fighting against the Texans were our people—our ancestors?

At least 5,000. There were 6,500 New Mexico volunteers fighting for the Union and most of them were our people.

I hope we have some proof of that? It would be important.

One thing you need to learn Hijo, is if I say something—Mike and I will have something to back it up. We might not always read what we have—but we'll have it if we need it. Here's an article that talks about Civil War Volunteers:

> By many the people are looked upon as foreign and not in harmony with American institutions. It is strange that this objective should arise in a land which absorbs half a million of foreigners every year, and which manages to assimilate the very worst elements of continental Europe. It should be remembered that New Mexico was acquired in 1848, that all of its inhabitants except the oldest were born on American soil, and that its people belonged to a sister republic with institutions similar to ours, and so needed no new education in free government. For almost half a century they have been electing their legislatures, making their laws, and carrying on their local government under the American system.

> The people have shown themselves as loyal as any in the nation. During the rebellion out of her total population of 93,567 she sent 6,561 into the army. Her volunteers fought at Valverde, Peralta, and on other fields; and at Glorieta, together with their comrades of Colorado, defeated the enemy and turned back the column which was advancing northerly from Texas with the intention of cutting

off the Pacific Slope from the remainder of the country. The value of that service to the Union cause can scarcely be overestimated. The total number of volunteers from the Territories now composing the six new States of North Dakota, South Dakota, Washington, Montana, Idaho, and Wyoming was 1,170. Colorado sent but 4,903, and Nebraska, Oregon, and Nevada, taken together, did not contribute but 6,047.

Sorry, Grandpa, but I don't really understand what was going on. New Mexico had 6,561 volunteers fighting for the Union—more than any of the states we'll be comparing yet our soldiers continued to be treated like they really didn't count. It sounds like the government hated our people so much that no matter what they did they weren't going to get any credit for it. Why were they disliked so much? They were fighting alongside the regular Army and were still being treated like foreigners.

I'm glad you said it that way. Here's something that you're going to find interesting. Start here—where I'm pointing.

If we look at the foreign element in the population we will find it smaller in New Mexico than anywhere else in the Country except in certain Southern States.

A comparison with Territories recently admitted is instructive in this regard. The figures are from the 1880 census, which are the latest we have.

New Mexico contained 7,219 foreign-born inhabitants to 100,000 native-born, or 7 to 100; Washington had 26 foreign to 100 native; Wyoming had 39 foreign to 100 native; Montana had 41 foreign to 100 native; Idaho had 44 foreign to 100 native; Dakota had 62 foreign to 100 native.

Even in the older States, New York and Michigan had 31 to 100; Massachusetts, 33; Rhode Island, 36; Wisconsin, 44; California, 51, and Minnesota, 52. So that New Mexico looms up as an especially Native American community.

But to the uninformed the large number of voters of Spanish descent is looked upon as a grave misfortune. There could not be a greater mistake. It is the possession of that conservative element in connection with the energetic and enterprising American from the East which gives New Mexico her special advantages as a self-governing community over most other Territories.

This makes me feel better, Grandpa—but at the same time it makes me feel a little sad. There's no excuse why our people were treated the way they were. At least Governor Prince was nice enough to show them some respect—prove they weren't really foreigners. But it's tough hearing how bad they were being treated. When you were saying that after the battle at Apache Canyon our people didn't go home— that they were sent out to protect the Santa Fe Trail and wound up protecting the lawyers, politicians, and speculators coming across the trail, only to have them turn around and steal from the grants—that's terrible.

You're lucky, really. I'd left out the part about how, when they were protecting the Trail, a lot of them died there; freezing to death in the winter and dying from the heat and a lack of water in the summer. It gets even worse when you realize that the ones that survived guarding the Santa Fe Trail found out later that the people they'd been ordered to protect were the very people stealing their land.

What we've said about the government really isn't anything. Wait until I get around to explaining how the government wound up with millions of acres of Treaty of Guadalupe Hidalgo protected land—and was bragging about it.

-5-

We Were Trespassers On Our Own Land

I'm glad we're back to talking about our family, what we were talking about last time was depressing. I hope today is going to be better.

Today will be better, Hijo, but, unfortunately, it will get worse—a lot worse—before we're through.

Can't we skip that part—just leave it out? Only talk about our family? I mean even the part about our family is depressing, except when you talked about things like drunk chickens.

No, Hijo, we can't leave that part out. It's at least as important as our family history, you'll see.

By the time I was fourteen my brothers and sisters were old enough to help with the farm and the animals, so I started looking for a job.

The first time I went looking for a job I went to Alamosa, Colorado with my sister and her husband. We got hired working on a farm that was owned by a real nice Japanese couple. I kinda remember that their names were George and Ruth Casimoro. I got along with them real good and it wasn't long before they took me out of the fields and gave me a job irrigating. They had me irrigate at night so it wouldn't interfere with the people hoeing weeds during the day. When I started irrigating they raised my pay from forty cents to a dollar an hour but they told me not to tell the other workers. Since I worked at night it was hard to sleep during the day because all the other people were around the shacks we lived in. Besides working nights they had me sharpening hoes at noon when the workers would stop for lunch.

The next year I went back to Colorado with some friends because that was the closest place where we might find work. We went to a company that

50

was cutting trees and sawing them into lumber. When we pulled up outside my friends said I should be the one to go in.

When I asked if there was any work, the girl handed me an application and told me to fill it out. I printed my name. Then it asked for my address and I put "Canjilón." When I looked at the next question I realized it wanted to know where I had worked before. I was so nervous I didn't even remember working in Alamosa. Even if I had remembered I wouldn't have known how to spell their name. After looking at the paper for a couple minutes I told the girl I would bring it back the next day.

I was embarrassed that I couldn't even fill out an application for a job. It hit me right then that I had messed up by not being able to go to school.

As I was walking out the door I realized my friends would ask me what had happened so as soon as I got in the car, before they could even talk, I told them there weren't any jobs—that we needed to go home.

I found a job a couple weeks later right there in Canjilón working for Howard Darnell, a logger. Since I was only about fifteen I had to lie about my age. I'm sure he knew I was to young—he could tell just by looking at me. But one thing that was on my side was that I was taller than all the other guys. After I had worked for him for almost a year he told me he liked the way I worked and asked me if I would become a crew boss. I told him I didn't want to but I didn't tell him why. It was because I knew if I took the job and the other workers would find out that I couldn't read or write too good they'd probably laugh at me. And at that time I had a bad problem. I couldn't talk right. When I would get nervous or be around someone I didn't know I'd stutter. Then I would get mad because I couldn't talk right and that would just make me start stuttering worse and pretty soon I couldn't sa-sa-say anything. See? Just talking about it made me do it.

By that time I was pretty good at fighting and had a little temper so I knew if the other workers would start laughing about the way I talked there'd be a fight and I'd probably win the fight but I'd lose the job. Since the job and the money were more important than kicking someone's butt for laughing at me I didn't take the position. He asked me a lot of times to be the boss, but I never did.

In those years I mostly worked for loggers. Besides Darnell, I worked for Bill Thomas, Leonard Jensen, and Ernie Darst. I was lucky that almost all the work I did for Darnell and the others was close enough to Canjilón that I could live at home. That was great because I didn't have to pay rent, I saved money on gas, and I could still help my mother and father.

I remember one time when I was about seventeen and had saved up some money I told my mother that I was going to put electricity in our house. She went into a panic, started saying, "No. No. Don't do it."

When I asked her why she said they couldn't afford the five dollars a month that it would cost. She was scared to death that if I put in electricity they wouldn't be able to pay for it.

Over the next several years I ran water to the house and added a bathroom and a new roof. There was no way my parents could have afforded it while raising all us children with their only income being from the crops, selling the lambs and calves in the fall and the wool in the spring. They were still having to trade with their neighbors for what they needed.

Those years I worked for the logging companies, cutting logs, planting trees, building roads—were good years. I made good money and got along good with Darnell and the others. I could tell they liked me, respected me. I could tell that they weren't prejudiced—they weren't at all like the bosses at the Forest Service.

That was the first time I had worked with Anglos and I was beginning to realize that they were good people. Once I got to know them I realized that they really weren't any different from us. They had their good days and bad ones—good weeks and bad—just like we did. They treated me just like they treated the Anglos that worked for them. I learned a lot about people during that time that I hadn't known before.

My father had told me a lot of times—since I was a little boy, how bad our family had been treated—how our land had been taken. Ever since I'd quit school I'd seen how he and the other Spanish people in Canjilón had been treated by the Forest Service. I had come to believe that that was the way we were going to be treated by all Anglos.

Now that I'm telling you about this. I can remember times when I would see my father with tears all over his face. He was a big man—strong, he wasn't afraid of anything in the world—other than the Rangers that had given him and his father—and the rest of the people, so much trouble that it had gotten to the point that he was always afraid what they might do to hurt our family. I even remember him saying that the way our families had been treated by the government over the years—we might as well have lived with our hands tied, it couldn't have been any worse. As I got older I started to see why he was so afraid of the people from the Forest Service. It was so bad that every time he would see a green uniform, green trucks, right away he'd get nervous. Since he knew how his father, grandfathers and great-grandfathers had been treated and how he'd been treated he was always thinking that someday the government would come to our house, like it had to his father's, and take everything we had.

He had heard over and over when he was growing up how the government had shown up in Cañones and told the families they only had 1,400 acres—that the 147,500 acres they had depended on for generations didn't belong to them anymore.

One morning when I was getting ready to leave for work I saw that he was acting real nervous. When I asked him what was wrong he said that a man was supposed to have come from Española the day before to buy our calves and that he didn't show up. I asked him why it made him so nervous and he said he needed the money to pay the bank —that he was going to be in trouble because he couldn't pay. I asked him how much he owed and he said $300. I took him to Chama and paid the bill and on the way back he had tears all the way home. He kept telling me, over and over, how sorry he was—how bad a father we must think he was that he couldn't even take care of his bills without our help.

I don't think I ever told you this, Hijo, but my father and mother never owned a car or truck before the late 50's when I bought an old pickup and gave it to them. As soon as my father saw it he asked what I was going to do with it. When I told him I'd bought it for him he said there was no way he was going to learn to drive. Sometimes, when I would get home early from work, and on weekends, I'd ask him to let me teach him how to drive and he'd always say no.

One day I finally talked him into getting behind the steering wheel and I showed him how to work the clutch and the gears. When he finally tried to drive he let the clutch out too fast and we started bouncing across the pasture. I could see he was heading straight for a ditch and I yelled for him to hit the brakes. He grabbed the steering wheel with both hands and started yelling, "whoa, whoa," and drove right off into the ditch. He never tried to drive again.

When I think about how hard life was for my parents it makes me sad. We need to change what we're talking about, discuss something else.

One day while I was leaning back against a tree eating my lunch, Bill Thomas, who I was working for at the time, came to where I was. I was eating some jerky and he asked me what kind it was. I told him it was elk. He said he loved elk meat and asked if I could get him some the next time it was legal to hunt. He said he'd even pay me for it. I told him I wouldn't take his money but that I would get him some. The next morning I told him I had killed an elk calf on my way home and had sliced it and put it out to dry—that I'd bring him some as soon as it had dried.

He said, "But, Juan, aren't you afraid of getting caught?"

I asked him why—I wasn't doing anything wrong, why should I get caught?

"But, it's not hunting season, Juan," he said.

I told him, like I said the other day, that my father and all the old timers around Canjilón used to say that our ancestors had been here for hundreds of years—that Spain had given our people the right to use the land long before the Americans had come—that the most we were doing was trespassing on our own land. He kinda laughed, shook his head, and walked away. After that he used to come by every once in a while—even after I had stopped working for him, an ask if I'd mind trespassing again—that his supply of jerky was running low.

I asked him one time if he had to ask permission to plant a garden behind his house and he said, "Hell no." Then I asked him why not and he said, "Damn-it, Juan; you know why—because I own the damn place."

"Well!" I said, "I don't have to ask permission to get meat from the forest either, cause we owned the damn place for eighty years, until the government came along and st, st, sto—took it."

Later on, when he was logging in an area that required him to drive by my house every day, he stopped by. "Damn big pile of fire-wood you have there, Juan," he said, "how may cords you guess you have?"

I told him I figured there were at least 350—400 cords.

"Musta been a hell of a piece of land your ancestors owned," he said, as he was driving off.

Grandpa I want to thank you for taking the time to tell our history. I know our family's going to appreciate it. There's no other way we could have kept our history alive without you sitting here telling it.

I'm happy to do it, Hijo. It's just that reliving my life makes me sad when I start remembering all the things that happened. Not everyone's going to agree with what I have to say—but it needs to be said.

I can tell from watching you as you tell it, how hard some of it must be. Can you answer one question for me before we stop for the day?

Sure.

I keep wondering about those chickens and how they acted when they got drunk. Did you ever feed your chickens mula when you were growing up?

Yeah—a time or two.

That's all, a time or two?

Well, let me put it this way, in order to be more accurate about how many times I gave mula to my chickens, I'd have to lie. And since I said when we started that I was only going to tell the truth, I'm not going to say anymore about that than I already have.

-6-
From 810,000 Acres To Less Than 5,000—
Overnight

Before I say more about when I was growing up I need to say what I know about the Juan Bautista Valdez and San Joaquín del Río de Chama Grants—and the grants around them.

My third great-grandfather, Juan Bautista Baldez, that's the way they spelled our name when he was born in Santa Cruz in 1749, he was already 58 years old when Spain gave him and the others the grant about nine miles west of Abiquiú—where Cañones is today. He and the other men whose names aren't on the grant papers—had already cleared about a mile of the land by the time the grant was made.

The grant papers described the boundaries as the Cañones Creek on the east, which was also the west boundary of the Polvadera Grant; the Martinez or Piedra Lumbre Grant as it became to be known, on the north; and the headwaters of the Cañones Creek, which was also the north boundary of the Baca Location Number One Grant, on the south. The west boundary was described as the Cerro Blanco, which meant white hill and which was a little over 20 miles west of Cañones. The grant was supposed to be three leagues, almost 8 miles, from north to south. (Fig.1; see also, figs. 7, 8, 9).

The Cerro Blanco was a well known feature, could be seen from miles away. The Surveyor General that had approved the San Joaquín del Río de Chama Grant on December 17, 1872, used the names Cejita Blanca and Cuestecita Blanca, which mean the same as Cerro Blanco, to describe its west boundary. The San Joaquín and the Juan Bautista grants had the same west boundary and even though slightly different names were used, they clearly identified the same hill. Even though the surveyor general was able to find and identify the Cejita Blanca and the Cuestecita Blanca as the west boundary of the San Joaquín Grant in 1872, the Court of Private Land Claims and the Corps of Engineers acted as though they had no clue where Cerro Blanco was twenty-seven years later. They identified a small hill within a mile of Cañones as the west boundary which caused it to be reduced from 147,000 to less than 1,500 acres.

Witnesses living on the Juan Bautista at the time of the hearing testified before the Court of Private Land Claims that the west boundary was ten to fifteen miles west of Cañones—west of the small hill the court used as the west boundary. The court ignored the testimony and the survey of the San Joaquín del Río de Chama and placed the boundary where it remains to this day, just west of Cañones.

Between the time the Juan Bautista Valdez Grant was established in 1807 and the final hearing before the CPLC in 1898, hundreds of people were living in four settlements on the grant, three of them west of the boundary the CPLC used. The original grant, like I just said, was for more than 147,500 acres but after the CPLC got through taking what it wanted the grant only had 1,468 acres. Our ancestors, and the other settlers who had lived on the Juan Bautista for over eighty years, were cheated out of more than 146,000 acres. But that's not really that bad when you consider that the people living on the San Joaquín had it a lot worse. There had been thirty-nine grantees named in the original San Joaquín grant in 1808 and even though the Surveyor General had approved it for 472,736 acres in 1872 the CPLC came along thirty-three years later and cut it to 1,423 acres—cheating the people out of more than 471,000 acres.

What were the names of the other settlements on the Juan Bautista at the time the court took the land, Grandpa?

Coyote, El Rito de las Encinias and Río Puerco—and that still doesn't include the families that were living outside the settlements. The 1880 U.S. census shows that there were over 250 people living in Cañones and Coyote, it was spelled Collote back then—more than 500 people living on the grant in 1880.

My father told me that when he was little he had heard that there were more than 400 people living on the San Joaquín when the government took the 470,000 acres, leaving the people with only three or four acres each at the same time it was giving away 160 acre homesteads to settlers coming from the east.

I need to read something an important government employee had to say about the amount of grazing land needed to survive during that time.

> The grass is so scanty that the herdsman must have a large area for the support of his stock. In general a quarter section of land alone is of no value to him; the pasturage it affords is entirely inadequate to the wants of a herd that the poorest man needs for his support.

> Four square miles may be considered as the minimum amount necessary for a pasturage farm, and a still greater amount is necessary for the larger part of the lands; that is, pasturage farms, to be of any practicable value, must be at least 2,560 acres, and in many districts they must be much larger.

Two years after John Wesley Powell wrote that, President James Garfield appointed him Director of the United States Geological Survey. I'd think a man that was that important would have been listened to, Hijo. If 160 acres was as worthless as John Wesley Powell said,—leaving our people with three or four acres each was—never mind—you'd just have to take it out.

Some people might say that if our heirs didn't like what the government was doing with our grants they could have applied for a homestead. But keep in mind what Powell was saying about 160 acres. There was no way our people could afford to move to a homestead. Once they'd apply they'd lose their interest in the grant—for a lousy 160 acres somewhere else—no way. And we've already discussed what happened when our people did apply for a homestead—how the General Land Office would cheat them out of the land; besides, we just got through reading where Powell was saying a family needed 2,560 acres—the amount of acreage in sixteen homesteads—just to survive.

We need to talk about how our grants wound up with less than 1,500 acres each while the Piedra Lumbre and Polvadera were approved for 49,748 and 35,700 acres. All four of these grants were next to each other yet two got more than they had claimed and our two were left with almost nothing.

To make it even worse the census records show that while there were settlements on our grants with hundreds of settlers—the Piedra Lumbre and Polvadera, which were grazing grants, had very few people living on them. (Fig. 15).

I don't get it, Grandpa, how could four grants in the same area wind up with such different amounts of land?

Before I try to answer that I need to talk about some of the other grants that existed at that time—talk about the Sanjon de los Moquelumnos, Santa Margarita Grant, Santiago de Santa Ana and Simi Grants in California. The government has said that Spain and Mexico had limits on the size of private land grants—that no one person could be granted more than eleven leagues of land.

The California Land Grant Commission confirmed the Sanjon de los Moquelumnos Grant with over 100,000 acres to the heirs of Anastasio Chabolla. Since the documents show that the land went to his heirs it's clear that other than the private lots granted to the individual heirs the remainder of the 100,000 acres were common lands available to the heirs like most of the grants here in New Mexico.

The Santa Margarita y Los Floresta Grant confirmed to Pio Pico in 1879 for 133,000 acres and the Santiago de Santa Ana Grant confirmed by the California Commission to Bernardo, et al., for 157,000 acres are examples of grants that were confirmed for more than 20 leagues each. In each case the families wound up with over 100,000 acres to be used by the heirs of the original grantees.

Now we can get to one of the most interesting grants we found in California—the Simi Grant. The Commission confirmed it in three different tracts to José de la Guerra y Noriega, all together the three tracts had 339,000 acres—but that's not all, de la Guerra also had eight other grants confirmed by the California Commission for a total of 538,000 acres. Like we discussed before, under the California Commission system grants were treated very different there than they were here in New Mexico.

It might help, Hijo, if we take a little time and name some of the Texas grants. Spain granted Juan José Balli the 127,000 acre Hinojosa de Balli Grant in 1790. Since the United States had given Texas millions of dollars to become a state and since it had already become a state, Texas wasn't required to have a surveyor general or the Court of Private Land Claims settle its Spanish and Mexican grants. Texas was allowed to set up its own system for settling grants.

Jose Narciso Cubazos received over 600,000 acres in grants from Spain, the largest being the El Agostadero de San Juan de Carricitos. All his grants were confirmed—but not by the United States—they were confirmed by the state of Texas.

Here's something else that we found interesting, Hijo. In 1821 Mexico won its independence from Spain and shortly after that it began allowing Americans to settle in the Texas territory and the Mexican State of Coahuila. Americans coming from the States were allowed 4,428 acres of grazing land and 177 acres of crop land upon their promise to obey the laws and Constitution of Mexico and become Catholic.

Later Mexico used an impresario system which allowed any person bringing a hundred families to Texas to have five leagues, 22,140 acres of grazing land and 885 acres of crop lands. Mexico even allowed women to have grants—something the Congress refused to allow in New Mexico until the Homestead Act was passed in 1862 and even then they couldn't have a homestead if they were married, but we'll talk about that later.

To add an insult to what was happening in New Mexico compared to what was happening and had happened in other states and territories, I need to read the first sentence of the Supreme Court decision in *Río Arriba Land and Cattle Company v. United States*:

> Assuming, but without in any manner deciding, that Gov. Allen-caster had full power to make the grant in any quantity and in any manner he saw proper, we think it clear that he did not, and did not intend, to make a grant of nearly half a million of acres to the original applicants, in common, and that the Alcalde did not so understand it, and did not attempt to deliver juridical possession of such

a tract, but only of the various allotments that were made petitioners in severalty.

The Supreme Court decided the *Rio Arriba Land and Cattle* case on the
same day it decided the notorious *Sandoval* case and kicked our people off
all but 1,422 acres of the San Joaquin that had been approved twenty-five
years earlier by the Surveyor General.

For the Court to be saying what I just read it had to know it was ignoring all the California and Texas grants we just talked about—ignoring that
the Maxwell Grant had been approved by Congress with 1,714,764 acres;
that the Sangre de Cristo had been approved with over 998,780 acres.
Ignoring that the Pablo Montoya was approved for 655,468 acres; that the
Tierra Amarilla had originally been granted over 500,000 acres and ignoring that the Preston Beck, Jr. had been approved for 318,699 acres.

Where were those justices, Hijo, when the 100,000, 300,000, 500,000
acre grants in California, Texas and New Mexico were being confirmed?
They were intentionally ignoring facts that they had to have known about
the size of the grants.

How could the justices of the Supreme Court say in the first sentence of
their decision say that it was clear that Governor Allencaster did not intend
to grant nearly 500,000 acres to the thirty-nine grantees of the San Joaquín
del Río de Chama Grant when there was all the evidence that we just mentioned about the size of the grants in California, Texas and New Mexico?

Hopefully, before we finish our history it will be clear why the Supreme
Court was willing to say and do what it did.

*But, Grandpa, that still doesn't answer how and why the Piedra Lumbre and
the Polvadera were able to keep their land while our grants were losing their land.*
(Figs. 14. 15).

I need to wait a while before I answer that. I don't have the complete
answer to that yet. But we'll find out why and I'll tell you when we do. I do
have something to say though about an excuse the government and the
GAO used to explain how the boundary descriptions in our grant papers
were impossible to follow. Here's one of those excuses they liked to use,
Hijo:

Land boundaries were defined with reference to terrestrial land-marks or the adjoining property, and because these markers were often difficult to locate, Spanish and Mexican land records some-times lacked the geographic precision of the U. S. system.

So far as the description of the Juan Bautista was concerned what we just read is nothing more than a wheelbarrow full of ah, ah,—bullshit. I'm sorry, Hijo, you better take that out. Anyway, all the boundaries of the Juan Bautista and the San Joaquín were easy to locate, easy to find. The government was able to find the boundaries of the Piedra Lumbre and Polvadera and our grants were right next to them—touching them. The government didn't want to find the Cerro Blanco—it's that simple. And, if the CPLC didn't want to find it—why should the GAO care where it was?

Now we need to turn to how unfair it was for the government to use the descriptions of the grants as an excuse. I'll use the boundaries of the Juan Bautista and the Piedra Lumbre to explain what happened since they're right next to each other and have a common boundary.

The west boundary of the Juan Bautista, the Cerro Blanco, was the only boundary that could have caused a problem. So the government jumped on that one, saying it must have meant a small foothill west of, and within a mile of Cañones, rather than the white cliff testified to by the witnesses as having been ten or fifteen miles in the direction that the sun goes down. To use the small foothill the CPLC not only had to ignore the testimony at the hearing it had to ignore the three settlements west of the little hill, and it had to ignore the 1880 census—even the 1870 census showed that more than 140 people were living on the Juan Bautista at that time.

Now let's look at the boundaries of the Piedra Lumbre. The grant document said the east boundary was "the stoney hill looking toward Abiquiú." You've been to Abiquiú a lot of times, Hijo, do you think you could find "the stoney hill looking toward Abiquiú?"

From all the stoney hills facing Abiquiú it would have been impossible for the government to know which one it was. There are stoney hills in every direction, two and three in some directions, it could have been anywhere.

The government didn't have any trouble finding the boundaries it wanted to find. The problem was that it only found the boundaries it wanted to find. It found the ones for the Piedra Lumbre—and the Polvadera—but couldn't find the ones for the San Joaquín and Juan Bautista.

The Piedra Lumbre description went on to say: To the west, "Mesa Prieta of the Río Puerco; "to the north," some small red bluffs;"to the south, "the hills of the Pedernal."

Using that description the surveyor general was able to carve out a 49,000 acre grant. But by looking at the plat of the Piedra Lumbre it only takes a second to see that the surveyor didn't really follow any particular boundaries.

The surveyor went back and forth wherever he wanted. For example, on the south side he was supposed to use the hills of the Pedernal. Once he found those hills, they were supposed to be the east to west boundary on the south side of the grant. They aren't. And on the north side—once he found the small red bluffs, you think, for the time it takes you to drink a warm beer, excuse me—for me to drink a warm beer, not you—that he followed them from east to west—on the north side of the Grant? Hell no he didn't. (Fig.14).

One other thing about the Piedra Lumbre. The case names the parties as Aniceto Martínez, et al., plaintiffs and the United States as defendant. But the decision has a different title. Next to the United States as a defendant, is added the names, Thomas B. Catron, et al. And the decision ordered that the plaintiffs and Catron—and his clients share the 49,000 acres.

There's something else I need to say about the San Joaquín and the Piedra Lumbre grants. We looked at how much the surveyors had charged for their surveys—the bills for the surveys. We tried to use them to figure how many acres had been surveyed—using the rates they used in those days.

The bill for the San Joaquín showed that it had run four lines, the north and south winding boundaries which were a mile and a half long, the west line which was five and a half miles long and the east boundary which was about six miles. If you average those out it seems like the bill was for a survey of about 5,000 acres not the 1,423 acres the government claimed was the size of the grant.

We did the math for the Piedra Lumbre survey, too. We took the north meandering boundary of twelve miles, the west grant boundary of seven miles, the south meandering boundary of eleven miles, and the east boundary of ten miles and figured the size of the grant at about 63,000 acres.

These totals are off some because of the wondering lines but not enough to throw the totals off as much as they appear. There's always the chance that the surveyors were lying about how long their survey lines were so they could make some extra money, but we don't have a way of knowing whether that happened or not. All we know is that the bills didn't match the size of the grants.

It's time to shift gears, Hijo. Talk about something else that has us upset—and that's all the problems we found with the Appendix in the GAO Report. It's clear from what the people writing the report left out that they either weren't interested in what they were doing or they were intentionally trying to hide something.

During the decades our people were living on and working their grants—and volunteering to fight and die for the Union Army—the government just couldn't wait to give away land to Anglo settlers in the hopes that someday they would outnumber our people. But that wasn't something the GAO cared enough about to mention. Here are some sentences that we think support what I'm saying:

> To every white male citizen of the United States, or every white male above the age of twenty-one years who has declared his intention to become a citizen, and who has resided in said Territory prior to the first day of January, eighteen hundred and fifty-three, and who may be still residing there, there shall be, and hereby is, donated one quarter section, or one hundred and sixty acres of land.

> And to every white male citizen of the United States, or every white male above the age of twenty-one years, who has declared his intention to become a citizen, and who shall have removed or shall remove to and settle in said Territory between the first day of January, eighteen hundred and fifty-three, and the first day of January, eighteen hundred and fifty-eight, there shall in like manner be donated one quarter section, or one hundred and sixty acres, on

condition of actual settlement and cultivation for not less than four years.

It is saying that the government was making land available for settlers coming from the states. All the settlers had to do was move to New Mexico and live on the land for four years. The government was willing to give 160 acres to total strangers who were just arriving—years before it got around to setting up the CPLC to take most of the land from our grants.

I need to clear something up before we move on. The government considered our ancestors as white at the time, so when its laws refer to "white" people that wasn't meant to exclude our people. But look at it this way: Spanish and Mexican settlers had been living here since the 1600's—since 1598 to be exact—living on land granted to them by Spain and Mexico and along comes the United States in 1848 and sets up its own rules which, unfortunately, just happened to benefit everyone in the Territory other than the Spanish, Mexican and Pueblo Indians who were supposed to be protected by a Treaty.

There was no way our ancestors could afford to apply for the 160 acre tracts and Congress knew it. If they applied for homesteads it would mean that they'd have to move to the land and by moving they would lose any interest they had in the grant because the minute they moved the government would say they were abandoning the grant—that they no longer had an interest in it.

I don't want to embarrass you Grandpa, and I'll take this out after we finish, but you already said that.

Sorry—I don't mean to repeat what I've already said but it's hard for me to remember everything I've said before. If I do it again let me know right away so you won't have to hear it all over again.

Anyway—like I was wanting to say, the Spanish settlers who lived in settlements other than in the grants, lived in Santa Cruz or Santa Fe, who didn't have any interest in the grants, they could afford to apply for homesteads since they'd have nothing to lose. But our ancestors and all the others living on the grants couldn't afford to. Now listen to this:

That in the case of townships heretofore surveyed in the Territories of New Mexico, Arizona and Utah, and the States of Colorado,

Nevada and Wyoming, all persons who, or whose ancestors, grantors, or their lawful successors in title and possession, became citizens of the United States by reason of the Treaty of Guadalupe Hidalgo, and who have been in actual continuous adverse possession and residence thereon of tracts of not to exceed one hundred and sixty acres each, for twenty years next preceding such survey, shall be entitled, upon making proof of such facts to the satisfaction of the register and receiver of the proper land district, and of the Commissioner of the General Land Office upon such investigation as is provided for in section sixteen of this act, to enter without payment of purchase money, fees, or commissions such legal subdivisions not exceeding one hundred and sixty acres …

Our ancestors had lived on their grants for over 80 years yet they weren't allowed to keep their land under what the government was calling adverse possession like the people who had been living on townships were.

The CPLC knew our people had been living on the grants for four times as long as was required for adverse possession. Why didn't it give each family patents for 2,560 acres like Powell had said was the minimum each family would need to survive? Why didn't the GAO say in its Report that adverse possession would have been a fair way to treat the people living on the grants? The government, by refusing to apply the adverse possession law to the people living on the grants, was treating them different—denying them what they were entitled too. Even if the government wasn't willing to live by the Treaty it should have at least lived by its own laws about adverse possession.

Now I need to read from a law that Congress used to start settling land grants in New Mexico. It's the 1854 law that set up the office of the Surveyor General of New Mexico. I'm going to be reading from Section 2:

Sec. 2. And be it further enacted, That, to every white male citizen of the United States, or every white male above the age of twenty-one years who has declared his intention to become a citizen, and who was residing in said Territory prior to the first day of January, eighteen hundred and fifty-three, and who may be still residing there, there shall be, and hereby is, donated one quarter section, or one hundred and sixty acres of land. And to every white male citizen of the United States, or every white male above the age of twenty-one years, who has declared his intentions to become a citizen, and who shall have removed or shall remove to and settle in said Territory between the first day of January, eighteen hundred and fifty-three, and the first day of January, eighteen hundred and fifty-eight, there shall in like manner be donated one quarter section, or one hundred and sixty acres, on condition of actual settlement and cultivation for not less than four years: ...

You can see from what I just read, what it took for someone to qualify for a 160 acre homestead in New Mexico: you had to be a white male citizen of the United States or white male over the age of twenty-one who had declared he was going to become a citizen.

Now that I read from the 1854 law setting up the surveyor general for New Mexico I need to talk about a 1850's law passed by Congress to deal with land in the Oregon Territory. We need to compare the laws—compare their differences.

In 1850 the Oregon Territory included what are today the states of Oregon, Washington and Idaho. It wasn't covered by the Treaty of Guadalupe Hidalgo, the United States got it as part of a settlement with England.

Section 4 of the law that applied to the Oregon Territory said:

... [B]e it further enacted, that there shall be, and hereby is, granted to every white settler or occupant of the public lands, American half-breed Indians included, above the age of eighteen years, being a citizen of the United States, or having made a declaration according to law, of his intention to become a citizen, or who shall make such declaration on or before the first day of December, eighteen hundred and fifty, and who shall have resided upon and cultivated the same for four consecutive years and shall otherwise conform to the provisions of this act, the quantity of one half section, or three hundred and twenty acres of land, if a single man, and, if a married man, or if he shall become married within one year from the first day of December, eighteen hundred and fifty, the quantity of one section, or six hundred and forty acres, one half to himself and the other half to his wife ...

Apparently, in 1850, Congress and President Fillmore believed women and Indians in Oregon Territory were only entitled to own land if the woman was married to a white person or half-breed Indian and if one of the Indians parents was white.

Just think—where you were born; whether you were a man or woman; whether you were a full blood or half-breed Indian; whether you were eighteen or twenty-one years old, what state or territory you were in—it all made a difference. Congress was willing to allow 18 year old white men and women and half-breed Indians in Oregon to have 320 acres each if single, or 640 acres if you were a married white couple. But in New Mexico, before 1862, only a white man could own land and then only 160 acres. Half-breed Indians and white women were out of luck in New Mexico—as well as in the pages of the GAO Report.

-7-
Recollections Of A Dreadful Past

Before we start, Grandpa, can I ask you something?
Yes.
I'm still trying to figure out why there would have been a still in Canjilón. I'm sure it wasn't just so kids could watch chickens get drunk. Did your father and his friends drink mula?

I'm glad you asked me that. It's as good a time as any to let you in on how I learned a lot of what I know about the San Joaquín and Juan Bautista grants—about our family history.

But first, I need to answer your question. They had a still in Canjilón because no one could afford to buy whiskey and besides there wasn't any place to buy it in Canjilón. To answer your other question, they didn't drink very often but when they did it wasn't hard to figure that they were drinking. Since, like I already said, there weren't any package liquor stores in Canjilón when I was growing up, mula and home-made wine were about all there was to drink—other than Diet Coke and Pepsi.

Come on, Grandpa!

Just keeping you off your heels. Mula was all my father and his friends could afford to drink and they usually had to trade something for it.

Sometimes—mostly on Sunday afternoons—my father's friends would stop by and they'd sit around and have a few drinks.

I can still see it. His friends would come to our house and he'd walk out to the wagon in the early years or a pickup in the later years and the first thing you'd see is the person closest to where my father was standing would pass him a bottle and he'd take a drink.

They'd visit for a while, talking, laughing, passing the bottle back and forth, and about the third or fourth time the bottle was passed around my father would invite his friends to get down.

They'd sit on the porch and visit—sometimes for hours and sooner or later they'd start talking about the past—about their ancestors and the land grants—and about the time they started talking about the grants they'd start talking louder. I'd hear "San Joaquín;" "Juan Bautista;" "El cabrón, Burns;" "damn thieves;" "thousands and thousands of acres;" "just think where we'd be today, compadre," and "if it wasn't for the pinche gobierno."

Should I take all that out, Grandpa?

That's not me talking—I'm just repeating what I heard.

Are you saying this is one of the ways you learned about land grants—about how our family had been treated? By listening to what your father and his friends would talk about?

Exactly! Those were the times when I would hear about our people—our family—when I would hear about the suffering our ancestors had gone through—the land they had lost. And it was about this same time that my father started to explain to me what our ancestors had gone through—telling me what had happened to our family and the others—what had happened to the grants. After that we talked about it for the rest of his life.

When they would start talking louder and louder we knew it wasn't going to be long before they'd all pile in the wagon—or the pickup, and head off for another bottle.

So a whole lot of what you heard about the grants—about the way our people were treated—the way the government treated our people, you learned from listening to your father and his friends during those Sunday afternoon fiestacitas?

They were the beginning of my education about the past.

Sometimes they'd talk for hours about Juan Bautista and our grant. Other times they'd talk about the San Joaquín—about the way the gringos, Burns, Catron, Bond—and the government had stolen our grants. Most of what I heard was really sad—but there were times when they'd say something funny. I remember one of them told a story that he'd heard when he was young about how the Indians would steal his great-grandfather's sheep every summer and the next spring his great-grandfather would go outside early in the morning and the sheep would be back. The Indians didn't want to be bothered when the lambs were coming so they'd bring the sheep they still had back to our people and steal them again in the fall.

I remember hearing about how the Forest Service would kill the wild horses they'd find in the forest—that there was a canyon where they'd killed so many—where there were so many bones—the people used to call it the Cañada de Los Huesos.

Would you mind telling some more of the stories you remember?

Not at all. What I used to hear on those Sunday afternoons was some of the most interesting, most important things I remember. I was hearing about our family history. That's why it's going to be bad when I'm finally gone, Hijo, there won't be anyone left to tell about our past.

We need to thank the Lord, Grandpa, that you're still able to tell our story.

One of the first things I remember my father and his friends discussing, probably when I was around nine, was how Juan Bautista and the other men in Cañones lived in those days—we're talking 150-200 years ago. I remember hearing that before Juan Bautista moved to Cañones he had lived in Barranca, just above Abiquiú—on the old road through the Chama Canyon from Abiquiú to Tierra Amarilla. I don't know how they knew all of it, but it was interesting.

I imagine they learned it just like you did—sitting with their parents and grandparents visiting with their family and friends.

I bet you're right. I'm sure that's the way history has been passed down for centuries. But one thing I don't know is if they had mula to drink while they were telling their history.

I'm sure they had something like that, Grandpa. They might have even had drunk chickens, who knows.

They said that at the time Juan Bautista died, in 1822, he owned more than 1,000 sheep and 200 hundred cows—and a Molino. They would talk about how the people from Abiquiú would bring their wheat and corn to Grandpa Juan Bautista's mill. And I remember, now that I mentioned the mill, that when we were reading the papers from the court hearing that one of the witnesses had even mentioned that he owned a mill.

I remember my father and his friends talking about how much land it took to graze cattle and sheep. They'd get real loud, real upset, when they'd talk about grazing. Someone would say that it would take at least sixty acres to feed a cow and that they could feed six sheep on the same amount of land it took for one cow; and one of them would say: "Hell, if Juan Bautista had 200 cows he needed more than a thousand acres—just to feed 'em." Then someone else would butt in, "and more than 5,000 for his sheep."

Then someone else would butt in: "And all the San Joaquín wound up with was 1,400 pinche acres—that wouldn't even feed twenty-five cows. Wouldn't even feed one cow for every ten families. How'd the government think our people were going to survive?"

I heard one old timer say that there were over 400 people living on the San Joaquín in 1875. Then someone else from behind the wagon where he was taking a leak, said "when there were still houses on the San Joaquín they found six skeletons in one of them—and they found another skeleton in the chimney."

One time I heard them arguing about how T. D. Burns would steal our land. He had a big store in Los Ojos and at least three other stores; one in Chama, one here in Canjilón, and another one somewhere else, maybe in El Rito. Anyway—I heard them say that he'd give our people credit through the year and in the fall when they sold their crops and their calves, and in the spring when they'd sell their wool, they'd go to his store to pay what they owed. One of my father's friends said that every time his grandfather would go to Burn's store to get something Burns would make him sign a paper for it and he'd say that he would tear it up when the bill was paid. That it was the only way the people could survive until they sold their cows, crops and wool—the only way they had of getting what they needed through the year.

But in the fall when his grandfather would go to the store to pay his bill Burns would say he was too busy to look for the papers. He'd take the money and say: "don't worry Amigo—I'll tear it up when I get through here." I've wondered ever since I used to hear that how Burns always knew how much the people needed to pay but he never knew where the papers were.

And I remember when my father and his friends would all start talking at the same time, each one trying to talk louder than the others: "The son of a bitch never tore up the papers—he kept 'em hid," one would say. "Then someone would butt in, "they weren't just papers, Viejo, they were god-damn deeds." And another one would yell out: "when a Viejo would die Burns would wait about a month after they put him in 'la Tierra,' and he then would go to the courthouse and record the paper and claim he'd bought the land." Then I would hear, " bet that's the way he got the San Joaquín, Amigo" and from around the corner of our house another compadre would say, "damn right, prim, you tell 'em."

After a few minutes while the bottle was making the rounds it would start all over again. "He wasn't the only son of a bitch to screw our people, Amigo. Bond did a good job of it, too," someone would say. Then another of my father's friends would butt in: "He use to tell my grandfather's Tío, Jesus that he could put his sheep on the Valle Grande but that he'd have to take care of some of Bond's sheep while his were there." "Que cabrón—he had thousands of sheep," one of them would say. And after another drink he'd continue, "Tío Jesús would take his twenty or thirty, or maybe thirty-four sheep to the Valle Grande and stay all summer watching them and watching after Bond's sheep." Then this friend of my father's that used to drink more than the others would make me laugh every time I would hear him. He's say the same thing every time: "Are you through with your bull-shit, Amigo, because I have something important to say." Then the one telling the story about his grandfather's Tio Jesús would say, "Just a damn minute, cabron, I have a little more to say." They he would say that when it came time to bring Tio Jesus' sheep down in the fall Bond would act like he had counted or had Juan Largo count his sheep and he would tell Jesus that he was missing twenty-five sheep and he would keep twenty-five of Jesus' sheep. "My grandfather said," he'd continue, "that there were even years when Jesús would stay all summer and come home with less sheep than he had taken to the Valle in the Spring." Then he'd say, "Okay, Cabron—I'm through—tell your important story," and someone else would say: "He can't say it—you talked to long—he went to sleep."

I can remember like it happened yesterday, Hijo, another way Burns would cheat our people. One of his favorite tricks was to tell all our people that went to his store in Los Ojos that he had a safe where he could keep their important papers—where they'd be safe. And our poor viejos would take their papers to him. Later when they'd ask for their papers he would say that they were lost or that he couldn't find them.

After my father and his friends would finish talking about Burns they would get around to talking about losing the grants. "My father told me," one of the men would say, "that his father told him, that one day around 1900 or there abouts, the government came along and told everyone to get their animals off the pastures, "that they didn't own it."

"I don't know if it's true they were told to leave," he'd continue, "but they left. Where the hell are all the houses, the corrales—the barns? Where's the school?" Our people lived there for no telling how long—three, four generations—and then they were run off the land. "Where the hell did they go?"

-8-
Oregon Territory And New Mexico—
A Preemption Comparison

Remember when I was saying that the Oregon Territory would allow white men or half-breed Indians eighteen years old or older to have 320 acres—and a white married man and his wife could have 640 acres? It wasn't right that an18 year old white married couple in the Oregon Territory was entitled to 640 acres while in New Mexico only U. S. citizens and white males over 21 were only allowed 160 acres.

We need to talk about the Homestead Act of 1862, Hijo. It was different from the other laws we've discussed when it came to qualifying for a home-stead. It allowed men and women to apply for a homestead so long as the person applying was the head of a household. It allowed thousands of peo-ple to settle from the Dakota Territory to the Pacific Northwest and across the Southwest after 1862. All a person had to do to claim 160 acres was be twenty-one years of age, prove that he or she was the head of a household, pay a small fee, and live on the land for a few years. Unlike the earlier law in the Oregon Territory where married women could claim 320 acres of land, the Homestead Act did just the opposite. If a single woman had chil-dren and qualified as the head of a household and got a homestead guess what could happen if she got married?

The way you asked the question, Grandpa—I figure she'd lose it.

You're right and for getting the answer right you just won the right to read this letter.

Sir: I am in receipt of a letter, dated the 5th instant, from Hon. Thomas Croxton, of the Committee of Private Lands, U.S. House of Representatives, requesting information bearing upon H. R. No. 161, for the relief of Mary C. Crosby.

The records of this office show that Mary C. Crosby filed pre-emption declaratory statement No. 20780 for the N. ½ of the S.W. ¼ section 3, township 106 north, range 62 west, Mitchell, Dak., April 14, 1883, alleging settlement April 3,1883.

It appears from correspondence on file that in October, 1883, Miss Crosby married, and thus, under the rulings of this department, was unable to complete her pre-emption entry, her application to make such entry having been refused by the register and receiver under the rulings referred to. It is held by such rulings that when a single woman marries before completing her pre-emption she loses her qualification to do so, being no longer a single woman or the head of a family.

If, therefore, any relief in the present case is deemed by the committee meritorious, I respectfully suggest that it extend only to the restoration of the pre-emption right, which it seems can now be exercised, as the party had, by divorce, again become qualified to make settlement and entry as a feme sole.

So there you have it—we've now discussed three different rules.

Before 1862, Congress allowed married women in the Oregon Territory to own 320 acres but denied women in New Mexico Territory the right to own land. Then along comes the Homestead Act and allowed single women who were heads of households to own land but refused married women the right to own a homestead.

Why do you think Congress had different laws for different areas, Grandpa? And why do you think it allowed what it called half-breed Indians to own land in Oregon Territory but didn't allow them to own land in New Mexico?

I don't know for sure, but it seems to us like the laws were intentionally different so the government could control which states and territories people could settle in; and which people could settle where the government wanted them to settle.

Wasn't there some place our people could go to challenge the way the government was treating them? Couldn't they go to a court, somewhere—anywhere, to get the government to treat them like it was treating the Anglos moving into New Mexico from the east?

Who came up with those questions—your teacher?

Well—after I told him what we'd be discussing today—what we'd already talked about—and after I told him about the different way other people were treated from the way our people were, he said that there was a world court; that when it comes to treaties the World court treats them like contracts—contracts between countries. He said the World Court was set up to settle problems between countries. Then he said the reason Mexico never challenged the way the United States was ignoring the Treaty was probably because it was afraid the United States might start another war—and take more land.

I guess it's almost time we talk about Treaties and the World Court,. but before we do I want to read four statements that were in the GAO Report and discuss them.

The first one says:

> As agreed, we do not express an opinion on whether the United States fulfilled its Treaty obligations as a matter of international law.

The second one said:

> As agreed, GAO does not express an opinion on whether the United States fulfilled its obligations under the Treaty as a matter of international law.

And the third:

> Any conflict between the Treaty and the 1854 or 1891 Acts—which we do not suggest exists...would have to be resolved today as

a matter of international law between the United States and Mexico or by additional congressional action. As agreed, we do not express an opinion on whether the United States fulfilled its Treaty obligations as a matter of international law.

And finally:

> While we do not suggest that any such conflict exists, as agreed, we do not express an opinion on whether the United States fulfilled its Treaty obligations as a matter of international law.

I don't know whether you caught it or not, Hijo, but the words, "as agreed," show up in every one of those statements. We couldn't believe the GAO would repeat the words "as agreed" four times by accident. There had to be a reason for it. We figured the GAO and Senators Domenici and Bingaman, who had requested the report, must have been up to something—come to some kind of agreement that the GAO was uncomfortable with and that it wanted to make it clear that what it had done or not done had been okayed by the senators. We finally figured that the GAO didn't want to admit that the United States had failed to fulfill its Treaty obligations .

By refusing to say whether or not the United States had violated the Treaty of Guadalupe Hidalgo the GAO was, so far as we were concerned—so far as the heirs of the grantees of the Spanish and Mexican land grants were concerned—refusing to answer one of the most important questions the government has refused to answer for over 150 years.

We figured that if we could prove that Senators Domenici and Bingaman had agreed that the GAO didn't have to answer the question the agreement itself would be proof that the GAO had come to the conclusion that the United States had violated the treaty. If the United States had fulfilled its treaty obligations as a matter of international law the GAO wouldn't have had any reason to refuse to answer the question. If the senators had been confident about the government's actions regarding the Treaty there would have been no reason for them to agree with the GAO that it didn't have to answer the question.

Mike sent the GAO a freedom of information request, a FOIA, in March 2009 asking for copies of all the correspondence between Senators Domenici and Bingaman and the GAO regarding the Senators request and the GAO's investigation. The GAO answered that it couldn't release the correspondence because it was privileged—that if we wanted it we'd have to get written permission from the Senators for the GAO to release the documents. Then we sent e-mails to the Senators requesting permission for the GAO to release the correspondence.

Senator Domenici's office answered right away—saying he was retiring and didn't have time to respond. Senator Bingaman answered some weeks later stating that he had no problem releasing copies of the correspondence; however—since there was another senator who had signed the correspondence it might not be possible to receive copies unless we got the signature of the other senator. Of course, he was talking about Senator Domenici whose office had already refused to cooperate.

All Senators Domenici and Bingaman had to do was agree for the GAO to give us copies of the correspondence—and if there was no agreement that would have been the end. By the GAO's refusal to cooperate it left us with no way to resolve the problem without putting more pressure on the GAO.

Grandpa, you said you believed at the time that the GAO and Senators Domenici and Bingaman agreed before the Report was written that the GAO didn't have to investigate whether the government had violated the treaty. It sure would be something if we could prove that the GAO and the Senators had had an agreement. That would prove the GAO's so called investigation had been a complete waste of time and money.

You're getting good at this. We may have to find a way to send you to college, maybe even law school. I have to confess though, that I've kinda been leading you along. We were able to get the GAO to admit that there had been an agreement between it and the senators. After a number of telephone calls and e-mail letters we received a letter in July answering the questions we'd asked in March requesting copies of the correspondence. We didn't get the correspondence but we did get a letter. Here's what it said:

Dear Mr. Scarborough:

This letter responds to your March 12, 2009, request for information related to the Government Accountability Office's (GAO) report, TREATY OF GUADALUPE HIDALGO: Findings and Possible Options Regarding Longstanding Community Land Grant Claims in New Mexico [GAO-04-59, June 4, 2004]. Specifically, you are seeking documentation relating to the statements in GAO's report (at pages 10, 48, and 142) that:[a]s agreed [with the congressional requesters of the report], we do not express an opinion on whether the United States fulfilled its Treaty obligations as a matter of international law.

It is GAO's longstanding practice not to make findings and determinations on U.S. compliance with international treaties, as the Department of State has special responsibility for and jurisdiction over such matters. Consistent with this practice, in discussions with the offices of Senators Domenici and Bingaman … regarding the scope of this engagement, it was agreed, orally, that we would not assess whether the U.S. complied with the Treaty as a matter of international law…

[W]e concluded on the basis of our independent historical, factual and legal research that the U.S. complied with the grant confirmation procedures established by 1854 and 1891 U. S. statutes implementing the treaty and that these statutory procedures complied with the Procedural Due Process requirements of the U.S. Constitution.

Do you believe the man when he says that it was agreed orally between the GAO and the offices of Senators Domenici and Bingaman that the GAO didn't have to assess whether the U.S. had complied with the Treaty as a matter of international law?

No! We think he was saying that to keep from having to admit there was a written agreement. We don't think Senators Domenici and Bingaman would even consider making that kind of an agreement without it being in writing—unless they were trying to hide something. Besides—if that's what really happened—why do you think Domenici refused to let the GAO send us copies of his correspondence?

I can't say for sure, Hijo. But it kind of reminds me of what happens when you go outside at night and you smell a skunk. You know it's there—you just don't know exactly where. That letter smelled an awful lot like a skunk to us.

-9-

Calves And Lambs—Crops And Chicos

I've remembered some more about when I was growing up that I forgot to mention before. I remember talking about our cows and sheep but I forgot to talk about the lambs we would get from Abel Trujillo, a sheep herder that watched over hundreds of sheep between here and Mogote Ridge. In the spring, when the lambs started to drop, some of the mothers wouldn't let them suck. When that would happen the lambs would die unless Abel could find another mother to feed them.

He had no way to take care of all the little ones so when it was time for lambing my father would saddle a horse, give me a gunny sack and some jerky for Abel, and tell me to go find him and I would usually run into him about ten miles east of here. If he had a lamb or two that weren't getting milk he'd give them to me and I'd put them in the sack and bring them home.

When I'd get here, if there wasn't a bottle handy, I'd cut a finger off an old leather glove and punch a couple small holes in the end of it, fill a bottle—like an old medicine bottle, with cow's milk, pull the finger over it and feed them. We'd keep feeding them that way until they were old enough to eat.

Another thing I remember was that people who didn't have any pasture, who I told you earlier would borrow our wagon to cut grass in the pastures, they would cut the grass along the road all summer, take it home and stack it on top of the barn for winter feed.

We had to spend a lot of time during the summer gathering hay, but it was a lot easier for us since because we had a large pasture. But even with

82

the pasture we couldn't afford to keep the calves and lambs through the winter. We could have eaten them but then we wouldn't have had enough money for spring planting.

Grandpa, I have a question about your garden now that you started talking about planting. Why do the squash you grow look like gourds and why is your corn black and real small? They're completely different from what they sell in the grocery stores in Española.

It's because I still use the same seed my father used—the seed we used when I was just a kid. I wouldn't be surprised if the seed I use today is the same seed Juan Bautista and his children and grandchildren used when they were living in Cañones—seed that had been passed down through the family from generation to generation.

For as long as I can remember, when our garden would start to turn brown in the fall we'd always bring the dried plants inside, separate the seeds and store them until the next year.

After you mentioned how the government would kill the wild horses, I saw an article that said that some people from around Albuquerque had checked the DNA of some wild horses that had been caught in the forest and once in a while they would find one that would match the DNA of horses from Spain. I wouldn't think it would be much different to check the DNA of your seeds—see if they could be traced back to Spain or Mexico—or one of the Pueblos.

Could you talk about how you'd keep your corn through the winter, how you and Grandma would make chicos?

In the fall we had two ways to save the corn. We could make chicos or grind it into meal. To make chicos we'd fill a fifty gallon drum with water and build a fire under it. When the water would start to boil we'd put the corn in the water.

Excuse me, Grandpa—didn't you take the dried husks off before you put the corn in the barrel?

No, we'd put them in the water with the husks.

Why'd you do it that way? It seems like it would be better to pull them off.

Because it would keep the flavor in better. We also left them on so that after they'd boiled we could tie four or five of them together and hang them out to dry. After they would dry we'd pull the husks off and store the kernels until we were ready to use them. It took less room if we took the kernels off after we boiled them rather than to wait until spring; besides, we could keep them away from the mice better.

Had the corn you took to the mill been boiled? When would you take it to the mill?

The corn we took to the mill was the extra corn we'd put out to dry that we didn't use for chicos. We'd take them to the mill in the fall after we'd finished getting everything ready for winter.

Sounds like it must have taken a lot of time to make chicos. You had to bring them from the garden, boil them, tie em together, hang em out to dry, take the kernels off after they'd dried—and store them. Can you talk about what you did when it was time to eat them?

Sometimes we'd cook the chicos with beans and meat and other times other times we'd grind them into powder, brown the meal on a grill or in a skillet and make little cakes by adding water and chokecherries. Sometimes we'd make atole by adding sugar and cream, boiling it down and drinking it for breakfast—or cook it a little longer until it was like oatmeal.

Awhile back you explained how you would get lambs from Abel Trujillo. Would you get calves the same way?

No, but for years—from when I was in my thirties—until ten or fifteen years ago I used to go every spring to a dairy in Los Lunas, south of Albuquerque, and buy four newborn calves. When I would get home I'd take them to the corral and put them with a Holstein cow and she'd feed them until they were old enough to eat by themselves.

Why would you do it that way? Wouldn't it have been easier to have five mother cows?

Sure. But we didn't have permits.

Now I get it. By using only one mother cow you were able to limit your trespassing.

And if I'd had a mother cow for each calf I wouldn't have had enough feed and I would have had to put all the cows on the forest every day. The way I did it I didn't have to put them on the forest except for a couple months in the fall. That made it harder for the Forest Service to catch me using our land.

I'm still interested in finding out what you did for fun—after all your work was done.

Forget fun, Hijo, that wasn't really a part of our life until we were older.

But you couldn't have just worked all the time, what'd you do besides work?

When I'd get in from work I'd have to go to the shop and sharpen my chain saws so they'd be ready for the next day. I usually took 4 or 5 saws with me every morning and they all had to be sharpened. That'd take 2 or 3 hours. I'd drink a few beers while I was working—maybe a few after I finished if my friends had come by. But, if there was a full moon—maybe I shouldn't tell you about the full moon.

Ah, come on, Grandpa.

Later—I'm too tired—we need to quit for today.

But—before we quit can you talk about Grandma—her family?

Thank you! Thank you! I should have talked about her a long time ago. Without her none of you would be here. Maybe I wouldn't either. I can't believe we waited this long to talk about your grandma, Rose—the most important woman in my life. Well—she's tied for the most with my mother. My mother was important too. But maybe you should leave that last part out, leave it the way I said it the first time, I don't want to hurt your grandmother's feelings. I'll tell you one thing for sure—your grandmother was a lot better wife and mother than I was a husband and father—and that's for sure. I feel bad about that, she deserved for me to be better. (Fig. 18).

Can you explain what you mean when you say she's a better wife and mother?

Sure. I guess the first reason is all the trouble I got in, with the Alianza—and getting in a few fights. And I was way too grouchy with her. I should have been nicer—and sometimes I drank too much. I mean—she was always here taking care of me and all our children—helping out with you grandchildren when you started coming along. I said it right when I said she was a better wife and mother, but I need to add that she was a better grandmother, too. She deserved for me to be better—but it didn't happen that way. I try to be as good as I can now—but that won't ever make up for when I was younger.

I need to tell you how we met. I met your grandmother in 1963—in Española. At that time I was living in Truchas and working as a logger in the Truchas Peak Wilderness Area and it was a Saturday afternoon and I had gone to Española for the weekend.

For me it was like a miracle that we met. Maybe not for her, but maybe so—the way everything's finally turned out.

She was born in Dixon and had lived there most of her life but after she finished high school she moved with her aunt, Mary Herrera—her father's sister, to San Francisco. She lived there for a couple years before we met. That's one reason I say it was a miracle—since she was only here visiting when we met. Another miracle is that I saw her again that night at a dance. Now that was a miracle by itself, because she told me later that she never liked to dance. And something else I almost forgot—she was at the dance with Teddy—your great-uncle Tony's wife.

We got married the next year and after that we've had eight children, counting your mother and you aunts and uncles. I guess I shouldn't say we had them because it was your grandmother that had them. I need to name them since years from now there will be relatives who might not know all of them. First was Juanita and then Deborah. Then your Tio, Amarante. Luisa was next and then Reyes. Then we had Vialquin, Tanya and Amada. And counting you, Hijo, we have about twenty-seven grandchildren—I can't remember for sure. And now the greats are starting to come along. The reason I didn't say which one was your mother is because we need to keep that a mystery. (fig.17).

You said Grandma did most of the raising of the children. Did she stay home while you were working?

Oh no. She not only raised the family she also worked for the County and had to drive back and forth, sixty miles a day all those years to Tierra Amarilla.

Now that we're talking about your grandmother let me tell you what she would do when I would tell her that Mike was coming to visit. She'd cook scalloped potatoes because one time years ago when he was eating with us and she had made scalloped potatoes, he had told her he loved them and she never forgot. Every time she would hear he was coming she would make those potatoes for him. He loved to eat here because of all the delicious things that your grandmother would cook—but I think he liked the potatoes best.

And something else—your grandmother is the hardest working woman I've ever seen. She goes to Española three times a week for dialysis—and it takes all day because she leaves here at five in the morning and doesn't get back until late in the afternoon. But, you know what, even though the dialysis makes her so weak she can hardly move, as soon as she gets home she starts cooking supper. I get upset with her for that, telling her one of the girls can do it. Sometimes, now that I'm older, I even try to cook some of the meals to help, but she says she wants to do her part and keeps cooking and working around the house—washing dishes and clothes—and cleaning house.

Can you talk about Grandma Rose trying to teach you to read? It's a funny story.

Sure. Before I met Tijerina—before we went to the courthouse—and after, your grandmother and I would sit at the kitchen table at night and on weekends and she would get a newspaper and use it to help me learn to read better. But after I got in all that trouble she quit using the newspaper and started taking out the Bible. One day I asked her why she was using the Bible—that it was harder to read than the newspaper—and that by reading the newspaper I could learn to read and keep up with what was going on at the same time.

She laughed, that little laugh she has, and said by using the Bible she was hoping that I could not only learn how to read better I might learn more than just the news; that she was trying to kill one bird with two rocks.

-10-
Cobell vs. A Hand—Picked Judge

Would it be alright to ask a couple questions before you start what you're going to be talking about?

Okay.

How do you feel about the way the government treats our people? Does it treat us better or worse than it did twenty or thirty years ago?

Now that you asked me, I remember something that happened last year that convinced me that nothing has really changed. For several years Mike and I have been talking about a lawsuit that 500,000 Indians had filed against the Government to collect money the government has cheated them out of for over 100 years—money the Government has been refusing to return, claiming I guess, that it doesn't exist. Here are some newspaper stories Mike gave me that talk about what you just asked. Read this one first:

> A federal appeals court took the rare step of removing U.S. District Judge Royce C. Lamberth from a long-standing legal battle involving billions in Native American oil and gas royalties, saying the judge appears to be biased against the Interior Department.

> The U.S. Court of Appeals for the District of Columbia Circuit cited Lambreth's own words to illustrate why he should be removed from the case, Cobell v. Kempthorne, including a July 2005 opinion in which he called the Interior Department "a dinosaur—the morally and culturally oblivious hand-me-down of a disgracefully racist and imperialist government that should have been buried a

century ago, the pathetic outpost of the indifference and anglocentrism we thought we had left behind."

I've discussed what you just read with some friends and we agree that the judge could just as well have been talking about the Department of Agriculture's taking of hundreds of thousands of acres of our land at the same time the Government was taking trust money from the Indians. I'll read the next part.

> The court said Lamberth's opinion extends beyond historical racism and all but accuses current Interior officials of racism ...

I don't mean to stop there but I want to say that I'm glad the Indians didn't waste their time asking for a GAO investigation. A claim of historical racism or any kind of racism would have wound up as a "collateral issue" and "beyond the scope of the investigation," as the GAO said in its Report. Anyway, here's the next paragraph:

> The ruling removes a sitting trial judge for only the third time in the D.C. Circuit and provides the latest twist in a contentious decade-long class action lawsuit filed by the Native American Rights Fund over the trust accounts, which were set up in 1887 to compensate Indians for the use of their lands. Since Blackfeet tribe leader Eloise Cobell filed the lawsuit in 1996, several independent investigations found that the Interior Department had never kept complete records, used unknown amounts of the fund to help balance the federal budget, and let the oil and gas industry use Indian lands at bargain rates ...

My friends and I agree that what the Government was doing with the Indian trust funds—and the Department of Agriculture was doing with our ancestors land wasn't that much different from what Congress has been doing with the social security funds for years —using it for everything but what it was supposed to be used.

The article goes on to say:

> In making the rare request to have Lambreth removed, the Justice Department said that besides using intemperate language,

Lamberth has ignored appellate rulings and accused the government of falsification, spite and obstinate litigiousness with no legal or factual basis.

There they go again, Hijo. Claiming like the Supreme Court did in the *Rio Arriba Land and Cattle* case that there's no legal or factual basis—I better move on before I start stuttering:

The appeals court's opinion quotes at length from Lamberth's July 2005 opinion, in which Lamberth writes that the entire record in this case tells the dreary story of Interior's degenerate tenure as Trustee-Delegate for the Indian Trust ... a story shot through with bureaucratic blunders, flubs, goofs and foul-ups, and peppered with scandals, deception, dirty tricks and outright villainy ... the end of which is nowhere in sight.

See what happens when an honest judge tells the truth, Hijo?
The article goes on to say that:

Although the July 12 opinion contains harsh—even incendiary— language, much of that language represents nothing more than the views of an experienced judge who, having presided over this exceptionally contentious case for almost a decade, has become "exceedingly ill disposed towards [a] defendant" that has flagrantly and repeatedly breached its fiduciary obligations. *Liteky*, 510 U.S. at 550, 114 S.Ct. 1147. We ourselves have referred to Interior's "malfeasance," "recalcitrance," "unconscionable delay," "intransigence," and "hopelessly inept management." *Cobell VI*, 240 F.3d at1096, 1109; *Cobell XII*, 391 F.3d at 257; *Cobell XIII*, 392 F.3d at 463.

That last paragraph is really interesting, Hijo. The appeals court is saying it can call the Department of Interior's actions "malfeasance," "recalcitrance," "unconscionable delay," "intransigence," and "hopelessly inept management," but how dare the trial judge who has been actively trying the case for over ten years say the same thing?
Do you have any idea what happened after that article came out?

A lot has happened since then. The first thing the three judges did was appoint another judge to finish the case—to protect the interests of the government. On August 7, 2008 after having been assigned the case for less than six months and after having surely reviewed each and every one of the 3,000 documents filed over the 10 years and having read every word on every page of all the records and studied all the exhibits—he made a ruling.

I can see by the look on your face, Grandpa, that there's something wrong with how the case was decided, what happened?

He ruled that the plaintiffs, all 500,000 of them, who had established that they were entitled to billions of dollars for royalties collected and unlawfully spent by the Interior Department since 1887 were only entitled to $455,000,000. That's less than a lousy $1,000 each, Hijo. Consider this, the $910 each one was awarded included the principal and over a hundred-twenty years of interest. The amount the judge awarded each plaintiffs was so small it wasn't even worth the time it would take to figure out how much was principal and how much was interest.

It sounds like he turned out to be just the judge the government would want in a case like this, Grandpa.

He ruled that the 500,000 plaintiffs were entitled to less than one percent of what they believed they were entitled to. Does that figure, "one percent," make the bell in your head ring, Hijo?

From what we've read I guess the only conclusion we can come up with is that there's nothing as unimportant as ten years of hearings, evidence— sworn testimony—to stop a hand-picked judge from deciding a case exactly the way the hand-pickers wanted it decided.

Before we read the next article I want to explain a little more about the case. The plaintiffs were saying that the Government had taken billions of dollars of oil, gas, grazing, timber and other royalties which were supposed to have been protected by the Interior Department since 1887; they were claiming that for over a hundred years the government had been cheating them out of money that had belonged to their ancestors—money that was supposed to have been held for them by the government. This next article proves the government doesn't mind kicking someone when they are down.

The government had proposed paying $7 billion partly to settle the Cobell lawsuit in March 2007 but that was rejected by the plaintiffs.

The Interior Department broke its customary silence on the case to praise the ruling. "The department is gratified that the court recognized the complexities and uncertainties involved in this case," said James E. Cason, associate deputy Secretary of the Interior.

The question that needs answering, is how could this Cason fellow, a high ranking employee in the Interior Department, have had the nerve to praise a ruling that only awarded the Cobell plaintiffs a lousy six percent of the amount the Government had already offered them—and then express gratitude to the court for its decision?

I see you're chewing at your bit to say something but you're going to have to wait a couple more minutes. I have more statements we need to read and while I'm reading them I want you to keep what I said a moment ago, that the Cobell case was claiming that the Interior Department started using the Indian's trust money for its own benefit in 1887, in mind. Here's the first part we need to read—it's what President Harrison was saying about what the Court of Private Land Claims had done about land grants here in the southwest:

The Court of Private Land Claims ... is making satisfactory progress in its work, and when the work is completed a great impetus will be given to the development of those regions where unsettled claims under Mexican grants have so long exercised their repressive influence. The government is making satisfactory headway with the claims under Mexican grants that have for so long exercised their repressive influence.

Just five years after the Government began collecting the Indian trust money President Harrison was saying that the government was making progress toward development of the regions where the Mexican grants were having a repressive influence on development of the region.

In his 1892 farewell address, after having just lost his bid to be reelected and while discussing Indian reservations, President Harrison said:

> When to these results are added the enormous cessions of Indian lands which have been opened to settlement, aggregating during this Administration nearly 26,000,000 acres, and the agreements renegotiated and now pending in Congress for ratification by which about 10,000,000 additional acres will be opened to settlement, it will be seen how much has been accomplished.

He was bragging that during his four years in office, between 1889 to 1893 his administration had opened nearly 26,000,000 acres of Indian reservation land to non-Indian settlement—taken it out of existing Indian reservations. And he didn't stop there. He went on to say that he was in the process of having another 10,000,000 acres of reservation land opened for settlement. Add that to a statement he made several years earlier— which we'll be reading later and you'll have a pretty good idea what the government and the Government were doing with Indian reservations, Indian trust funds —and Spanish and Mexican land grants in the 1880's and 90's.

The question that we need to keep in mind is, whether it was just a coincidence that millions of acres were being taking from our land grants at the same time Presidents Cleveland and Harrison were stealing Indian reservation lands and trust funds?

I'm going to make it easy on you, Hijo, and say that it wasn't just a coincidence. During the 1880's and 90's the government was intentionally taking as many resources as it could from all of us.

We need to change the subject, Grandpa—talk about something else. I've had it with President Harrison, the Interior Department—the judges in the Cobell case: with all of them. If you keep bringing up all this bad news, I'll probably start stuttering right along with you.

A few days ago you compared the San Joaquín and Juan Bautista Valdez Grants with the grants around them. Maybe we could talk some more about them?

I'll be glad to but we'll need to describe some maps as we go along so whoever is listening can follow along.

At the time we were discussing these grants we were comparing the descriptions of the boundaries of the Juan Bautista grant with the Piedra Lumbre grant to see if they were treated different and if they were, how it was done. (Figs. 14, 15).

The first grant we need to discuss is the Piedra Lumbre. Take this piece of paper and find where it shows how many acres the Piedra Lumbre Grant had. What does it say?

It says 48,336 acres, Grandpa.

When does it say it was surveyed—who was the surveyor?

October 18, 1878, by Charles Fitch.

Now look at this other paper of the Piedra Lumbre—how many acres does it say?

49,748.

How much difference is there—in acres?

1,400—wait a minute—1,400 acres more. That's the same amount of acres the Juan Bautista and the San Joaquín wound up with, Grandpa.

And the La Petaca. (Fig. 14).

I don't remember you talking about the La Petaca before. Where was it? Why are you bringing it up now?

The La Petaca Grant wound up with roughly 1,400 acres—just like the San Joaquín del Río de Chama and the Juan Bautista Valdez. (Fig. 14).

We can talk about the La Petaca later—right now we need to talk about the four grants around Cañones. (Figs.1, 14).

What's the date on the second map of the Piedra Lumbre and who was the surveyor?

It says: Surveyed between November 14 and 28, 1897 by George H. Pradt. That's 20 years later, Grandpa, why would they wait twenty years to do another survey?

I'll show you later—but wait until you see what they did to the San Joaquín.

Can we do that next?

No, we need to do the Polvadera. Here's the plat—what does it say?

It says it was done in June 1883 by John Shaw, U.S. Deputy Surveyor; 35,024 acres.

Here's another plat of the Polvadera, what does it say? (Figs.12,14).

It says: Plat of the Polvadera Grant in Río Arriba County, New Mexico by Clayton G. Coleman—August 11 through 17, 1898—35,761 acres. That's sixteen years later. And like you said the other day, Grandpa, they increased the acreage of the Polvadera by 737 acres.

I bet you didn't notice, Hijo, but the first maps for the Piedra Lumbre and the Polvadera were done by the Surveyor General and the later ones— the ones increasing the acreage were done by the Court of Private Land Claims.

I hadn't seen that. Why do you think they were allowed all the land they claimed? And more?

We believe it was because there was so little forest on the Polvadera and no forest on the Piedra Lumbre—the government wasn't interested in them.

It's time to look at the map for the San Joaquín, the grant Tijerina claimed the government had stolen. What does it say at the top of the map? (Fig. 14).

It says: Plat of the San Joaquín Grant for Francisco Salazar, et al.

Who does it say was the surveyor—and what was the date it was approved?

Stephen C. McElroy, Deputy Surveyor—May 1878.

Tell me what it says over to the right.

It has the names of the grantees, let's see—there were thirty-nine of them. It also says, Grant Dated, August 1806, Grant Approved, December 17, 1872, Acres: 472,736.

Here's another plat of the San Joaquín. How many acres does it show were in the grant?

It only shows 1,423 acres, Grandpa.

When does it say it was surveyed?

It says:

> Map of the San Joaquín Grant, surveyed September 20-30, 1901.
> Then it says: Corrected survey of South Boundary, May 27, 1902
> under Supplemental Order of U.S. Court of Private Land Claims
> dated April 2, 1902.

So this is what you were talking about when you said they'd reduced the San Joaquín from 472,736 to 1,423 acres—that the government took more than 471,000 acres from the people whose families had been living on the grant since 1806?

That's right. These maps support what I told you the other day and what's even worse—the government used a law passed in 1891, a law passed nineteen years after the grant had been approved by the Surveyor General, to reduce it. (Fig. 14; see also figs. 6, 9, 12 and 15).

We couldn't find a map showing whether the surveyor general had ever approved the Juan Bautista. This is the only plat we found for it. What does it say at the top?

It says it was surveyed in November and December 1899 with 1,468 acres. Exactly what you said happened.

By the way, I need to remind you of something I said earlier about the Juan Bautista west boundary—that the description in the grant papers themselves said that Cerro Blanco was the west boundary. And the San Joaquín west boundary was the Cejita Blanca to the south and Cuestecita Blanca to the north. The surveyor for the San Joaquín had no problem finding the Cejita Blanca and the Cuestecita Blanca but for some reason the surveyor of the Juan Bautista didn't find the Cerro Blanco. (Fig. 14; see also, 6, 7, 8, 9, 15).

Just to repeat—to make sure our heirs don't miss it—the grantees of the San Joaquín del Río de Chama, Juan Bautista Valdez and La Petaca and their heirs had been living on these grants for over 80 years by the time the CPLC took over 800,000 acres from them.

-11-
A Trip To Canjilón Lakes

You told me the other day that you'd be talking about how important a full moon was, Grandpa. What about it?

The full moon can be very useful—can have a lot to do with what happens in your life and when it happens. How the moon looks at any one time is important. For example—the moon is important when you need to irrigate. With a full moon you can see better to irrigate—use the reflection to tell when to change from row to row. A full moon also gives you a better chance to borrow water from a neighbor that has a habit of borrowing it from you.

Just so I understand what you're saying when you use the word borrow, Grandpa, you're really talking about using water that hasn't been assigned to you by the majordomo, Right? Like when the government borrowed millions of acres from our grants, borrowed billions of dollars from the Indian Trust Funds?

Yes. If the Majordomo has said, "Juan you can use the water tonight," and while I'm using it the level of the water slowly begins to drop until it gets to the point there isn't any water left in the ditch—I would need to walk toward the head gate and find out whether my dam had washed out or beavers had torn it out—or someone had borrowed it. Now, if it turns out one of my neighbors had borrowed it—I simply borrow it back. Of course there's no way we can borrow our land back from the government. We can trespass on it but as far as getting it back—unfortunately, that can never happen. All we can hope for, is that one day, the government will get a conscious and decide to return it.

Then the next time that person is using the water, if he's the kind of person that's always borrowing his neighbors water, I might want to return the favor—borrow some from him. But, Hijo, in a dry year, I wouldn't recommend spending any time playing that game because it can get dangerous—real dangerous. In fact, in real dry years, especially after it has been dry for several years, people borrowing water have been known to have very serious accidents while irrigating.

But there are other times when you can take advantage of the full moon, too. Let's say you have a customer who wants to buy 1,000—2,000 latillas. On a clear night with a full moon it's possible to cut a few hundred latillas or aspen poles and get them home before daylight. Now I'm not recommending you do it, but if 20 years ago, say—when I was younger and in good health, I found a place in the forest that had previously been granted to my ancestors—but "borrowed" by the government and being treated like it was a National Forest—I might have trespassed—for latillas.

But something I definitely wouldn't recommend, Hijo, is going into the forest in the middle of the night to cut down a snag, a dead tree, for firewood—especially if it's windy. You need to understand, Hijo, what I'm about to tell you is actually from an experience.

One night about 15 years ago, around three in the morning, five or six miles from here, I misguessed the height of a tree, the speed of the wind, and how close I had parked my pickup to the tree. As I was just about to cut through the tree the wind shifted and the tree twisted just enough as it was falling that it landed right in the middle of the hood of what had just minutes earlier been my brand new pickup. And that's not all—your Grandmother's brother, Larry, was in the truck when the tree hit and that's all he could talk about as we were stumbling along in the dark trying to get home.

I know you spent a lot of time over the years in the forest, Grandpa, but you haven't said anything about going out at night for an elk or a deer.

As I'm sure you know, there's so many elk and deer around here you don't have to wait until dark to get one. In fact I can't remember the last time I even went out at night to get one. I bet it's been twenty or thirty years; besides, I ate so much jerky when I was growing up—and when I was working in the forest, I don't really care for it anymore. About the only time I shoot at anything these days is when I find 'em having dinner in the garden or relaxing in the pasture.

One time last fall when there was a full moon I went outside to see what the dogs were barking at and I bet there were 150 elk laying down in the pasture after having grazed all night. It's possible I shot one, but as old as I am—I can't remember for sure. I do remember firing a shot to run them off, though. When elk lay in a pasture late in the summer, when the grass is tall and damp, they can ruin it.

I remember you telling me about fishing at the Canjilón lakes in the fall. Can you talk about that?

Okay, but I'm getting tired sitting here. Why don't we drive up to the lakes and I can show you where we used to fish. You can use that recorder in the truck, can't you?

Sure.

Maybe if you take your camera you can get some pictures for your grandchildren so they'll be able to see what this country looked like when you were a kid—before the Forest Service allows it to be clear cut—mined—or burned to the ground.

Let's take my Mom's pickup.

There you go—trying to use your mother's pickup without even asking permission, shame on you. We need to go in the Pedo Express—it's been a while since we used it.

Pedo Express? You're not talking about that old pickup next to the barn, are you? The one with the different colored finders? Come on, Grandpa, we can't take that, it's a piece of junk. Besides—when did you start calling it the Pedo Express? What's that all about?

Mike started calling it the Pedo Express after we spent an afternoon driving it around in the hills behind the old house. After we get started I'll tell you the story.

Why you handing me the keys, I don't want to drive that thing.

You need to be good for something, Hijo.

But Grandpa—the floorboards are all rusted out—and besides, it stinks when the motor's running.

Can you imagine what my father would have said if he told me to take the wagon and horses and go to the neighbors to pick up some wheat and I had said, "but Papa I don't want to take the wagon, every time I take it, the horses are always farting." Why he'd have kicked my butt if I'd talked to him like you just talked to me.

I'm surprised you'd even say what you just said, Grandpa.

Well—I guess I probably shouldn't have said it that way, but saying it like that got your attention—didn't it?

You want me to take it out?

Sure. You think I would have said it that way if I thought you'd leave it in?

I still can't believe you said it. But I get what you're saying—that it's called the Pedo Express because it stinks when the motor is running.

Exactly. But be careful—the brakes don't work very good.

And the windshield's so busted I can barely see—and there's a spring pinching my butt. You said when we were walking out here you were going to tell me about when Mike started calling it the Pedo Express.

It was last year in October when he was up here hunting. He only hunts during the season since he's a gringo and his family never got permission from Spain or Mexico to use the forest.

We were headed out for a ride one afternoon and I handed him the keys, like I just did with you, and told him to drive. We went out through the back there, to the north—behind the old house. He was driving along being careful not to scrape any branches and when we got to a place where the trees were real close together he started to back up but I told him he had to drive between them. As he was driving through the branches were scraping both sides of the truck and making a lot of noise.

After we got to the other side and had gone a little ways, I said, "I guess I'm going to have to sue you."

And he said, "What the hell do you mean—sue me?"

I said, "You just scratched the hell out of my pickup—ruined a perfectly good paint job."

He raised his voice a little and said, "how the hell can you say I ruined the paint job? There's not a inch of this truck that isn't rusted or busted—and the fender's are all different colors—the glass in the mirror's the only one that's not broken."

"I don't care," I told him, "you have to learn to be responsible—learn to respect other people's property."

He was quiet for a while and finally said, "If this pickup is that important to you I'll drag the damn thing to Juarez and get it painted."

"No way in hell you're gonna take this classic pickup to Mexico. It needs to be repaired by professionals."

"If that's the way you feel go ahead and sue me, cabrón. I'm not going to pay $1,500 to repair a damn $63 pickup."

After we'd gone a mile or two, he said, "You know what Juan—you've been one of my best friends for years. Such a good friend—I'm even willing, if you really want to sue me, to represent you—for free."

I thought about that for a minute and said, "I really don't think that would be a good idea—maybe you'd lose my case on purpose."

"What do you mean, I'd lose on purpose? I can't believe you'd say that— even after I promised to do it for free." After a couple minutes passed he said: "Well, go ahead—sue me—if that's what you want. At least I won't have to hire a lawyer—and besides—if you sue me I'm going to file a counter-claim against you."

Then he said, "We really shouldn't be making idle threats or rash decisions, amigo. Why don't we just relax, have a beer before we discuss this any further? It'll be a while before the elk will be coming out in the pastures— what you say we pull over here. Wait—thirty—forty-five minutes. Give you enough time to pee."

I told him that that was mean—that since I was older he should treat me with more respect.

Then I, asked him, "Why would you file a counter-claim against me I haven't done anything to you?"

"The hell you haven't," he said, "having to drive this piece of junk has caused me to suffer brain damage—serious brain damage—having to smell all that—exhaust. I'm sure by now it's a permanent impairment."

They I told him I hadn't caused his problem, that he'd had the mental condition he was complaining about for years—that a judge would say it was a pre-existing condition—that driving my pickup hadn't caused his problem.

How'd you come up that, with "pre-existing condition," Grandpa, that sounds more like something Mike would say?

What can I say, Hijo—I've heard them talking like that for years. I was bound to remember a few of their words.

So, anyway—it was when we were driving in the hills that he called it the Pedo Express.

We're almost there, you need to slow down and begin turning left. But then after you turn you need to speed up because it's steep and we need to get there with enough time to get home before dark—the lights don't work to good.

No, no, no—don't park there—it's too level. You need to park on a slope in case it won't start. Keep going—we need to stop at the top of the lake where the water comes from the spring. Hurry—but be careful.

So this is where you fished in the winter when you were young. I've been here a lot but I never realized you used to come to this end of the lake.

Yeah, the natives, the cut-throats—they come together just before it freezes. Hundreds come to this end of the lake. When they're here they make the water look like it's boiling. We used to come up here on horseback, bring gunny sacks, fill them with fish and take them home. After we'd clean the fish we would tie the sack in a tree and leave them there until they froze—then we'd have fish to eat for weeks.

Did you ever consider getting the fish that way might be against the law? Were you trespassing on our property?

This is a little too far east to be in any of the grants, Hijo. But I figure if I got caught I could argue that since the government took our grants—ran us away from the Chama River—maybe—no, I don't think that would work. I guess on those occasions I was just ignoring the law.

-12-
According To The GAO We Are Non-Indians

The other day you handed me the GAO Report and told me to turn to look at
Table 27: Non-Indian Community Land Grants.

Excuse me for interrupting but one of the reasons I showed it to you was
because it not only referred to our ancestors as non-Indians, like we had discussed before, but it has information about some community grants. What's
the title say:

> Table 27: Non-Indian Community Land Grants with Original
> Confirmed Acreage and Currently Held Acreage.

What does it say are the numbers for the Town of Abiquiú Grant?
There are three different sets of numbers, Grandpa. The first says, original
acreage confirmed, 16,708, then it has current community acreage owned, 16,425.
Then it says, acreage difference, 283.

So it shows that the Town of Abiquiú hasn't lost too much land. Look
further down the list; tell me what it has for the Juan Bautista Grant.
It says, original acreage, 1,468 and shows that it still has the same number of acres.
How about the San Joaquín del Río de Chama?
It doesn't show a community grant for the San Joaquín.
What about the Piedra Lumbre?
It doesn't say the Piedra Lumbre was a community grant.
And the Polvadera?
That wasn't a community grant either.
Before we go on we need to discuss the Juan Bautista some more. Dur-
ing the time the government was deciding how much land the grants should
have—how much they were entitled to—it said that only Juan Bautista's

heirs were entitled to land since the other people on the grant hadn't filled claims for their land.

In 1897, the Supreme Court in *U.S. v. Sandoval* ruled that there was no such thing as common land in the grants—that Spain and Mexico had never meant for land they had set aside for everyone to use belonged to the people they gave the right to use it. What it sounds like the *Sandoval* case was saying, Hijo, was that even though Spain and Mexico had said the land was for the use of the grantees, they really hadn't meant it: that the settlers had their own little plots of land where they built their houses and since Spain and Mexico really hadn't granted the common lands to the people like it actually did—the common land had really belonged to the United States since the treaty was signed—since February 2, 1848.

The *Sandoval* case makes one thing clear—that even though the United States signed the Treaty it was never serious, before, during or after it signed—about protecting the grantees rights.

We'll come back to that later, but for right now I want to talk about how the government was required to give the grantees notice anytime their cases were scheduled for hearings.

Read these pages, Hijo.

> The U.S. Supreme Court issued its first decision discussing what constituted due process under the Fifth Amendment in 1856, and it has been clear since that time that due process does not necessarily require a formal court proceeding. Rather, as the Supreme Court explained in 1877, where there is notice that a property interest is at stake and opportunity for a proceeding that is appropriate to the nature of the case, the judgment in such proceeding cannot be said to deprive the owner of his property without due process of law, however obnoxious it may be to other objections. As the Supreme Court commented in the early 1900's, the fundamental requisite of due process of law is the opportunity to be heard.

> As time has progressed, the Supreme Court has clarified that the opportunity to be heard must be afforded at a meaningful time and in a meaningful manner.

As discussed below, we conclude that the Surveyor General of New Mexico procedures met both of these fundamental due process requirements as the court defined them at the time and even today.

Even under modern-day due process standards, we conclude that the Surveyor General's newspaper notice was sufficient because it was reasonably calculated under the circumstances to apprise interested parties of the pendency of the Surveyor General process.

Now this is where it gets interesting. We found some information the GAO either didn't know about or didn't want to admit it knew about it. Read the underlined part on the second page.

Due notice by publication, in both the English and Spanish languages, as provided for by section 10 of the Act of Congress, approved March, 3, 1891, was ordered on April 23, 1900, and publication once a week for four consecutive weeks, was made in two newspapers, one El Boletin Popular published weekly at Santa Fe, New Mexico, the Capital of the Territory, and the other, the Bland Herald, published weekly at Bland, New Mexico (the latter being the newspaper published nearest the grant surveyed), notifying any and all persons claiming any interest in the tract embraced in said grant, or any part thereof, that they would be required to file in the Surveyor General's Office, objections in writing, setting forth the interest of the objector and the grounds of the objections, with such affidavits and other proofs as they desired to produce in support thereof, within the period of ninety days from the date of the first publication of said notice.

Now read the part that's inside the parenthesis—again.

"The latter being the newspaper published nearest the grant surveyed."

Do you know where Bland is—was, Hijo?

I have no idea. (Fig. 1).

I didn't either until I saw the maps. It was a mining town nine miles northwest of Cochití Pueblo—in the Cochití Mining District. To get there from Santa Fe you had to take a wagon or go on horseback on the Camino Real for two or three hours to the southwest; cross the Río Grande at Cochití Pueblo, and then go west another nine miles up a small canyon. That would take another hour or two and once you got there you'd be at Bland. There were no roads or trails from Bland to Cañones—from Bland to the Juan Bautista Grant—without going back through Cochití and Santa Fe. Once you got back to Santa Fe you'd have to go north about twenty-five miles to Santa Cruz and northwest another twenty miles to Abiquiú. At Abiquiú you had to take the wagon trail southwest another nine miles to Cañones.

The people in Cañones who wanted to know if they had been scheduled for a hearing were apparently expected to send someone to Bland every week to search the notices they didn't know about and couldn't have read if they'd known about them—just to find out whether they had to be in some court, somewhere, some day.

Would you like to know more about the Bland Herald, and the El Boletin Popular?

Not really.

Well, I'm going to talk about them anyway. When we started our history you said your teacher said that I need to tell everything, even if you know it already. I believe he also meant for me to say what needs to be said even if you don't want to hear it. Read this letter:

> Dear Sir: In reply to your request of the 23d inst. The Bland Herald has been published under the present management regularly every Friday since July 3, 1896, or one year, ten months and two weeks to date. Some seven months prior to the present management taking hold of the Herald, the paper was published under the same name but different management. The Herald's present circulation is general, 310 copies being sent weekly through the Bland Post office to bona fide subscribers.

I had you read that to show what kind of newspaper the judge had ordered the notice for the Juan Bautista Valdez Grant to be advertised in. It was being advertised in a weekly newspaper approximately seventy-eight miles from Cañones that only had 310 subscribers who received their copies through the mail. So if the newspaper mailed out all the copies there wouldn't have been any copies in Bland if someone from Cañones had made the trip to get a copy.

We need to read part of another document before we say anything else about the one we just read. While I'm reading remember that the San Joaquín is just north of the Juan Bautista—remember that they had a common border.

> Due notice by publication, in both the English and Spanish languages, as provided by the Act of Congress approved March 3, 1891, and amended June 6, 1900, was ordered by office letter dated August 15, 1902, and publication once a week for four consecutive weeks was made in [the] "El Republicano" published weekly at Tierra Amarilla, New Mexico (the newspaper published nearest the grant surveyed), notifying any and all persons claiming any interest in the tract embraced in said grant, or any part thereof, that they would be required to file in the surveyor-general's office, their objections in writing, setting forth the interest of the objector and the grounds of the objections, with such affidavits and other proofs as they might desire to produce in support thereof, within the period of ninety (90) days from the date of the first publication of said notice ... (Figs. 1, 14).

Why you looking so upset, Hijo?

You really want to know why, Grandpa? In the first order we read the surveyor general said Bland was the closest newspaper to the Juan Bautista Grant but in the second one the surveyor said the San Joaquín was closest to Tierra Amarilla. From the maps we've looked at Tierra Amarilla was closer to both grants than Bland was. You'd think government surveyors would be able to measure distances better than these two did?

When Mike and I went over this I asked him what he thought and he said the only excuse he could think of was that maybe the Republicano wasn't being published in Tierra Amarilla in 1900—or the Bland Herald wasn't published in 1902.

He was right about the El Republicano because it didn't begin publication until 1901 but wrong about the Bland Herald. But then he told me that that wasn't the only problem.

He said the order for the San Joaquin only required the notice to be published in the Republicano but that that was probably okay since it was published in English and Spanish. But, if it was okay to publish it that way then the judge in the Juan Bautista Valdez case should have ordered the notices to be published in Santa Fe since it was actually the closest town where a newspaper was being published and that if it was published in Santa Fe it should have been published in the *New Mexican* in English and the *Nuevo Mexicano* in Spanish rather than publishing in the El Boletin Popular and the Bland Herald.

But Grandpa, we've even heard before about newspapers that were caught printing a legal notice in a single copy of a newspaper—leaving it out of the rest of the copies. How—if the surveyors general were required to put the notices in the newspapers, could they get away with putting a legal notice in only one newspaper—or putting notices in newspapers like the Bland Herald that were so far from the grants that the people never would have know about them?

That had to have been what the government and the speculators were up to, Hijo, because during the times the surveyor generals had to publish notice for the Juan Bautista and the San Joaquín the two papers I just mentioned were being published in Santa Fe and they would have qualified to print the notice for both the grants. But you need to keep in mind that it was risky for the court to require the notice to be published in a Santa Fe newspaper—because the grantees and their heirs might accidentally have found out about it. And it was too risky for the GAO to bring it up—because then the world would have found out what was going on.

To make it even worse, the notice laws in New Mexico in those days required that notice be published in both languages in both newspapers. The Juan Bautista notices were not published in English in the El Boletin Popular, which was actually a scandal sheet, not a newspaper—or in Spanish in the Bland Herald.

-13-

Reies López Tijerina And The Alianza

I guess it's time we talk about what led to us going to the courthouse, Hijo.

Finally! I've been waiting for this since we began. I can't believe you're finally going to talk about it.

I first started hearing about Tijerina and the Alianza in 1963. I'd hear Reies talking about the land grants in Northern New Mexico on the radio. I was a little bit interested but didn't pay much attention to what he was saying until one day my father told me that he thought Tijerina knew a lot about our history. I told my father I'd heard him but asked how could he know about New Mexico history if he was from Texas—then I said that he was probably just doing it to make money.

Then my father said that Tijerina was the first man he'd ever heard talk like he did about the grants—that he seemed to know more about them and how our families had been treated than a lot of the old-timers that had been around forever.

The more I began to listen the more I got interested in what he was saying and it wasn't long before some of my friends, including my cousin Moisés, became interested. I remember that some of us even went to Albuquerque to meet him. By then I was starting to realize that he knew what he was talking about and the more I listened the more I became interested in what he had to say.

On July 4, 1966, after Tijerina and a couple hundred of his supporters had walked for three days from Albuquerque to Santa Fe they showed up at the capitol to protest the treatment our grants and our people had gotten and to complain about the way we were being treated by the Forest Service.

I didn't go on the walk because I was working but I showed up at the capital where he was explaining about the treatment our people had been getting. When I saw that the governor, Jack Campbell, didn't even bother to come out to meet with Tijerina after he and the people had walked for three days, I got pretty upset. I couldn't believe the Governor wouldn't even come out of his office to listen to what Tijerina had to say. After a while one of his flunkies came out and said a few words, but then he spun around and went back inside.

Tijerina impressed me when he and most of the people who had walked from Albuquerque set up a camp and refused to leave. I realized when they didn't leave that Tijerina was serious about what he was saying. Realized that he was going to keep up the pressure until something was done about our treatment and the treatment of our grants—about the Forest Service treating our people like it was.

About a week later Governor Campbell finally invited Tijerina and some of us to his office. I got embarrassed when we were there because some of our people were acting pretty bad—not showing any respect for where we were. I'm sure it was because they'd been camped out, waiting for a week for him to show up and were getting tired of the way they had been treated—but they should have shown respect for the place.

At the end of the meeting Campbell promised to contact some people in Washington on our behalf, but I don't think he ever did. After that, besides listening to Tijerina on the radio and talking with my friends about what he was saying—and paying a few dues—I really didn't plan on doing anything else.

Three months later a couple hundred heirs of the San Joaquín del Río de Chama showed up at the Echo Amphitheater—which was under the control of the Forest Service at the time, and took it over for several days. (Figs. 1, and 18—at T 25 N, R. 4 E).

I wasn't there that time because I was working. But the next weekend over 100 of us showed up and took over the Amphitheater again. It was on a Saturday and I remember "Gorras," that's what we called Baltazar Martínez, was there and had a rifle. Most of the others also had pistols and rifles. But all I had were my boots.

What do you mean all you had were your boots?

I'll tell you in a little while. During the week between the first and second time our people showed up at the Echo Amphitheater the Forest Service people were on the radio every day saying that anyone that went to the Amphitheater would be kicked out unless they had a permit. It was like they were inviting us to try and take it over again—so we did.

We were in a long line of cars and trucks with our horns blasting as we came up the highway and turned into the parking lot. There were cops, FBI agents, Forest Rangers, even Captain Martín Vigil and some other State Police officers were there—all waiting to see what was going to happen. The first thing we did was place two Forest Rangers, Phil Smith and Walter Taylor, under citizen's arrest for trespassing since the Echo Amphitheater had been part of the San Joaquín Grant before the Court of Private Land Claims took it.

There was an Anglo with us, Jerry Noll, who'd been saying that he was an attorney. I don't think he was but anyway Reies appointed him judge and as soon as the two Rangers were placed under arrest, Judge Noll—he liked for us to call him judge, climbed up on a picnic table and announced that the trial was going to begin. I know it sounds ridiculous now but it was serious business back then. After a quick trial Noll—Judge Noll, I almost forgot, found both of the Rangers guilty of trespassing and ordered each one of them to pay a fine of $500.00 and to spend eleven months and twenty-one days in jail. How he came up with that penalty has always been a mystery to me but I never asked him how he decided on it. After he announced the sentences he suspended them and told them they were free to go. Some of our members set up camp and stayed around a couple days until one day two car-loads of federal, state and Forest Service police showed up and ordered everyone to leave.

You still haven't told me why you mentioned your boots, Grandpa.

I'm getting there, Hijo, you still need to learn to have more patience. Like I was going to say before you interrupted me, there was something I did at the Amphitheater that I'm not real proud of—but at the same time— now that it's over—I'm glad I did it.

After we made the citizen's arrests of Smith and Taylor and they were being held on the ground in front of the table, I went over to where Phil Smith was and kicked him in the butt.

111

Why'd you do that?

He was the Ranger that was always giving my father trouble about our cattle and sheep being on the forest. My Father had died the year before and I was still mad about how he'd been treated all his life—so I kicked Smith in the butt to get even for everything he'd done to make my father's life so hard.

What'd he do when you kicked him?

He grabbed my legs but I broke loose and kicked him again. Then I thought if I could just talk about it with my Father I would tell him that I was getting even for the way Smith had treated him all those years.

-14-
The Pueblo Lands Board Indian And The Indian Claims Commission

Before I talk about going to the courthouse we need to discuss some more political history— talk some more about what we've found that proves that the GAO was trying to hide information—and then I want to say a little about what I've been told about the Constitution and international law.

All the time I've been talking about our past I've been saying that I don't have a problem with all the good the government's done for the Pueblos. We're glad the government passed the Pueblo Lands Act in 1924 and the Indian Claims Commission in 1946 to protect the Indians property rights, but, at the same time, we wonder why Congress didn't pass the same laws for our people. The 1924 law made the United States responsible for its failure to protect Indian property rights and gave the Pueblos the right to file claims for their losses. By passing the law Congress was admitting that the government had failed to protect Indian property rights and that something needed to be done about it.

The GAO Report says that between the confirmation of the Pueblo Grants and 2004 the government gave the Pueblos $130,000,000 and 1,757,000 acres of additional money and land. We've also found out that since the 2004 Report the government has given the Pueblos millions of additional dollars and tens of thousands of additional acres—and that there are still claims that haven't been settled. And during all that time the government has given the Spanish and Mexican grantees and their heirs "0"dollar and "0" acres since "borrowing" 30,000,000 acres of Treaty grant lands.

We're happy the government has admitted it didn't act fair with the Pueblos and that it is making an effort to make up for the way it had treated them. What bothers us is that the government has been willing to admit its mistakes when it comes to the Pueblos but to this day refuses to admit that it has made serious mistakes regarding the Treaty of Guadalupe Hidalgo and the Spanish and Mexican grants.

We believe the GAO should answer a question we have about all our people who are not only part Spanish and part Mexican—who are also part Indian? Everyone that talks about our past says that after all these years we're all mixed blood—cousins. Why can't the government protect the part of us that is Indian? I know that may sound strange but it isn't any stranger than what the GAO wants us to believe. I mean—how'd the government decide who was Indian and entitled to help and who was non-Indian and not entitled to help?

Maybe the government should do DNA tests, Grandpa—settle the question, like my teacher says: scientifically.

No one can say that we didn't live side by side with the Pueblos for hundreds of years, or that our people didn't intermarry over and over again and after all of that the GAO comes along and says that those who were living in Pueblos in 2004 were Indians and the rest of us—were non-Indians.

In saying the government has a duty to the Pueblo Indians the GAO wants us to believe that the government's duty comes from somewhere other than the Treaty of Guadalupe Hidalgo—that it comes from laws that existed before the Treaty was signed.

Let me give you an example of one way GAO has been intentionally dishonest. Open the GAO Report to page 186—where it says Appendix VII, Sec. 12. Do you see that Sec. 12 only has five lines and ends with the word "barred" and four dots?

Yes.

Take this copy of the Court of Private Lands Claim Act. It's the complete law—not just the part the GAO wanted us to see.

But, appendix VII says it's only excerpts from the 1891 Act establishing the Court of Private Land Claims. Why are handing me a copy. of the law when Sec. 12's already in the Appendix?

Because, Hijo, I'm handing you what a man I used to listen to on the radio when I was a teenager would call "the rest of the story." You're going to see when you start comparing them that the part the GAO left out was far more important than the part it left in.

Read the part of Sec 12 in the GAO Report after where it says: "and shall be forever barred...."

That's all there is. The word "barred" is the last word.

Now take the Act and—starting at the bottom of page 859, the sixth line of Sec 12 after the words "and shall be forever barred," and after the four dots, read what it says?

Well, right off it doesn't have the four dots. It has a colon. Then it says:

> *Provided,* That in any case where it shall come to the knowledge of the court that minors, married women, or persons non compos mentis are interested in any land claim or matter brought before the court it shall be its duty to appoint a guardian ad litem for such persons under disability and require a petition to be filed in their behalf, as in other cases, and if necessary to appoint counsel for the protection of their rights.

We believe the part you just read—that the GAO left out of its Report—is one of the most important parts of the law. It shows that Congress was ordering the Court of Private Land Claims—at least as far as children, married women and persons non compos mentis were concerned—to protect their property. A question we want answered is why—considering what you just read—why the GAO was claiming that the government didn't have a duty to protect the rights of non-Indians—the Spanish and Mexican grantees and their heirs. The part you just read, Hijo—that the GAO left out—shows that Congress was at least ordering the Court of Private Land Claims to protect the rights of non-Indian children, married women and the persons non compos mentis. What Congress was saying in section 12 of the act wasn't that only the rights of the Indian children, Indian married women and Indian persons non compos mentis were to be protected—it was saying the rights of "all" minor children, married women and persons non compos mentis, should be protected. It was saying the government had a duty to protect the rights of all children, all married women, and all people non compos mentis who might have some interest in the land grants.

What does non compos mentis mean, Grandpa?

Mike told me it means people who were incompetent—not able to care for their rights.

Unfortunately, "Sec. 12" wasn't the only section the GAO "overlooked." Here's another one:

> It shall be lawful for and the duty of the head of the Department of Justice, whenever in his opinion the public interest or the rights of any claimant shall require it, to cause the attorney of the United States in said court to file in said court a petition against the holder or possessor of any claim or land in any of the States or Territories mentioned in this act who shall not have voluntarily come in under the provisions of this act, stating in substance that the title of such holder or possessor is open to question, or stating in substance that the boundaries of any such land, the claimant or possessor to or of which has not brought the matter into court, are open to question, and praying that the title to any such land, or the boundaries thereof, if the title be admitted be settled and adjudicated; and thereupon the court shall, on such notice to such claimant or possessor as it shall deem reasonable, proceed to hear, try, and determine the questions stated in such petition or arising in the matter, and determine the matter according to law, justice, and the provisions of this act, but subject to all lawful rights adverse to such claimant or possessor, as between such claimant and possessor and any other claimant or possessor, and subject in this respect to all the provisions of this section applicable thereto.

Congress meant for the justices of the CPLC, the United States Department of Justice and the United States Attorney, Matt Reynolds, to protect the rights of the Spanish and Mexican grantees and their heirs the same way the Pueblo Indian's heirs rights were to be protected.

Congress wasn't saying that the CPLC, the Department of Justice and Reynolds were only required to protect the rights of Pueblo Indian children, married women and incompetents. It was clear from what was said that the Spanish and Mexican heirs rights were to be protected.

And when Congress was requiring the CPLC and Reynolds to file claims for settlers who had not filed claims it was clear that it was talking about the Spanish and Mexican heirs because individual Pueblo Indian settlers didn't have private claims.

Before we move on let me give you another example why we think the part of the law requiring the Court to protect the rights of the children was important. We found a census document that showed a house where there were six women and four children living alone. The record showed that all six of the women were widows—that they had all lost their husbands within the year before the census.

The law we were just talking about required Reynolds and the CPLC to protect the property rights of married women and children, protect any right they may have had in the grant. The law required Reynolds to find out whether any of men who had died owned any part of the grant and if they were the fathers of any of the children. We couldn't find anything indicating that the CPLC had appointed guardians for the children or done anything to protect any property rights they might have had. In fact the GAO, other than intentionally leaving the part of the law we are talking about out of its report, didn't bother to even mention that Reynolds and the CPLC had ignored the rights of the children, the women or the incompetent settlers. Let me say that again—the GAO not only left the part of the law protecting children, married women and incompetent grantees and heirs out of its report, it ignored that part of the law completely.

We never found a single document showing that a single guardian had ever been appointed to protect the rights of any of the people Congress said should be protected—not a single court order giving President Roosevelt the right to take real property from any minor, any married woman or any incompetent settler.

The other section we read required the U. S. Attorney to file petitions on properties where settlers had not filed claims to determine who owned the land. That never happened. Of the hundreds of people living on the Juan Bautista grant only the Valdez family succeeded in receiving any land since none of the other people filed claims. If the CPLC had filed on those claims like the act required, those people might have been able to keep the land they had lived on for generations. By Reynolds and the CPLC ignoring the law any claims they might have had are apparently lost forever.

The GAO didn't bother to mention that Reynolds had apparently refused to protect persons who had failed to file claims and to protect the property rights of minor children, married women and incompetent heirs.

Now that we've discussed some of what Congress ordered the CPLC to do to protect the interests of the minors, married women and incompetents, we need to read another part of the same law that ignores the parts we just discussed . Even though Congress appeared to be concerned about the rights of some of the people living on the grants it didn't have the same concern for the land they may have owned. The section we're going to read and talk about next actually allowed the government to do whatever it wanted with any of the land in the grants—no matter whether it belonged to minors, married women, incompetents—no matter who it belonged to; no matter what the treaty had said.

That sounds confusing, Grandpa. Are you saying that after Congress ordered the Court to protect the property rights of minors, married women and incompetent settlers, it turned right around and said the government could do whatever it wanted with the land? I don't get it.

To say the truth, I don't either—here's what it said:

> If in any such case, a title so claimed to be perfect shall be established and confirmed, such confirmation shall be for so much land only as perfect title shall be found to cover, always excepting any part of such land that shall have been disposed of by the United States....

Congress was saying that even though a claimant, any claimant, could prove he had perfect title, the United States could ignore the Treaty, ignore the perfect title—do what it wanted with the land.

That's not in the same law as the other parts you just read is it?

Yep!

What did the GAO have to say about that?

Are you kidding—the GAO didn't even bother to mention it.

Before we go any further, Hijo, we need to take a break from all the bad news and talk about some good news. I just heard on CNN this morning that the government has settled the Cobell case for $3,400,000,000. That's $2,950,000,000 more than the hand-picked, substitute judge had awarded. Congress still has to agree to the settlement but Cobell and the 500,000 plaintiffs appear close to getting back maybe ten percent of the trust funds they were claiming the government had cheated them out of. Just think, the case had been going on for over 12 years and in less than a year the administration has agreed to a settlement giving the Plaintiffs about seven times as much money as they had been awarded.

We need to talk about another important problem. A problem the GAO by its agreement with Senators Domenici and Bingaman didn't have to bother looking into, and that's international law. I won't be saying a whole lot about international law or the Constitution since I don't know anything about them other than what I've been told. The way it was explained to me was that when one country forces another country to sign a treaty, the one that used force was violating the laws about treaties. I'm sure it was explained to me the way it was because I wouldn't have understood what was going on if it had been explained the way lawyers talk to each other.

To start with, I was told that a treaty is like a contract. Mike used an example of a partido contract to explain it because I know what they are.

He said it's like if someone needs another person to watch their animals or grow their crops they'd try to come up with a fair agreement for the work to be done.

So, Hijo, if a person that owned cows or sheep would make an agreement with someone to take care of them while they were in the mountains and while the calves and lambs were being born the person taking care of them would have to protect them from wild animals and people trying to steal them. In the fall when he'd bring the cows or sheep back from the mountains the owner would count them and give the person who had taken care of them a share of the calves or lambs or a share of the crops as payment for the work he had done. The agreement was to share in the profits and, unfortunately, to share in the losses—which was usually the way most of the agreements around here turned out. Sometimes the agreements were in writing but since most of our people couldn't read or write they were usually done by shaking hands. One difference with treaties is that they needed to be in writing.

He explained that every country that enters into a treaty, like everyone that signs a contract, has duties they have to do for the contract to work.

Countries that sign treaties have certain things they are expected to do and if there's a problem with the way they treat each other, the way they have acted is compared to what the treaty expected them to do. For example, the parties to treaties are expected to have signed the treaty freely. In other words they're not supposed to have signed under a threat.

If one of the countries can prove that it wouldn't have signed the treaty without being threatened—that it was forced to sign—the treaty could be declared to be no good. Like a sheep herder who watches sheep only because the owner threatened him, made him do it—that wouldn't be fair and the person making the threat wouldn't be allowed to enforce the contract.

Mike said that every country that signs a treaty is expected to act in good faith and that a country that signs a treaty is believed to have acted in good faith until the other country proves it didn't. He said that sometimes it's hard to prove whether a country has acted in good faith—that it's easier to prove someone acted in bad faith if it can be shown that a country that started a war started it so it could take the other country's land. That if after a weaker country surrendered it was forced to give up some of its territory that would show that the country that forced it to give up some of its land hadn't acted fair and by not acting fair it was violating the treaty.

Do you have any articles or documents that back up what you just said? I don't think we should try to get away with just saying that's the way it works.

Listen to this:

> A treaty is void if its conclusion has been procured by the threat or use of force in violation of the principles of international law. A treaty shall be interpreted in good faith in accordance with the ordinary meaning to be given to the terms of the treaty in their context and in light of its object and purpose.

That was given to me as an example of what a court would look at when it was trying to figure out whether a country had acted in bad faith or whether a treaty was unfair. Mike didn't want to have me say for sure whether what I just read would apply to the Treaty of Guadalupe Hidalgo because what I was reading didn't become a law until after the Treaty of Guadalupe Hidalgo was signed. But he said it is important because it says that starting a war—like the United States did with Mexico—to take half of Mexico's territory—wasn't right.

I remember when Senators Domenici and Bingaman announced that they and Congressman Udall were going to ask the GAO to look into how our government had acted regarding the Treaty of Guadalupe Hidalgo, my friends and I got pretty excited—believing that finally, after more than a 150 years, the government was finally going to decide whether it had—just a minute I have what I want to say written down here somewhere. Here it is: "we were excited that the government was finally going to answer the question whether the United States had fulfilled its obligations under the Treaty as a matter of international law." As it turned out their announcement was just one more bull crap statement that, like all the others, turned out to be nothing more than another nightmare.

Sorry, Grandpa, but I'm pretty sure you had already said that, but I didn't want to interrupt you, because it seemed important for you to say it.

I think, even if I had said it before, it was worth saying it again. There was no way, really, looking backwards at it, that we should have expected the GAO would admit that the government had violated a treaty.

But what keeps me upset is that there's nothing in the Treaty of Guadalupe Hidalgo that says that our Spanish and Mexican people and Pueblo Indians should be treated different than any other citizens of the United States—treated different from the people in California, Texas or Colorado—or the Oregon Territory. Or that we and the Pueblo Indians should be treated different from each other.

By signing the Treaty the United States was supposed to be accepting the responsibility to treat all people who stayed here after the war no worse or better than the native Americans coming here from the east.

I've been told that even after the GAO and Senators Domenici and Bingaman agreed that it didn't have to investigate whether the U. S. had violated the treaty it still should have looked into whether the way our ancestors were treated violated their constitutional rights of due process and equal protection—whether, when their land was taken, they should have received money for it.

An example of something else that the GAO ignored was why the pre-emption laws available in New Mexico before the Homestead Act of 1862, were different from the ones in the Oregon Territory and whether, since they were different, they were violating our ancestors right to be treated equally.

And it's sad that in all the years the GAO claimed it was researching the treaty it never once tried to determine whether changing from a surveyor general to the Court of Private Land Claims to settle the land grant claims in New Mexico was fair.

When we were researching why our people were treated different than the people in other states and territories it became clear that a lot of the prejudice against our people must have been, like I said before, because the government was upset that our ancestors refused to leave their grants and go to Mexico.

Do you have anything to support that, Grandpa?

Yes, quite a bit, but one of the main statements that comes to my mind is something Senator Albert J. Beveridge, Chairman of the Senate Committee on Territories had to say about our people. His argument, which he didn't mind stating before Congress was that the Spanish and Mexican residents of New Mexico and Arizona:

> … [W]eren't equal in intellect, resources, or population to the other states in the Union. Nor, said he, were they sufficiently American in their habits and customs.

Beveridge's dislike for our people was so strong that he held up our becoming a state for nearly 10 years.

What would happen today, Hijo, if a Senator like Beveridge stood up in the Senate and said African-Americans, or Native Americans, or Spanish or Mexican Americans—or Italian Americans or Japanese Americans—or Polish or Irish Americans—are not equal in intellect, resources and population to Anglos? What would the news media say? No one could get away with saying it today, but he said it about our people, and the Spanish people in the Philippines and nothing was ever done about it.

Before I quote him again I want to mention something about the sixty years between 1850 and 1912.

Do you know how many territories became states between 1850 and 1912—between when California and New Mexico became states?

I wouldn't have known if you and I hadn't talked about it a couple weeks ago. I kind of remember that there were fourteen.

It seems like, after we compared the information about all the territories the only reason it took sixty-two years for New Mexico to become a state was because Congress didn't want New Mexico and Arizona to become states, Hijo.

After we found what Beveridge was saying about New Mexico not being equal in population to the other territories we looked up the populations of the territories. In 1850 when California became a state New Mexico had 61,547 residents. Ten years later our population was 95,500. New Mexico had more residents during the time Beveridge was saying we didn't than all the other territories that were granted statehood between 1850 and 1912—other than Kansas.

In 1850, Minnesota had a population of 6,100, Nevada had 6,857, Nebraska had 29,000, Colorado had 34,200 and South Dakota had 48,000. North Dakota had less than 2,000 and Montana had less than 10,000; Washington only had 1,200. Idaho had less than 10,000 and Wyoming had less than 5,000. Utah had 11,380 and Oklahoma had less than 30,000. Even though New Mexico had more people than all the territories other than Kansas—every single one of them became states before New Mexico and Arizona did.

There's another point I need to make. Between 1850 and 1900 New Mexico had more natural resources, including coal and timber, than most of the territories granted statehood during that time, certainly more than North and South Dakota; Nebraska, Wyoming Idaho, Montana and Nevada and at least as many as Oklahoma, Kansas and Colorado. New Mexico had four times as much coal as California and Oregon together.

Unfortunately, the one "natural resource" politicians in Washington believed New Mexico lacked was the one they considered the most important—Anglos. It's clear from the statements coming out of Washington between 1891 and 1910 that we weren't going to be given statehood as long as the majority of our residents were Spanish, Mexican and Pueblo Indian.

Here are some more of Senator Beveridge's statements that support what I've been saying.

> When in the early fall of 1902, his [Senator Beveridge's] committee took up the question of admission, he and a subcommittee made a whirlwind tour of the three Western territories. From the questions he asked it was clear that he liked "American" Oklahoma, but that he was acutely hostile to the idea of statehood for "frontier" Arizona and "Mexican" New Mexico.

> [I]t appears that Beveridge's real reasons were not economic or reformist but cultural. He returned to Washington believing that the Spanish-speaking residents of the Southwest were at best second-class citizens, passive, pliant, and uneducated. Beveridge and his supporters were to argue for the next eight years that the Spanish-Americans were not at home with United States law, its court and school systems, or even with the English language.

> WASHINGTON, Dec. 5. Senator Beveridge is preparing an exhaustive report on the Statehood bill to present to the Senate before next Wednesday, when it will be taken up as unfinished business and considered until voted on unless Senator Quay is sidetracked by Senator Hale and the other parliamentarians of the Senate who are opposed to admitting the three Territories of New Mexico, Arizona and Oklahoma.

> As to Arizona and New Mexico, it will be urged by the committee who visited the Territories that in parts of both the native American citizen sometimes feels that he is in a foreign country. Spanish is spoken and in some places public business is conducted in Spanish. The sub-committee that went out there recently found Justices of the Peace that tried cases in court in Spanish and spoke no English.

Did you catch where it said, the native American citizen sometime feels that he is in a foreign country?

Yeah! But why was it saying there were parts of Arizona and New Mexico where the Indians were feeling like they were in a foreign country?

It wasn't talking about Indians.

You need to read it closer, Grandpa. It said the native American sometimes feels that he's in a foreign country.

It's talking about settlers coming to New Mexico and Arizona from the east. Saying that the Anglos in the east were the first native Americans.

Why would the government be calling the settlers coming from the east native Americans? Other than the Indians, who were here first, our people had been American citizens for over fifty years by the time Beveridge was saying what he did?

Simply because of prejudice, Hijo—simply because of prejudice. In fact, like I just said, our ancestors, having been born here, were native Americans. And, according to Article VIII of the Treaty they had been, like you just said, citizens for over 50 years. The statement I just read was the reason I was making it a point to mention the term "native" Americans. That's where I got it. The first time I read it, I was just like you, wondering why it was being used the way it was.

We need to read the second paragraph of Article VIII of the Treaty. It says:

> Those who shall prefer to remain in the said territories may either retain the title and rights of Mexican citizens, or acquire those of citizens of the United States. But they shall be under the obligation to make their election within one year from the date of the exchange of ratifications of this treaty; and those who shall remain in the said territories after the expiration of that year, without having declared their intention to retain the character of Mexicans, shall be considered to have elected to become citizens of the United States.

Unfortunately, I'm not quite through reading what senator Beveridge had to say back in those times. There are still a couple of his statements we need to read. I'll read the next couple so you can hold your nose while I read:

> Senator Albert Beveridge gave this speech on the Senate floor, arguing in favor of annexing the Philippines and against granting

Filipinos self-rule, an issue that had much importance during President William McKinley's administration. Beveridge believed the Filipinos and Asian people in general were incapable of governing themselves by democratic rules. He based this belief on a conviction that Anglo-Saxons were racially superior, an attitude reflected in his speech. At the same time, Beveridge's views more generally demonstrate that territorial expansion by the United States at the beginning of the 20th century was closely related to racial bias and to the belief that white men had a burden to civilize a barbarous world. In his speech, he said: "But, Senators, it would be better to abandon this combined garden and Gibraltar of the Pacific, and count our blood and treasure already spent a profitable loss, than to apply any academic arrangement of self-government to these children. They are not capable of self-government. How could they be? They are not a self-governing race. They are Orientals, Malays, instructed by Spaniards in the latter's worst estate. They know nothing of practical government except as they have witnessed the weak, corrupt, cruel, and capricious rule of Spain. What magic will anyone employ to dissolve in their minds and characters those impressions of governors and governed which three centuries of misrule has created. Savage blood, oriental blood, Malay blood, Spanish example ... are these the elements of self-government?"

And here's another one,

The opposition tells us that we ought not to govern a people without their consent. I answer the rule of liberty that all just government derives its authority from the consent of the governed, applies only to those who are capable of self-government. We govern the Indians without their consent, we govern our territories without their consent, we govern our children without their consent. How do they know what our government would be without their consent? Would not the people of the Philippines prefer the just, humane, civilizing government of this Republic to the savage, bloody rule of pillage and extortion from which we have rescued them?

The reason we're reading about the Philippines is because our government had captured it during the Spanish-American War and we wanted to show how the Chairman of the Committee on Territories—who was responsible for holding up New Mexico's request for statehood, felt about Spain and Spanish people in the late 1890's and early 1900's. The Spanish American war brought back the governments fifty year old hatred of Mexico. It had been forty-eight years since California had become a state and most of the territories had become states and once again there was an increase in hatred for anything Spanish. The Spanish American War moved New Mexico and Arizona to the back of the line for statehood.

We need to stop for today but before we do I want to read something about Beveridge that I saved for last—something he did in desperation to prevent a statehood vote for New Mexico. It shows the extreme he was willing to go to, to deny statehood once he realized that there was enough support in his Committee to send the bill to the full senate and a sufficient number of votes in the full senate to grant New Mexico statehood:

> Beveridge was not to be defeated. After mobilizing many other senators and using filibustering techniques, he resorted to an unexpected device. For reasons of courtesy no vote could take place without his presence as chairman of the Territorial Committee. At the crucial moment he hid on the third floor of Gifford Pinchot's home for a week and the time passed when a territorial bill could be considered in 1903.

Remember the name, Gifford Pinchot, Hijo, you'll be hearing it again. And again.

Four years after Beveridge hid in Pinchot's house, he switched to the position that New Mexico and Arizona should be considered together, as one state, where Arizona would be its name and Santa Fe would be its capital.

After the "one state" theory was defeated in an election Marcus Smith, an Arizona politician, was quoted as saying about Beveridge that he had proceeded, "from his own argument on the principle that one rotten egg is bad, but two rotten eggs would make a fine omelet."

-15-
The Attempted Arrest Of Alfonso Sanchez Goes Terribly Wrong

It's time we talk about why we went to Tierra Amarilla and what happened while we were there.

Great!

To begin with I want to make one thing clear—we did not go there to raid the courthouse, like the newspapers and radio and television people wanted everyone to believe—we went there to make a citizen's arrest of Alfonso Sánchez, the district attorney.

Why would we raid a courthouse where we knew all the employees? Where everyone knew us? Where most of the employees were land grant heirs like we were? The people working in the courthouse were our friends—our relatives. It doesn't make any sense that we would have even thought about "raiding" our own people.

The story that "a group of revolutionaries raiding a courthouse in Northern New Mexico" got a lot more attention than it would have had it been reported that we had gone there to arrest the District Attorney. Can you imagine how big the story would be today, the way CNN, FOX and Telemundo carry on when they have a story they can make sound important?

We weren't a bunch of revolutionaries like Alfonso Sánchez wanted everyone to believe—we were just a group of land grant heirs trying to get the government's attention. All we wanted was a chance to explain how the government had mistreated our people and taken millions of acres from land grants our families had lived on for generations.

I know from all that's been said since 1967 that there are still people who believe that we were a bunch of radicals trying to start a war. That's why it's so important that we tell the story from beginning to end. It's important to prove that we had real claims, honest claims, to hundreds of thousands of acres illegally taken by the government from our ancestors.

On the morning of June 5, 1967 about 30 members of our group, the Alianza, and our families, got together for a picnic at Tobias Leyba's ranch here in Canjilón to discuss what we were going to do about Sánchez trying to keep us from having meetings and discussing our problems. I had come from Española where I was living and Reies, his daughter, Rosita and his son, Hugh had come from Coyote. Some of the people had come from as far away as Albuquerque.

We had talked a few times before about arresting Sánchez for interfering with our right to have meetings. On June 2nd, the night before a meeting we had scheduled for Coyote, Sánchez had about eleven of our members arrested, including two of Reies' brothers who were arrested while they were on their way to Coyote for the meeting the next day. On June 3rd we figured that since Sánchez had the police arrest some of our members there might be a hearing at the courthouse on Monday so we made plans to meet at Tobias' ranch in Canjilón on Monday to talk about what we should do next.

While I was on my way to Canjilón that morning I kept hearing on the radio that Reies' brothers and the others were going to be arraigned that afternoon and when I got to Tobias' everyone was saying that they had heard the news and we agreed that if Sánchez showed up that would be a good time to try an arrest him.

We already had some experience in making citizen arrests since the October before when, like I said before, we had arrested the two Forest Service employees at the Echo Amphitheater. The only reason we had arrested them at that time was to try to push the government into taking us to Court and getting an order to stop us from making arrests. We'd been told by some lawyers that if the court signed an order stopping us from meeting or demonstrating we might be able to go to court and tell our story about how years earlier millions of acres of our land grants had been *borrowed* by the government and *converted* to public property.

The government was way too smart for that, Hijo. Rather than getting a restraining order to stop us from taking over the Amphitheater they arrested some of our people for kidnapping. By that time some of the local newspapers and radio and television stations had started giving us publicity about how our people had their grants stolen by the Santa Fe Ring and converted to public property by the federal government, but we still needed for the whole country, the world, to know about our problems. In order to get the word out we needed to present our story in court. We had already figured out that there wasn't a judge in New Mexico that would allow us to explain our history unless we were getting national attention. So here we are, Hijo, forty-three years later—telling the whole story for the first time about what really happened to our land and our people.

We agreed at Tobias Leyba's that if we caught Sánchez at the courthouse we'd put him under arrest, take him to Tobias' and have a trial. If he was found guilty, which he would have been, we would sentence him and place him in a small shed and leave him there for a couple hours to sweat it out and then we would let him go.

While we were making plans to go to Tierra Amarilla, I said to Reies that if we took pistols and rifles there might be shooting—somebody could get hurt. He got mad when I said that. He never liked anyone saying anything about what he was saying. After I mentioned that someone might get hurt he said that we didn't need to worry—that once the people saw us coming toward the courthouse they would give up—that no one would try to stop us. That it would be like it was the year before at the Echo Amphitheater, that no one got hurt there. Then he said we should all wear masks.

I asked him why should we wear masks—we were land grant heirs not a bunch of robbers. We knew everyone in the courthouse, Benny Naranjo, Eulogio Salazar, the jailor; the County Commissioners were even there having a meeting. The Clerk was there, and the Treasurer and County Assessor—and all the employees.

Then I told him that if we wore masks everyone would know who we were anyway and they'd think we had gone crazy. I asked him what we had to be ashamed of—the only reason we were going there was to arrest Sánchez—that wearing masks could even make it worse because if there were police they would start shooting at us—we could all wind up dead.

Everyone except Reies agreed that we shouldn't wear masks.

Then someone asked who was going to be the first one to go in the courthouse and no one said they wanted to go first. I didn't want to because your grandma was going to have a baby any day—and because I might get shot. Since no one would agree to go first and we weren't getting anywhere talking about it someone said I should go first and before I could say anything, everybody agreed—it happened so fast I didn't even have a chance to say no.

Reies was quoted after it was all over saying that he had had his daughter, Rosita, dress up in her finest clothes so she could go in before the rest of us and look around and then come out and tell us if there were any police. Rosita was quoted later saying that she didn't have any idea why we were even going to the courthouse until we left the ranch and that she hadn't talked about it with her father. I don't know which one was telling the truth but I think it was Rosita because she wasn't all dressed up in fancy clothes.

While we were making plans, my cousin, Moisés, was told to drive to Tierra Amarilla and check out the courthouse and to let us know if there were any cops. He called back once he got there and said there were no more police than usual and it didn't look like they were expecting trouble.

We left Canjilón around three. I was in the front in my pickup and there were three cars behind me. We left about five minutes apart so when we would pass the Ranger Station the people wouldn't get suspicious. The best I remember, Gerónimo Barunda, we called him "Indio," was in front with me and there were some others under a tarp in the back. The ones I remember going to Tierra Amarilla that day were my brother Tony, Indio, Ezequiel Domínguez, Ray Morales, Tobias Leyba, Ventura Chávez, Baltazar Martínez, Baltazar Apodaca, José Madril, Salamón Velásquez, Rosita and Hugh Tijerina, Rosita's boyfriend Fabián, Alfonso Chávez and Reies.

Rosita has said that she and her boyfriend were in my pickup with me and Indio, but I don't remember. I kept thinking on the way to Tierra Amarilla about what would happen if the police started shooting and about your grandma going to have a baby any day. Then I'd think about my father and how bad the Forest Service had treated him all his life. I had a pretty tough time driving to Tierra Amarilla.

I heard later that Rosita has said that I was very quiet on the way to the courthouse which I'm sure I was since I was thinking about what might happen. In one story she was saying that her boyfriend started singing about what was going to happen when we got to the courthouse. I don't remember that since I don't remember him even being in my truck on the way the courthouse.

It took about thirty minutes to get there and after I had parked across the street from the courthouse the others parked next to me.

Benny Naranjo, the sheriff, was quoted a few days later saying he saw my brothers Tony and Elizardo in the parking lot. Tony was there but he didn't go in the courthouse. Elizardo wasn't there. I had told him to stay in Canjilón.

As I was crossing the street to the front of the courthouse and opening the front door I was hoping there wasn't going to be any trouble.

Everything changed the second I stepped through the front door. I had a .45 caliber pistol and had just taken a step inside when I saw Nick Saiz, a state policeman, to my left looking at a bulletin board. When he saw me, saw my pistol, he started going for his pistol. I told him to put his hands up that someone would take his pistol—that no one was going to get hurt. But I knew when he kept reaching for his pistol that I was in trouble. I had no intention to shoot him but there was no way for him to know. There wasn't time to explain that we were only there to arrest Sánchez—wasn't time at that point to do anything other than to shoot or get shot. I had put myself where I had no choice—unless I was ready to die—and I wasn't. It came down to I shoot him or he was going to shoot me—so I pulled the trigger. Lucky for both of us he didn't die. The bullet hit him in his left arm and chest and the shot knocked him back about ten feet where he fell to the floor. I felt terrible that I had shot him but I had put myself where I didn't have time to do anything else—it was my mistake.

Rosita said later that she and Fabián, her boyfriend, had followed me into the courthouse and that when they saw what happened they ran outside and told the others that I had shot a policeman. I never saw them in the courthouse. But the way she said it, it could have happened because they would have been behind me, where I wouldn't have seen them.

As soon as I fired the shot, "Gorras," Baltazar Martínez, who had come in right behind me with a 30-30 carbine, yelled for me to move so he could finish Saiz off. I told him no, that he was already shot—to leave him alone. He yelled again for me to move and I turned around, standing between him and Saiz, and told him that if he was going to shoot Saiz he had to shoot me first.

Almost immediately Benny Naranjo, his deputy, Pete Jaramillo and Tommy Cordova, the Justice of the Peace, came around the corner from the Sheriff's office. When they saw Saiz on the floor and saw me with the pistol they got down on the floor and Benny pushed his pistol toward me. Tobías, who had come in after Baltazar, picked up the pistol. After that I remember Reies, Moisés, Ventura Chávez and Indio all came in. Reies was wearing a handkerchief tied behind his neck and holding it in his teeth covering his chin. He either hadn't believed me when I said we shouldn't wear masks or thought by wearing one he wasn't going to be recognized. Baltazar made Benny, Pete and Tommy go to a back room where all the employees were and made to get down on the floor. The rest of us started up the stairs to the courtroom where we figured Alfonso Sánchez would be.

When we got to the top of the stairs and started into the courtroom we could see that it was empty. As I went was going through the door I looked to both sides to see if the doors were open. The one to the left was to the judge's office and it was closed. The one to the right was to the jury room. As we turned to the right I heard the door close. Just before we got to it two or three shots were fired through the door from inside the room. Lucky for us the shots missed. At that time Reies raised the machine gun he was carrying and fired a blast through the door. After he stopped shooting the knob and the wood around it fell to the floor.

I don't remember who went in first but whoever it was spotted Dan Rivera, the Under-Sheriff, with his pistol back in the holster. Someone, I don't remember who, grabbed Dan and pulled him through the door into the courtroom. As he was being taken toward the door going out of the courtroom Ventura hit him in the back of his head with the steel butt of a rifle. I was behind both of them and saw it happen. It was terrible. The skin split from the bone and blood went everywhere. Dan fell to his knees and his hands hit the floor in front of him. Ventura raised the rifle back like he was going to hit him again and I jumped between them and told him not to hit Dan again.

I had known Dan since I was a teenager and had always gotten along with him even though he had arrested me a few times for fighting. He was a good man. I wasn't going to just stand there and let him get hit again. Even though I did what I could to stop Ventura, Dan believed for the rest of his life that I was the one that hit him. But I don't blame Dan for thinking that I hit him because I was behind him when he got hit and there was no way for him to know who did it.

I don't remember going across the courtroom to the door on the other side of the courtroom, but I heard later that the judge, J. M. Scarborough, Mikes' father, was in a storeroom with his court reporter, Mike Rice, Monroe Fox, a blind lawyer from Chama and his wife—and his seeing-eye dog.

They all said later that they'd heard a machine gun. Judge Scarborough was quoted saying he knew what a machine gun sounded like because he had fired one in the army and that the shots he heard were from a machine gun. Even Larry Calloway, an Associated Press reporter who was in a telephone booth right inside the front door of the courthouse when I shot Saiz, and who was kidnapped later that afternoon by "Gorras" and Baltazar Apodaca, said he had no doubt that the noise he heard coming from upstairs was a machine gun.

I found out later that when the judge and the others who had been in the courtroom had heard the first shot while they had been visiting in the courtroom immediately headed for the judge's office. Dan had been talking with them and Judge Scarborough asked him to go with them but he went across the courtroom to the jury room. Maybe he thought it was somebody looking for the judge and he didn't want to be around if there was going to be any more shooting.

The Río Grande Sun and some of the books that were written about what happened that afternoon have said that Mike Rice called the Governor's Office to report what was going on and that the person on the other end of the phone had hung up. Other people have said that he had called again and held the telephone to the window so they could hear the shooting. After his second call the State Police and the National Guard were told by Lt. Governor Francis to head for Tierra Amarilla.

When we got back downstairs I was glad to see that Saiz was still alive. The whole time I had been upstairs I was thinking about how stupid I had been to believe that if we walked into the courthouse with pistols and rifles no one was going to do anything—that it was going to be like the day we were at Echo Amphitheater.

If there's one thing I want you to learn from all of this it's that if you have some doubt whether you should do something that could turn out bad—don't do it. That's what happened to me and I've had to live with it for over forty years. Every time I think about Saiz—about what happened—how he has suffered—I want to spin around and kick myself in the ass. And you need to leave that in, it's the truth.

Once we got downstairs I saw Angie Zamora, the ambulance driver, and Tommy Córdova, and Nick Salazar, one of the county commissioners, loading Saiz in the ambulance.

When I went outside I saw "Gorras" reach in the ambulance, grab the keys, and throw them across the parking lot. I watched where they landed and went after them. I'm pretty sure I handed them to Angie but some of this is hard to remember because I was so upset about what I had done. I wanted to do anything I could to help get Saiz on his way.

Someone told me later, and it was in the Río Grande Sun, that while we were upstairs, "Gorras" went around pulling telephone wires out of the walls and threatening people, including the sheriff—and that later he was shooting in the air and at police cars. I also heard that someone had gone into the treasurer's office and dumped all the money on the floor. I was glad when I heard later that when the employees counted the money not a penny was missing. It would have been terrible if one of our people—on top of everything else that happened—had stolen money.

When we got ready to leave we couldn't find "Gorras," and Reies was yelling for us to leave without him. I didn't want to but since we couldn't find him we left.

I think "Gorras" did most of his shooting after we left because I didn't hear any of it. I remember as I was walking out of the courthouse, seeing a state policeman running across a field by the old high school and I heard later that after we left two state police cars had driven up and someone, probably "Gorras," started shooting to keep them away. It wasn't until a few days after that when I heard that "Gorras" and Baltazar Apodaca had taken Larry Calloway and Pete Jaramillo as hostages and driven them to Canjilón in Pete's car.

On the way to Canjilón Reies told me that Eulogio Salazar, the jailer, had been shot trying to jump out of a window in the Sheriff's office. He said he and "Gorras" had run after Eulogio and tried to convince him that no one wanted to hurt him. He was also quoted later saying he tried to get Eulogio to come back to the courthouse because he didn't want anyone leaving who might tell the police what was going on. I never saw Reies go outside from the time he followed me up the stairs until we left together so I don't know when he and "Gorras" could have run after Eulogio like he said they did.

Moisés told me later that evening that when Eulogio was jumping out a window he was hit by a ricocheting bullet. I never saw Eulogio the entire time I was at the courthouse so I can't say who shot him or how he got shot.

As we were passing the Canjilón Forest Service Office heading for Tobias place he, Tobias, told me to pull over that we still had some unfinished business. When I told him I wasn't going to pull over he grabbed the steering wheel and tried to turn my truck, but I didn't let him.

There were still a lot of people at the ranch when we got back. While we were talking about what had happened I began to hear sirens coming toward the ranch and realized we had to get out of there.

From the moment I shot Saiz, until right now I've felt bad about shooting him—and for what happened to Dan and Eulogio—and for scaring all the people at the courthouse that day. It wasn't what we went there to do. When we left Canjilón, none of us, so far as I know, believed that we would be hurting anyone. What happened is an example of what can happen when someone comes up with a stupid plan and tries to carry it out. The only reason we went was to arrest Alfonso Sánchez and look what happened, we wound up hurting our own people—good people—people who had lost their rights to the land just like our ancestors had.

Can you explain how you kept from being caught? How you escaped?
Sure.

My teacher and I were talking yesterday about what you might say and he said of all the newspapers and books he's read no one has ever explained where you all went once you left the Leyba ranch. The only thing I remember Tijerina saying about it in the English translation of his book was that after you left the ranch and were going through the forest he could see the lights from the plaza in Tierra Amarilla. But that would have been impossible because T. A. was more than 20 miles away—on the other side of T. A. Hill.

I think he just got it mixed up. From where we were he had to have been seeing the lights in Canjilón and maybe thought it was Tierra Amarilla.

After we started seeing flashing lights coming toward the ranch from near the church we knew we had to get out of there quick . Since we hadn't even thought about having to run we weren't prepared. Once Tobias' wife and the other women had heard we were about to take off they gave us some sardines and tortillas that were leftover from the picnic. We didn't realize until a couple hours later, when we were already in the forest, that we didn't have any water. I guess it's because we hadn't even thought about taking water since it was raining.

We ran to the fence, crossed it, and headed southeast into the forest. There were six of us. I was in front and Reies, his son Hugh, Indio, Moisés, and Jerry Noll were all following. (Fig. 17).

After about a mile we turned south and a couple miles further we turned more to the west. After another mile or so we crossed the Canjilón to El Rito road and headed toward Montoya and Blas Canyons and the Chama Highway. After we crossed the road to El Rito we were south of Placita García where Ernesto and Geraldine Garcia live. I learned a few days later that two of Ernesto's brothers, Leroy and Danny and a friend of theirs, Ramoncito Baldonado were putting gas in Leroy's car there in Canjilón when "Gorras" ordered them to drive him and Pete Jaramillo, who he had taken hostage at the courthouse, toward El Rito. When we left Canjilón we had two rifles, some pistols, a battery radio, and a pair of binoculars that Reies lost during the night. Several years later Ernesto found them in Blas Canyon. (Fig. 17).

It was raining so hard that when it started getting dark it was almost impossible to see where we were going. Besides the rain and getting dark we were having to stop every 20 or 30 minutes for Jerry Noll to catch up. He was so out of condition that there wasn't any way he could keep up with us. After we'd stopped three or four times I told him I was sorry but we had to keep moving and if he couldn't keep up maybe he should go back. I felt bad leaving him out there but I was afraid the police might catch up with us if we had to keep waiting for him.

After we'd walked a few hours Reies said we should stop until it got light so we could see where we were going. We stopped until just before daylight, listening to the radio, and trying to stay warm without a fire. (Fig.17).

While we were stopped I found a Los Angeles radio station and we listened to what they would be calling "breaking news" today. First there would be a story about a war in Israel and then it would switch to the revolution in New Mexico. The stories kept going back and forth—back and forth. I was hoping to hear that Saiz was still alive but they never said anything about him.

When it started getting light we could see that we had stopped just before we had come to a cliff. If we'd kept walking we probably wouldn't have seen it and since I was in front I might have walked right over it.

About a half hour after we started walking again we came to a ridge on the east side of Navajo Canyon where we could look down at the highway that runs from Española to Chama. It was getting light enough to see everything that was going on. We stayed there for a while, watching jeeps, trucks, and busses heading north that looked like they were carrying soldiers. I heard later that they were full of National Guard troops.

We left the rifles and radio under a big rock since it would have been hard to go down the ridge, cross the highway, and climb up the other side carrying them—and we figured if the police saw us with rifles they would be more likely to shoot at us.

We walked south along the ridge until we were across from the Grotto on the west side of the Chama Highway—the one they call "La Virgen." (Fig. 17).

That's where we crossed the highway. The best I can remember Moisés was the last one to cross and when he got across to where I was he said that while he was trying to hide from a police car that was going by he thought the officer had seen him but kept going.

A couple days later I found out that Jerry Noll had kept walking in the same direction we were going and had come out to the Chama Highway at Banco del Burro about a mile south of where we had crossed the highway. I don't know how he made it because there were a lot of cliffs between where we left him and where he came out to the highway. Considering how dark it was—and how hard it was raining, he was lucky he didn't fall over a cliff.

From "La Virgen" we climbed southwest up a steep canyon almost to the top of Mesa de las Viejas. (Fig. 17).

We walked all day just below the ridge—a couple of hundred feet below the top—so we couldn't be seen from the top or from the road. We followed the ridge for miles until we were above the Chama River. It took us all day because we'd have to stop and hide under the trees or behind rocks every time we saw police cars, jeeps or airplanes. There were times when the airplanes were even lower than we were.

Our food lasted all day but it was hard walking because we didn't have any water. As long as we were just below the top of the mesa we would drink from what they call baños de parajos—birdbaths—lava rocks that have holes that fill up with rain water. Later, when we started going down toward the Chama River, there were times when we were so thirsty we would drink from hoof prints in the clay.

After we'd climbed down almost to the Chama River we stopped to rest under some trees. One of the times we stopped Reies crawled under a tree to rest and there was a canteen on the ground right in front of him. We drank the water and took the canteen with us, filling it up when we were crossing the River. (Fig.17).

About a week later I saw Salomon Velásquez and he said he'd been arrested the morning after we were at the courthouse and while they were taking him to Española he said he heard on the police radio that they had spotted us walking along the ridge. None of the cars or airplanes we saw ever looked like they knew where we were. We even watched airplanes dropping some kind of white powder over Mesa de las Viejas but we never found out what it was.

What were you thinking—talking about?

I was worried about your grandmother—and about Saiz. I was hoping he was still alive and I was worried about your grandmother having the baby, hoping that what had happened wouldn't cause her to have any problems. I didn't talk much with the others because I was feeling so stupid for putting myself where I had to shoot somebody just to stay alive. When we did talk it was mostly about the cars and airplanes we were seeing. I think Moisés asked me a couple times what I thought they would do if we got caught. I don't remember what I told him—but it couldn't have been good.

Can you tell the part about crossing the Chama river? It was scary the first time you told me about it.

It was almost dark when we started to cross. Since it was early in June the water was running real fast and was cold from the snow melting. We crossed at a place where the river had to be turning back toward the east because the further we went in the river the deeper it got and the faster it was running. Moisés and I didn't know how to swim and we yelled to the others to help us. Indio got a hold of Moisés and Reies grabbed my arm. The water was up almost to my chest and very fast. We might have drowned if Indio and Reies hadn't been there to help us.

After we got out of the water we stayed under some trees for a while because it was still light and it would have been easy for the police to spot us climbing out of the canyon. Later—after we had walked a few miles, Reies started getting tired so Moisés and Indio took off ahead to get some horses but we got to Celestino Velasques's cabin before they got back. Uvaldo, Celestino's son was there and said we could stay in the cabin.

The next day, around noon, Reies told us that a reporter was going to be coming to the cabin and after dark three people showed up in a pickup. There were two Anglos and a Spanish guy that I saw. They were Peter Nabokov, a reporter with the New Mexican, I think. And a man called Clark Knowlton, who was a professor that said he was from El Paso. And Joe Benitez was with them. I think there was someone else driving the pickup. Maybe it was Reies' brother, Cristobal, but I can't say for sure.

Nabokov and Knowlton stayed talking with Reies until almost daylight. In fact, Indio was the one that told them they'd better leave when it was about to be light. The one named Nobokov had a typewriter and he spent the whole night asking Reies questions and then typing. They had some newspapers with them and Moisés and I looked through them to see if there was anything about Saiz—but there wasn't. Other than what we heard on the Los Angeles radio station and read in the newspapers they had with them we didn't hear any other news while we were out there.

One of the stories in the paper said that the police had El Rito and Vallecitos surrounded. I knew when I heard that, that the police and National Guard thought we had headed for El Rito because we had gone to the southeast when we left Tobias' house. They never figured we'd turn west and head toward Youngsville. Actually—east had been the only way we could have headed into the forest from Tobias' house once we saw the police coming. We were being given credit for being good at hiding in the forest while we weren't anywhere near where they thought we were.

Reies and his son left a couple days later—after Reies had told us they were going to Albuquerque to contact the police and tell them that the only way they would turn themselves in was if the police would agree not to charge any of us with any crimes. From what I've heard since then I don't think that's what he was planning to do. I think he was trying to get to Albuquerque so he could claim that he and his son hadn't even been at the courthouse. One reason I feel that way is because during his trial he testified that although he was in Tierra Amarilla on June 5th he hadn't gone to the courthouse until after everything was over. I found out when I turned myself in that they were arrested before they even got to Albuquerque because Reies had been spotted getting out of a car at some business and a roadblock had been set up to catch them.

Moisés, Indio and I stayed at the cabin for three or four days after Reies left and one night we walked to a bar in Youngsville where Nasario Barela from Coyote picked us up and took us to Española. He had let me out where your grandmother and great-grandmother were living—where I was living before we had gone to the courthouse.

When we got to Española I found out that Luisa had been born two days after we'd been to the courthouse and that Saiz was alive and expected to live.

Your grandmother gave me a piece of paper with a telephone number and a note saying for me to call if I wanted to turn myself in. I called the number and it was a State Policeman named Romero. I met him and he took me to the penitentiary where I had to stay for several months.

When the guards took me to the maximum security part of the prison everyone started yelling and clapping. Some of the prisoners had even written songs and were singing about what had happened at the courthouse.

Reies, Moisés, Indio and some of the others, who had already been arrested, including my brother, Tony, were already there when I got to the prison.

At first I felt good about all the attention but when I figured that the only reason they were acting the way they were was because I had shot a policeman I realized they were happy about something that made me feel sad. But I knew better than to tell them how I felt about what I had done.

It wasn't until some years later that I heard that Saiz was going to have problems with his arm for the rest of his life and I knew when I heard it, that it was because I'd been stupid enough to put myself where I had to shoot him. The point I keep trying to say is always take time to think about what could happen before you haul off and do something stupid. I didn't go to the courthouse to hurt anyone. My big mistake was that I let Reies convince me that no one was going to get hurt. But I can't blame him for that. After all—I was old enough to know better than to go to the courthouse with a pistol.

While we were still being held at the prison Indio came to me and said that he wanted to claim that he was the one that shot Saiz since he was single and because I had a wife and four children. I told him no, but he did anyway. He even took a lie detector test and passed it.

After Reies had represented himself and testified that he wasn't at the courthouse until after the shooting and the jury found him not guilty I decided to tell a different story myself.

But it didn't work for me. Saiz testified that Indio didn't shoot him, that I had, and the jury found me guilty. Then later the government filed charges against Indio for lying and he went to prison for a year and a half.

I felt real bad for him having to spend time in prison for trying to help me.

About three weeks after I had turned myself in the police brought "Gorras" to where we were. He told me that he'd spent most of the time hiding behind our house, my mother's house, here in Canjilón.

He said he would stay in the hills during the day and come in after dark and then he would leave before it got light. He told me that he'd gone through the mountains to El Rito a couple times. He also told me that he and my sister Gertrudes had decided to get married when he got out.

He said the reason he'd turned himself in was because his mother had talked Governor Cargo into giving her the $500 reward he had offered if she would turn him in and that after Cargo had agreed she had promised that if he turned himself in she would give him the money so he could get married.

Sure enough, when we were released his mother gave him the money and he and my sister got married. Your grandmother and I went to the wedding—and the wedding dance. Guess who showed up at the dance?

I know because you told me before, but you need to say it anyway.

Freddy Martínez and Carlos Jaramillo, the two State policemen that had been chasing us after we had gone to Tierra Amarilla. I really don't know why they came because they weren't invited but it seemed like they had a good time.

A few months after I got out on bond and when I was driving home from work there was a roadblock between the Chama Highway and Canjilón. The policeman that was in the road waived for me to go through and I did. A little while later the same two officers that had come to the dance, Freddie and Carlos, showed up at my house and told me I had to go with them— that Eulogio had been murdered and I was under arrest.

Since I'd just come from work I asked them if I could take a shower and change clothes. They said I could but that they had to take the clothes and boots that I had been wearing. After I took a shower and got dressed we went to their car and they said for me to get in the back seat. They didn't even handcuff me. Within the next couple days everyone that had been arrested before was back in the maximum security part of the prison again.

I've been thinking ever since you told me last week that today was the day you were going to talk about going to the courthouse, how important it could be if we could find something in the old newspapers quoting witnesses who'd seen you at the courthouse—see if there's anything officer Saiz has said about it. It'd probably take a miracle to find something that agrees with the way you say it happened but it wouldn't hurt to look through the old papers.

After we talked about it last week I got to thinking the same thing. I figure after you hear what we found since we talked you might want to start believing in miracles.

First, I want you to read what Larry Calloway said on June 5, 2007 forty years after we were at the courthouse. He'd written some of it for a magazine right after it had happened:

> I do not think shots fired in anger at T. A. involved an intent to kill. State Police Officer Nick Saiz was shot once through a lung and upper arm when Juan Valdez panicked, thinking he was going for his gun.

There you have it, Hijo. An Anglo reporter that was there and saw what happened says he didn't think I was shooting to kill—that I was thinking he was going for his gun. It can't be much clearer than that. And if someone hears what I just said and still doesn't believe me—needs more evidence, here's what Officer Saiz had to say 20 years after it happened.

> [Saiz] says raider Juan I.[sic]Valdez covered him with a .44caliber pistol and demanded [Saiz] turn over his handgun. According to Valdez, however, Valdez told the officer to put his hands in the air.
>
> "Maybe I moved a little too fast," the captain said. "Being that I was young and so on, I was probably going to outdraw him."

In another newspaper Saiz was quoted saying:

> "Juan Valdez had a weapon on me; he had a pistol," [Saiz] told the Journal. "He asked me for my gun and when I went for it—I don't know, maybe I moved fast to give the gun to him or maybe I was going for my gun. That's been 20 years ago."

Then the article went on to say:

> [Saiz] now serves as captain of the State Police in Socorro. He continues to feel some pain from his wound, which left his arm 1 1/2 inches shorter. But he said he doesn't think much about the raid these days.

Even Saiz has sympathy for the land grant families in Northern New Mexico:

"I think these poor people lost their land by not being educated, and that the U.S. government should have recognized that these lands were given to these people just the way Indians were given their reservations," [Saiz] said.

He added: "The overall goal ... I can identify with, but not with the way they went about it."

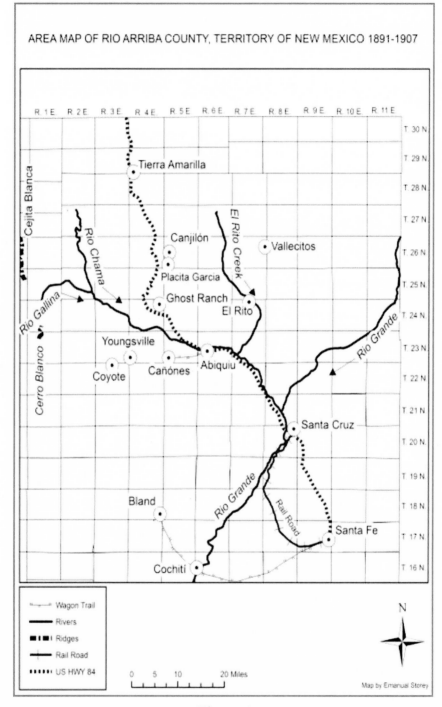

Figure 1

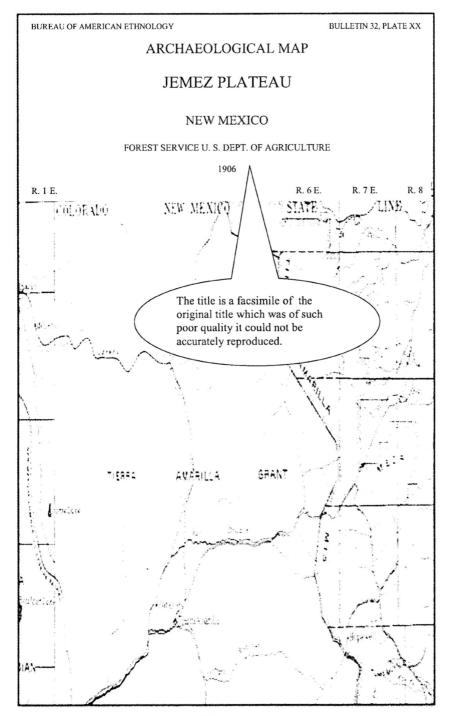

BUREAU OF AMERICAN ETHNOLOGY

BULLETIN 32, PLATE XX

ARCHAEOLOGICAL MAP

JEMEZ PLATEAU

NEW MEXICO

FOREST SERVICE U. S. DEPT. OF AGRICULTURE

1906

The title is a facsimile of the original title which was of such poor quality it could not be accurately reproduced.

Figure 2

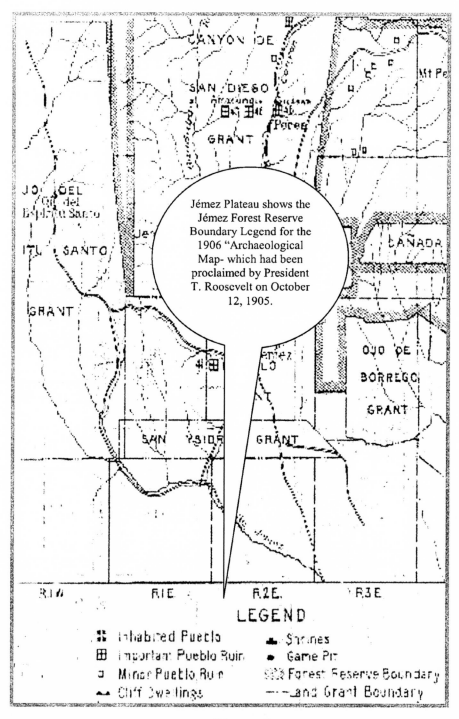

Jémez Plateau shows the Jémez Forest Reserve Boundary Legend for the 1906 "Archaeological Map- which had been proclaimed by President T. Roosevelt on October 12, 1905.

Figure 3

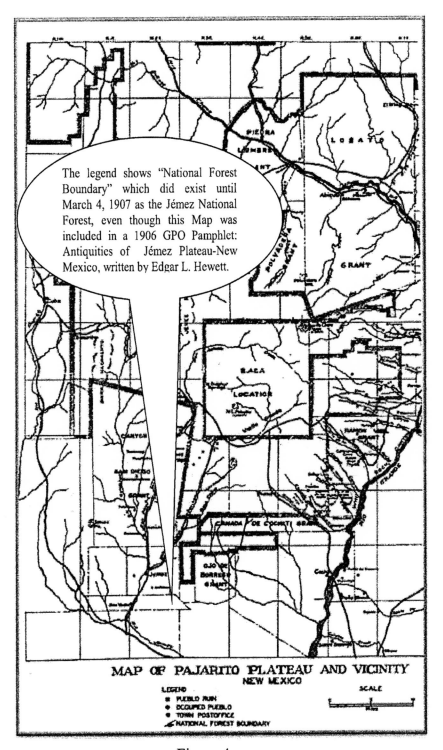

Figure 4

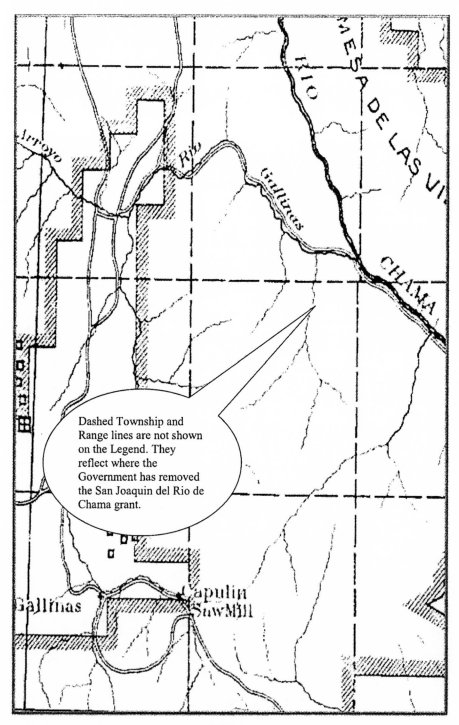

Figure 5

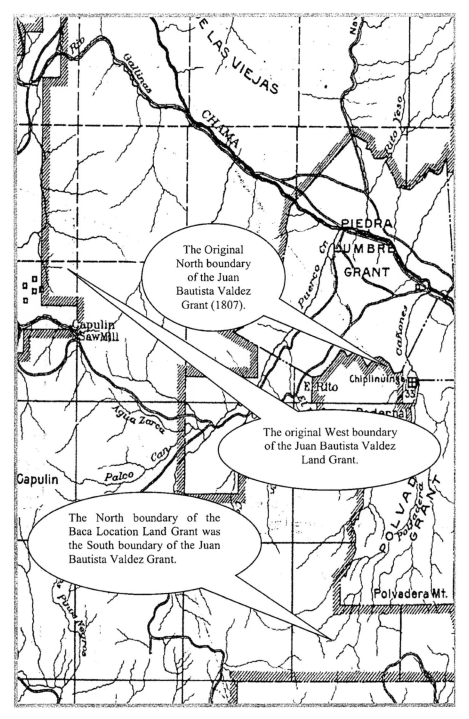

Figure 6

Mike Scarborough

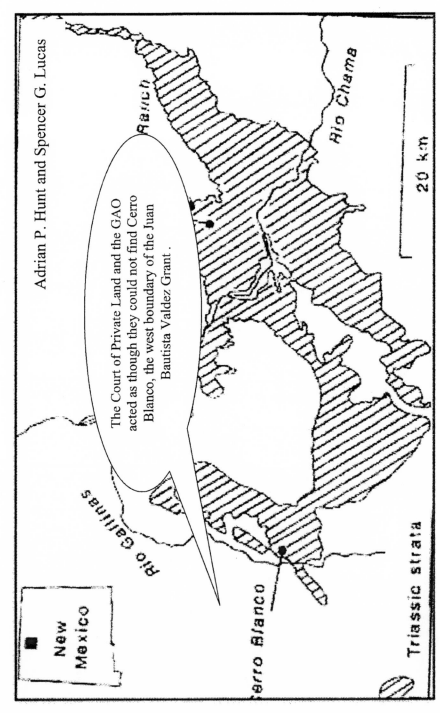

Figure 7

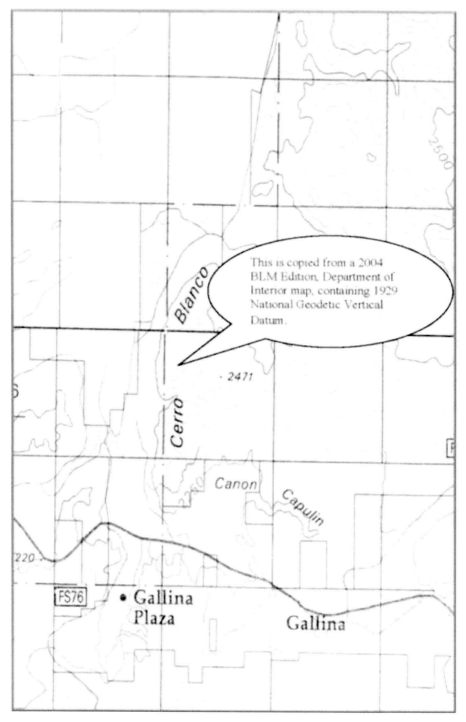

Figure 8

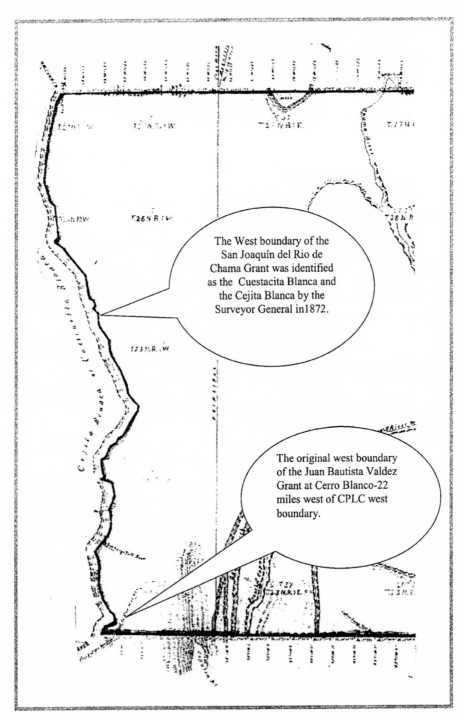

Figure 9

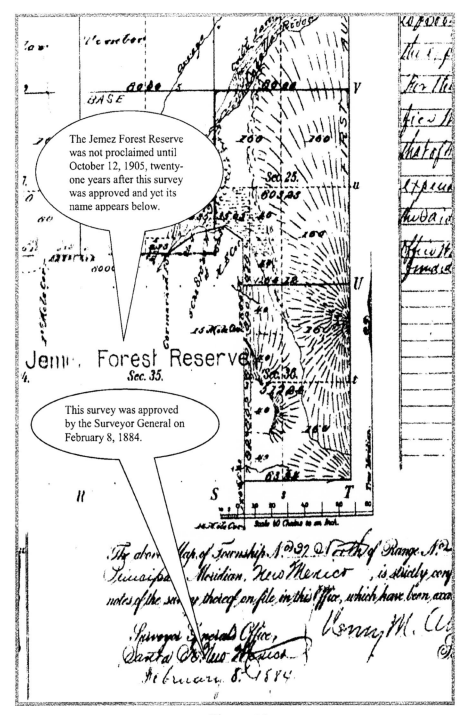

Figure 10

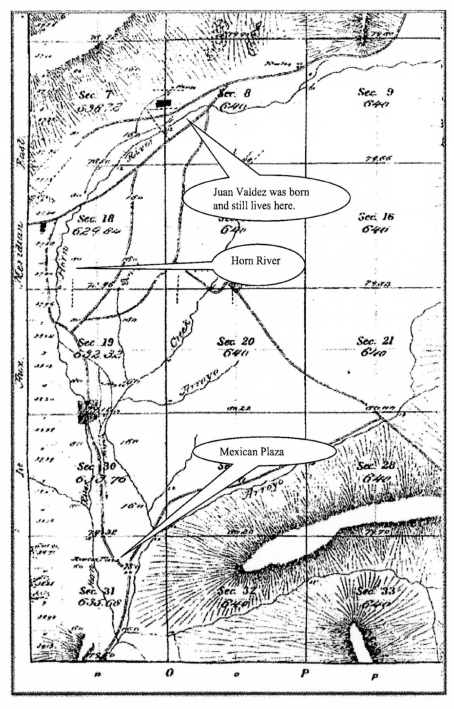

Figure 11

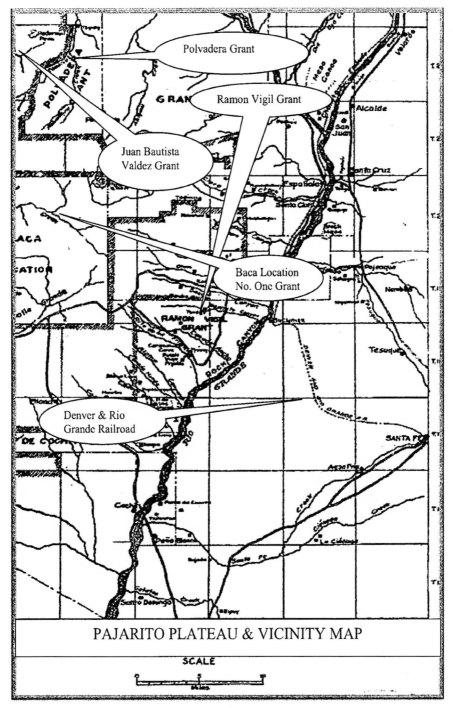

Figure 12

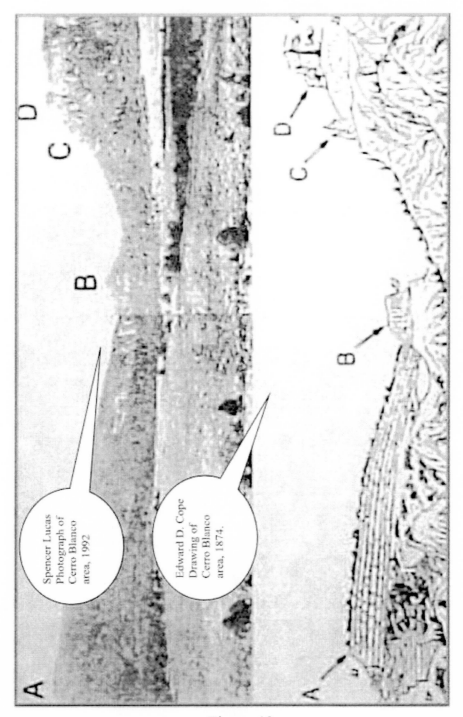

Figure 13

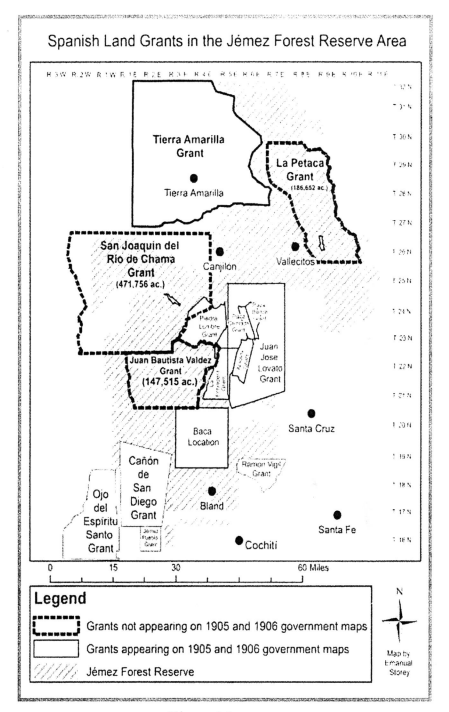

Figure 14

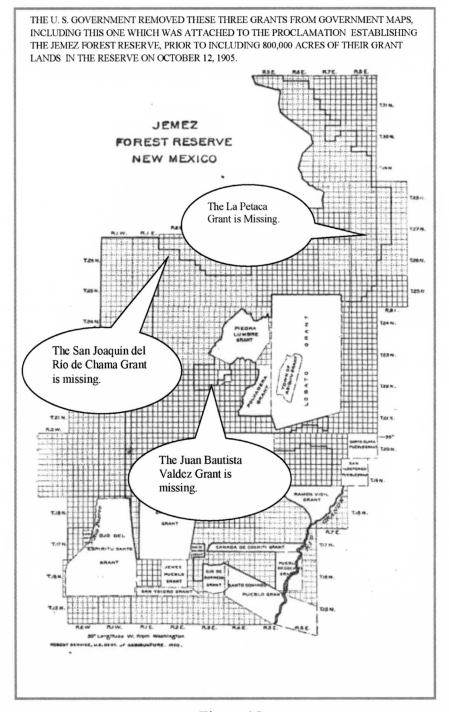

Figure 15

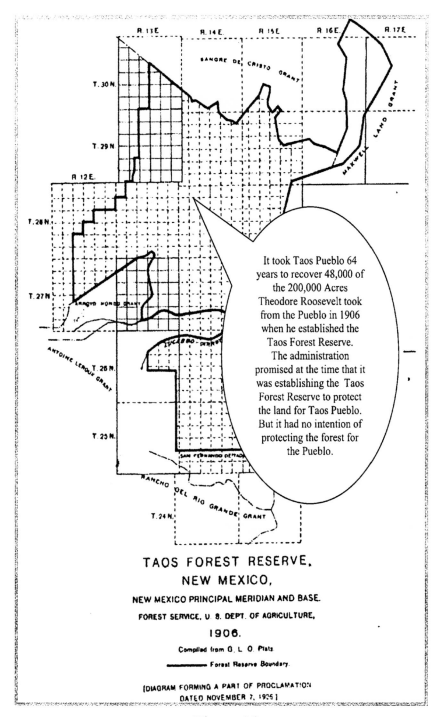

Figure 16

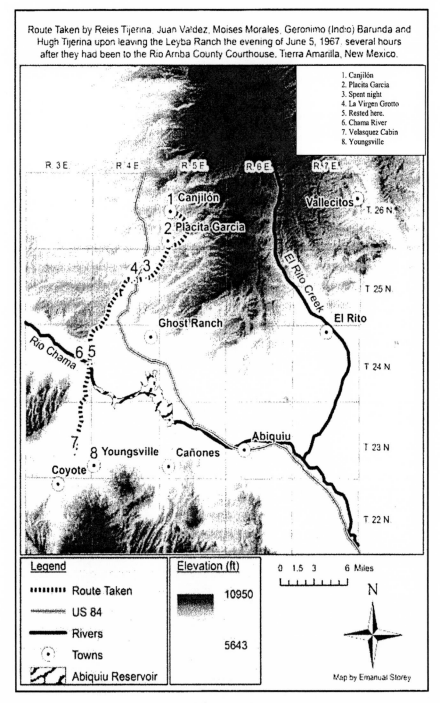

Route Taken by Reies Tijerina, Juan Valdez, Moises Morales, Geronimo (Indio) Barunda and Hugh Tijerina upon leaving the Leyba Ranch the evening of June 5, 1967, several hours after they had been to the Rio Arriba County Courthouse, Tierra Amarilla, New Mexico.

1. Canjilón
2. Placita Garcia
3. Spent night
4. La Virgen Grotto
5. Rested here.
6. Chama River
7. Velasquez Cabin
8. Youngsville

Figure 17

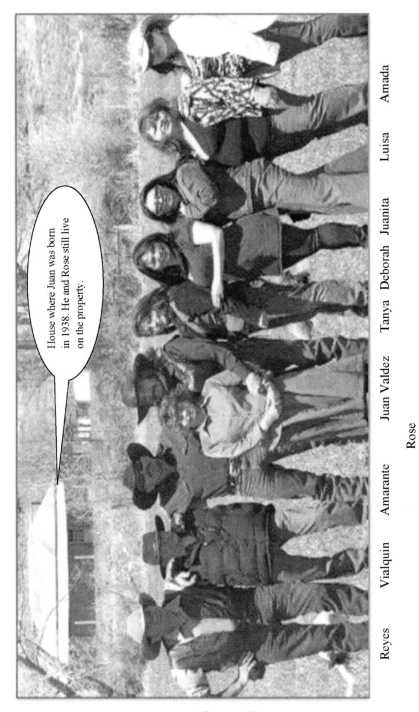

Figure 18

-16-
The Pajarito/Jémez Plateau—Hewett And The Forest Service

Today I'll be talking about a man named Edgar L. Hewett; about the Pajarito and Jémez Plateaus; and then about the Jémez Forest Reserve.

Then I'll be talking some more about why and how the San Joaquín del Río de Chama, the Juan Bautista Valdez and the La Petaca Grants wound up reduced from over 800,000 to less than 5,000 acres while at the same time the grantees and heirs of the nearby Piedra Lumbre and Polvadera grants wound up with more land than they'd claimed.

I'm going to start with Hewett. He was an archaeologist in Colorado before he moved to New Mexico because of his wife's health. After moving here he became interested in trying to save the Indian ruins around where Los Alamos is today. Shortly after he got here he began calling the place Pajarito Plateau and started trying to convince the federal government to make the area into a national park. In order to keep the attention of people in the Government and members of Congress he would tell them that the Government owned or controlled most of the area. He'd figured out that so long as he was saying the government had control of the property the right people would continue to listen, so he kept saying it even though it wasn't true.

Hewett's Pajarito Plateau dream didn't last long though because as soon as the federal government heard about it and became interested in the area it changed the name to the Jémez Plateau and increased it to four times its original size. Rather than just being the east side of the Jémez range as

164

Hewett had wanted, the government extended it west to the Continental Divide and north to the Colorado border. (Fig. 14).

Early government maps of the Pajarito and Jémez Plateaus contained a number of Pueblo, Spanish and Mexican grants within their exterior boundaries including the San Joaquín del Río de Chama, Juan Bautista Valdez and the La Petaca Grants; as well as the Tierra Amarilla, Piedra Lumbre, Polvadera, Juan Jose Lobato, Baca Location No. 1, Town of Abiquiú, Ramon Vigil, Canyon de San Diego, Ojo del Espíritu Santo, Ojo de San José, Ojo de Borrego, San Ysidro, Jémez Pueblo, Santo Domingo Pueblo, Pueblo de Cochití and the Cañada de Cochití Grants. But the first three grants I mentioned, the San Joaquín del Río de Chama, Juan Bautista Valdez and the La Petaca were missing from some of the government maps. (Fig. 15).

The first two maps with the three grants missing were the Archaeological Map-Jémez Plateau which claims to be a Department of Agriculture Forest Service map with a date of 1906; and the Pajarito Plateau and Vicinity map, which doesn't have a date on it. (Figs. 2, 4).

We couldn't find an explanation why the Archeological Map-Jémez Plateau has the date 1906 because—for one thing—the area had been renamed the Jémez Forest Reserve by President Roosevelt the year before, on October 12, 1905. There are a few other points about the two maps that we need to discuss, Hijo. One is that both maps are claimed to be Forest Service, U. S. Dept. of Agriculture, 1906 maps. But, if you'll look at the top left corner of the Jémez Plateau map you can see that it says, "Bureau of American Ethnology," and on the top right it says, "Bulletin 32, Plate XX." (See Fig. 2).

Even though the map that has the name Pajarito Plateau and Vicinity doesn't say it's a Forest Service map or that it was prepared in 1906, there is a pamphlet from the Bureau of American Ethnology, with the title, *Antiquities of the Jémez Plateau*, which was written by Edgar L. Hewett and is referred to as Bulletin 32, has a copy of the map in it as plate XVII.

Since Bulletin 32 was printed by the Government Printing Office (GPO) in 1906 we know one thing for sure—the map could not have been prepared later than 1906. Here's some more information that helps us identify that map:

The ruins referred to in this bulletin are distributed as shown on the map (pl. XVII). In many cases locations are only approximate, owing to the lack of authoritative surveys. The map was prepared by the Forest Office, the data being furnished by the Forest Service of the Agricultural Department, the General Land Office and the Geological Survey of the Interior Department and by the War Department, with corrections and additions by the author …

Nothing you just read talks about the Pajarito Plateau and Vicinity map, Grandpa?

Sorry. I forgot to tell you that "pl. XVII," that's mentioned in the paragraph I just read, is the plate we copied from the *Antiquities of the Jémez Plateau* pamphlet: the Pajarito Plateau and Vicinity map. (Fig. 4).

The description in the pamphlet, that I just read, is hard to follow because Hewett starts out saying it was prepared by the Forest Office in the Department of Interior. That would mean that it had to have been drawn before July 1, 1905, the day the Forest Office was transferred to the Department of Agriculture and renamed the Forest Service.

Hewett then says that the data was "being furnished by the Forest Service," which wasn't in existence before July 1, 1905. If we are to believe what Hewett is saying then the Pajarito Plateau and Vicinity map could not have been a 1906 Department of Agriculture, Forest Service map as he says it is.

Now let's put these two maps side by side and compare them. The first thing you see is that both maps are divided into townships and ranges except for the areas that are shown as land grants. What's strange about the Jémez Plateau and Vicinity Map, (Figs. 4, 6), is that the township and range lines where the San Joaquín del Río de Chama Grant was supposed to be are dashed lines that are not mentioned in the legend. Neither the boundaries or names of the San Joaquín del Río de Chama, Juan Bautista Valdez or the La Petaca Grants appear on either of the two maps, Figs 4 and 6, or on President Roosevelts Jemez Forest Reserve Proclamation map. (Fig. 15). All three maps appear as though the three grants were intentionally removed from them.

Do you have any information that any of those maps might have been made before 1905?

Compare what the two we're discussing say at Township 18 North, Range 8 East, Hijo. What does it say?

It says "Denver and Río Grande R. R." on the Pajarito Plateau and Vicinity Map and "Santa Fe Southern" on the Jémez Plateau map.

The Santa Fe Southern Railroad ran between Espanola and Santa Fe between 1887 and 1896 and after that it was bought by the Río Grande & Santa Fe Railroad Company and the name was changed to the Denver and Río Grande Rail Road. Since the Santa Fe Southern went out of business in 1896 it doesn't seem to us that a map maker would have used a ten year old name on a 1906 Department of Agriculture—Forest Service map. And it doesn't seem right that the Department of Agriculture would have had a map drawn in 1906 with the name "Jémez Plateau," for an area that had been re-named the Jémez Forest Reserve in 1905. (Fig. 2).

If the maps were drawn before the CPLC had ruled on the San Joaquín, Juan Bautista and La Petaca Grants it would mean that they could not have been drawn after 1894—the year of the CPLC order reducing the San Joaquín del Río de Chama Grant from 472,000 to 1,423 acres.

Regardless of when the three grants were actually removed from the maps they had to have been drawn at a time when the government believed the CPLC was going to take the land from them and erase them from existing government maps—making them a major part of the Jémez Forest Reserve. The map attached to the Jémez Forest Reserve Proclamation signed by President Roosevelt on October 12, 1905, which I mentioned a minute ago—is the third map that is missing all three grants. (Fig.15).

Another difference in the two maps we are comparing has to do with the size and shape of the Ramon Vigil Grant which is at Townships 18 and 19 North—Ranges 6 and 7 East. With the two maps side by side it's possible to see that the grant has two different sizes and shape—and even the Forest Reserve boundaries around them are different.

The last important difference in the maps is that the legend on the Jémez Plateau map refers to the boundary claimed by the government as the "Forest Reserve Boundary," (Fig. 3),while the legend on the Pajarito Plateau and Vicinity map claims the government boundary is the "National Forest Boundary." (Fig. 4).

There was no National Forest in the Jémez area in 1906 when the Government Printing Office published Bulletin 32, *Antiquities of the Jémez Plateau—New Mexico*, yet Plate XVII clearly states in its legend that there was a National Forest Boundary on the map. (Fig. 4).

We've mentioned the Court of Private Land Claims and the Forest Reserve Acts so many times it's about time we talk about how they became law.

As Congress was nearing the end of its 1891 session it became clear to President Benjamin Harrison that nothing regarding forest reserves was going to be introduced so he pressured both houses of Congress to appoint a committee with three members from each house and advised them to come up with a forest bill. After the members were appointed and a meeting held both houses advised that the issue had been settled. That an omnibus bill, a bill used at the time to gather a bunch of bills together at the end of a session was going to include a section establishing the right of the president to withdraw or reserve forest areas anywhere in the country.

Congress had been trying to pass laws to control the forests for over 20 years by the time Section 24, the last section of the bill and the only section that had anything to do with forest was added to the omnibus bill.

Arguments broke out in both houses during debate about the new section with the members against it arguing that the supporters were trying to force a vote on something that had not been printed or read, saying there was nothing to consider but the words of the conference members.

Ignoring the arguments against passage, the President's supporters were able to force the law through congress and President Harrison signed it into law on March 3, 1891, the last day of the session. Here's what it said:

> Sec. 24. That the President of the United States may, from time to time, set apart and reserve, in any State or Territory having public land bearing forests, in any part of the public lands wholly or in part covered with timber or undergrowth, whether of commercial value or not, as public reservations; and the President shall, by public proclamation, declare the establishment of such reservations and the limit thereof.

Unfortunately, the Court of Private Land Claims Act became law the same day and the two acts, used together, became a very serious problem for Indian reservations across the country and land grants throughout the Southwest, particularly in New Mexico. The CPLC immediately began to change the way land grants had been confirmed by surveyors general since 1854.

The Court of Private Land Claims Act required President Harrison to appoint five justices and a United States Attorney who would decide the future of Spanish and Mexican land grants that had been around for decades and that had not yet been confirmed by Congress. It became clear almost immediately that the two acts were going to be used to ignore the Treaty of Guadalupe Hidalgo and to remove millions of acres from the grants and convert them into forest reserves and, subsequently, into National Forests.

On March 30, 1891, just twenty-seven days after President Harrison signed the two acts into law he began establishing forest reserves by proclaiming the 1,240,000 acre Yellowstone Park Timber Reserve. In October, seven months after the Acts became law, he established the 1,200,000 acre reserve in Colorado known as the White River Plateau Timber Reserve. It was clear from the beginning that they were going to be federal timber reserves, otherwise, why name them timber reserves.

Guess where and when President Harrison established his third reserve, Hijo?

The way it's going, I wouldn't be surprised if it was somewhere right here in New Mexico.

You got it. He established the Pecos River Forest Reserve on January 11, 1892.

The Jémez Forest Reserve which we have been talking about and will be discussing a lot more contained 800,000 acres of the San Joaquín del Río de Chama, Juan Bautista Valdez and La Petaca grants was established by President Theodore Roosevelt on October 12, 1905.

It didn't just happen in 1905. It had been considered for reserve status and withdrawn two years earlier as the Río de Jémez Forest Reserve. Less than three weeks after it was named the Río de Jémez Withdrawal in 1903, the Commissioner of the General Land Office (GLO) ordered the same acreage withdrawn again on September 1, 1903, this time as the Jémez and

Nacimiento Country Withdrawal, covering the same 1,252,000 acres as the previous Río de Jémez Withdrawal.

When the Jémez Forest Reserve was finally proclaimed it contained just 14,798 acres less that it had when it was named the Río de Jémez and Jémez and Nacimiento withdrawals. The only reason we found that the General Land Office had withdrawn it as the Río de Jémez and as the Jémez and Nacimiento Country Withdrawal was to make doubly sure it was completely protected from settlement until President Roosevelt could get around to establishing it as the Jémez Forest Reserve two years later. The reason the government believed the area was so important was explained in President Roosevelt's Proclamation:

> The tract reserved contains much valuable timber that it is the purpose of the Government to protect for further uses.

The government wasn't taking any chances that the "valuable timber" might remain in the San Joaquín, Juan Bautista and La Petaca Land Grants or be settled by "native" Americans arriving from the east

Now is a good time to do another comparison, Hijo—comparing our three grants with the Piedra Lumbre and the Polvadera.

But we already talked about that, Grandpa.

I know. But what I'm going to do now is mention information we haven't discussed before—information about why those grants were treated differently—evidence about why we lost 800,000 acres while the government was adding land to the Piedra Lumbre and Polvadera claims.

We need to start by comparing where Hewett had been saying the Indian ruins were compared to where the grants were. And figure out where the forests were compared to where the grants were.

The Indian ruins north of Abiquiú, most of them, had been within the original boundaries of the San Joaquín and Juan Bautista Valdez Grants. The land taken from our grants contained those Indian ruins—in addition to over 600,000 acres of prime forest. Before we lost our grants more than half of the San Joaquín, ninety percent of the Juan Bautista and sixty percent of the La Petaca had been forest lands—but after the government got through converting the land it wanted to the public domain none of the forest land or Indian ruins remained in the 5,000 acres our three grants wound up with.

Remember earlier, when I was saying that the Piedra Lumbre had no forest and that the Polvadera hardly had any—that the part of the Polvadera that was covered with timber was steep—rough country?

Yeah!

We found what we believe is the evidence why the Piedra Lumbre and Polvadera got to keep all of the land they had claimed while ours lost virtually all of their land. The decision wasn't based on whether the grant papers were correct or the boundaries were easy to find—the grants were being approved or disapproved based on the location of the forests and the location of the Indian ruins. You may not recall when we were reading from Matt Reynolds' 1894 Annual Report—where he was bragging about saving the mines in the Cochití Mining District—and taking enough land to pay for the expenses of the Court of Private Land Claims, but we now believe that what he was saying then also applies to what happened to the San Joaquin, Juan Bautista and La Petaca grants.

I do remember how he was excited that two of the four grants lost all of their land and the other two only got a small part of their grants.

What the CPLC did to our grants was no different. It let the Piedra Lumbre and Polvadera grants, which were grazing grants, with very few, if any settlers on them keep all their land—receive extra land—and at the same time took all the timber lands from our grants—left the Piedra Lumbre and Polvadera with all their common lands and took all of our common lands—because the land the government wanted, our land, was covered with timber.

We don't believe the decisions of the Court of Private Land Claims or the Supreme Court were ever based on land grant issues—they were based solely on the existence of natural resources. By the end of our story there shouldn't be any doubt that that is exactly what the government relied on to make its decisions about which grants would keep their land and which ones wouldn't.

We need to move on, look at a map of Township 26 North, Range 5 East. Do you see the river there—running across the top and down the left side? (Fig.11).

Yeah.

What does the map say is the name of the river?

It says—Horn River.

Look at the bottom left side, where it says Sec. 31, you see that?

Yeah.

Right above where it says, Sec. 31—what's it say?

Mexican Plaza.

Do you know where that is?

No.

That's Placita García, Hijo.

Wait a minute—Placita García—Horn River. That means this is a map of Canjilón. WOW!

If we were to compare this map with the one for Township 27 North, Range 4 East, Hijo, you'd see that Canjilón was actually within the original San Joaquín del Río de Chama Grant. Since the Spanish description of the San Joaquín said that the "Rito de Cebolla" was the northeast boundary of the grant that would have put Canjilón within the grant—if the government hadn't cheated on the boundaries.

So when I was talking about trespassing on our own land, I was, like I've said before, using land that had belonged to our family for almost a century before the CPLC and President Roosevelt "borrowed" it.

-17-
Guilty—Sentenced—Pardoned

I need to finish talking about what happened after we had gone to the courthouse in Tierra Amarilla—after the jury found me guilty and the judge sentenced me to prison. When it was time for me to turn myself in, Emilio Naranjo who had been the U.S. Marshal in '67, and was once again the Sheriff, called me and said I had to be at his office the next day so he could take me to Santa Fe—to prison.

Before we got off the phone he said he was going to talk to the Governor and see if he could get him to give me a pardon. The next morning, since I hadn't heard from Emilio, I kissed your grandmother good-bye and took off for Española. When I got to his office he told me that Governor King had signed a pardon—I was free to go home.

I went back to work hoping my troubles were finally over—and they were—for a while. But then came 1978 which has to have been the worst year of my life other than '65 when my father died. My sister, Julia, her son and daughter, Ruben and Lorencita, and my sister Gertrudes' son and daughter, Gary and Lydia, were all killed when a drunk driver ran head-on into their car between here and Española. Then later that year a tree I was cutting twisted as it was falling and a huge branch pinned my legs to the ground. I had to have operations on both ankles and both knees and they've giving me trouble ever since. Sometimes they swell up and look like pink balloons. The doctors drain my knees but all I can do is stay in bed until the swelling goes away. One time I couldn't get out of bed for two months—not even to go to the bathroom.

After the operations I tried to go back to logging but I had to quit because I couldn't stand up all day. Some days, in the winter, we'd have to stand in as much as two or three feet of snow, like I'd been doing for years but there was no way I could do it anymore. After I gave up being a logger I started bidding on tree planting contracts. It was at a time when the Forest Service was being pretty good with our people and I won a few contracts. Each time I'd win a contract I would hire crews from around Canjilón and we'd plant thousands of trees. It was a lot easier for me, because all I had to do was tell the workers where to plant the trees. When I go through the forest these days I always look for the places where we planted trees. It makes me feel good to know that I was one of the people that helped plant all those trees.

Other than the planting contracts I made most of my money selling firewood and latillas. Over the years my legs have gotten so bad I don't even cut latillas anymore.

Your grandmother and I still plant a little garden every spring. We still plant in the same place where I've been planting for over 60 years. The same place where the little children used to crawl down the rows looking for something their mothers could cook for them. Other than planting a garden, I don't do much of anything. I even had to get rid of my cow and calves when I got to where I couldn't go to pasture to get them anymore.

There are times, Hijo, when my legs are hurting so bad that it makes me I start thinking about Saiz—wondering if he's in as much pain as I am. I hope he doesn't suffer like I do because if he does it's all my fault. Of course, it's my fault my legs hurt too, but that's different. Maybe I got hurt because of what I did to him—but only God knows the answer to that.

Did you have other bad years—after 1978?

Oh yeah, but not that bad. One time that comes to my mind was in the late 1980's—in October. I was in Española and Eddie Maes, a friend of mine, called me at my daughter's and told me that my barn was burning. It was a real bad time for the barn to burn because we had just cut the pasture and put all the bales, about 1,200, in the barn. It burned clear to the ground—we lost every bale. Sometimes the fire makes me think about how my ancestors had to live after the government took their land. I get mad at myself for even thinking about the fire I had compared to everything they had to go through.

Didn't you have insurance?

With all the fires we were having around here in those days—with all the buildings that were burning—no company was going to sell us insurance for a barn full of hay. I had about $5,000 worth of hay and that's not including the cost to build another barn. It would probably have cost that much for insurance.

Can you talk about how the Forest Service treated the people in Canjilón after you had gone to the courthouse?

For about the next ten years afterwards the Forest Service treated us like we should have been treated all along—like humans—like the "native" Americans that came here from the east.

During the years after we went to Tierra Amarilla the Rangers didn't follow us everywhere we went—didn't impound our cattle and sheep every time they caught them in the forest—didn't harass us like they'd done forever. The one thing I kept thinking about during those years was my Father—how he hadn't lived long enough to see the change.

But after treating us better for eight or nine years the Forest Service started going back to its old ways, rounding up our cattle—making us pay for firewood, vigas—latillas. It's never gone all the way back like it was before though, because after 1967 the government started hiring local people and putting some of them in positions where they could be involved in making decisions. Times had changed enough that it'll never be able to go all the way back to the way it was before.

I remember one time about twenty-five years ago some of my friends who'd been in the Alianza were at the Mel Patch Lounge in Española. I wasn't there but they told me about it later. They were upset that the Forest Service seemed like it was going back to the way things had been before. While they were talking about how things were changing one of my friends said that maybe it was time for another "chingacita," but no one jumped in and said they were interested in doing it.

Here's something we ran across that you should find interesting, Hijo. It's what Nick Salazar, one of the County Commissioners that was at the courthouse that afternoon in '65, the one I mentioned earlier that had helped put Nick Saiz in the ambulance, well here's something he had to say—twenty-five years later.

State Rep. Nick Salazar, then a Río Arriba county commissioner says he believes far-flung news of the raid led to a needed influx of money to the North. "I look back now and think to myself and I wonder if we would have made a difference in Río Arriba County if that had not happened."

… Salazar said money is precisely the eventual harvest Río Arriba reaped from the raid. "The government finally realized the frustration felt by the people in Northern New Mexico" he said. "If we had taken a plane and dropped money on the community it would have been better than the "War on Poverty," he said referring to President Lyndon Johnson's much-criticized social programs of the period.

Because of the raid, Salazar said the federal government turned over money to build Clara Peak Road, to conduct a feasibility study for the eventual construction of the Española vocational college and to bring 1,300 housing units to the north.

Funds also flowed into the state for weatherization, housing rehabilitation and water and sewer projects, Salazar said. Money to expand Española Hospital and bring health clinics to other parts of Río Arriba also came in the aftermath of the raid.

"I think it had its benefits," Salazar said. "It isn't a thing you condone. But, on the other hand, it's helped Northern New Mexico. I have to wonder if any of those things would have come about if not for that."

At least one politician was willing to say that some good might have come out of our trip to the courthouse. But we shouldn't have had to do what we did just to be treated like ordinary people.

-18-
The Court Of Private Land Claims

Grandpa, I told my teacher what you had told me about the size of the San Joaquín del Río de Chama, Juan Bautista Valdez and La Petaca Grants before the government took the land and how many acres they wound up with. I told him you had mentioned so many numbers I was having a hard time remembering them and he suggested we could make it easier to understand if we divided all the acres you talked about by 640, the number of acres in a square mile to try and make it clearer how unfair the government had been. I divided all the acreage we've been talking about and it made a big difference for me. Can I go over the numbers before we move on to something else?

Sure.

I'll start with some of the grants that received patents from Congress before the Court of Private Land Claims got involved.

The Maxwell and Sangre de Cristo Grants were supposed to be limited under Mexican law to eleven square leagues or approximately 153 square miles each. The Maxwell Grant wound up with 2,679 square miles—2,527 more than it was entitled to and the Sangre de Cristo received 1,562 square miles—1,408 more than it should have had.

The Pablo Montoya and Preston Beck, Jr. Grants were only entitled to 76 square miles each yet the Pablo Montoya received 1,024 square miles and the Preston Beck, Jr. wound up with 498.

Those four grants together were entitled to 358 square miles and they wound up with 5,762—5,300 square miles more than they were supposed to have.

The grants on page 113 of the GAO Report, the Cañón de Carnué, Cañón de Chama [San Joaquín del Río de Chama], Don Fernando de Taos, Town of

Galisteo, Petaca, San Miguel del Bado and the Santa Cruz were treated just the opposite—they were entitled to 1,776 square miles. Guess how many they wound up with, Grandpa?

How many?

They only wound up with 26 square miles. The remaining 1,750 square miles wound up belonging to the government..

Did you figure the square miles for the Juan Bautista Valdez?

Sure did.

We used an estimate of 147,500 acres for the Juan Bautista. If the government had confirmed all the acreage Spain actually granted to the San Joaquin, the La Petaca and the Juan Bautista Valdez there would have been approximately 810,000 acres—that means they should have received over 1,266 square miles.

How much did they actually get?

Six and a half square miles, Grandpa—6.5 of the 1,265 square miles they had been granted forty years before the United States even claimed to have any interest in New Mexico.

After we'd done the math, my teacher pulled out a copy of the census for the San Joaquín del Río de Chama that showed there were more than 400 people living there in 1880—in more than 140 homes. He said, like you had said earlier, Grandpa—they even had a school and a cemetery, but that all there is now are a bunch of National Forest signs—no houses—no schoolhouse, no cemetery—just Forest Service signs. The settlement that had been there for over 80 years is nothing but dust.

Last Monday my teacher brought a copy of the Sunday Albuquerque Journal to class. After he read an article about what the government is doing at a cemetery at Fort Craig, near Socorro, he told us that it's interesting how the Bureau of Reclamation can spend hundreds of hours and tens of thousands of dollars at a Cemetery recovering the remains of more than60 men, women and children—promising to provide them decent burials at the National Cemetery—but at the same time it won't spend a dime fixing up the San Joaquín del Río de Chama Cemetery—and the other land grant cemeteries around the state.

I saw the story you're talking about, Hijo. It was interesting to compare what the government was willing to do at Ft. Craig with what it isn't willing to do for our grants. When you stop to think about how the Forest Service has ignored the condition of the land grants it becomes clear how unimportant our ancestors are to the government.

To make it even worse many of the men who were born, lived and are buried on the San Joaquín and the other grants—fought as volunteers for the Union during the Civil War. They were veterans like the government claims some of the remains at Ft. Craig were, yet our volunteers continue to be ignored.

From what the article said, Hijo, the remains the government was finding at Ft. Craig weren't even Civil War casualties—a lot of the ones they identified didn't even get to New Mexico until after the battle at Glorieta, after the end of the Civil War.

Here's something I think our heirs will find interesting. It's a comparison of President Roosevelt's 1905 Proclamation establishing the Jémez Forest Reserve with the one President Harrison used to set aside the Pecos River Forest Reserve in 1892.

The first difference was that Harrison's proclamation number 316 had a township and range description of the land being withdrawn while Roosevelt's Jemez Forest Reserve proclamation didn't have a description—just a simple grid map, but that's not all. Harrison's proclamation had a paragraph that read:

> Excepting from the force and effect of this proclamation all land which may have been prior to the date hereof embraced in any valid Spanish or Mexican grant or in any legal entry or covered by any lawful filing duly made in the proper United States land office ...

Roosevelt's proclamation for the Jémez Forest Reserve skipped that paragraph. Even though the San Joaquín, Juan Bautista and La Petaca grants had been removed from the government maps they still physically existed. Since Roosevelt wanted all of the land in the three grants he probably left that paragraph out intentionally so questions about our grants wouldn't slow him down.

But you better believe that both proclamations say the same thing when it comes to timber. The words are slightly different but they make the same point. President Harrisons proclamation for the Pecos River Forest Reserve had this to say:

> And whereas the public lands in the Territory of New Mexico within the limits hereinafter described are in part covered with

timber, and it appears that the public good would be promoted by setting apart and reserving said lands as a public reservation.

Now listen to how that part of Roosevelt's Jémez Proclamation read:
And whereas, the public lands, in the Territory of New Mexico which are hereinafter indicated, are in part covered with timber, and it appears that the public good would be promoted by setting aside said lands as a public reservation ...

Both show how important the timber was—and that the forests should be placed in public reservations.

Before we go to something else I want to read a Joint Memorial the New Mexico Legislature passed on February 4, 1905 and sent to Congress.
To The President of the United States Protesting Against
The Creation of the Río De Jémez Reserve.

That the said reserve has been established and set apart without the several thousands of people who live within the boundaries thereof and are mostly affected thereby, ever having any notice of the intent to establish it, and without being given any opportunity to protest against the same.

That the said reserve embraces a section of country almost as large or larger in area than the state of New Jersey ... and including within its outer boundaries large tracts of land that are absolutely non-forest in character, and valuable only for mining, agricultural and grazing purposes, besides fifteen or more towns and villages and a large number of farms and stock ranches ...

Your memorialists further represent that New Mexico's chief industry is that of sheep raising and that the territory has within the last four years, advanced from the fourth to the first place in the nation as a wool producer, and that a large portion of the country so included in this forest reserve has been for nearly a half a century last past the principal grazing ground for a large number of flocks [sic] of the territory and from which grazing ground all sheep will be thereby excluded, thus irreparably injuring the owners thereof as well as the territory at large.

That the establishing of this reserve practically amounts to the confiscation of all the ranches and homes of the people living within the boundaries thereof, and although they established themselves there more than fifty years ago and endured the great hardships and risks in the accumulation of the property they possess, they are to be driven out to begin life anew....

Wherefore, your memorialists respectfully and earnestly pray that all that portion of the Río de Jémez reserve that lies within Taos and Río Arriba counties, may be restored to the public domain and consequent location and entry, relieving the people who will suffer thereby so much in consequence of the establishment of said reserve over such a large area of land of non-forest country: ...

I'm glad we found that memorial, Grandpa, it makes it clear the New Mexico Legislature was against Roosevelt setting up the Río de Jémez Reserve. Do we have any other information that President Roosevelt was setting up reserves the people didn't want?

Here's one we can start with:

In January 1907, there was considerable opposition to a Presidential proclamation that reserved thousands of acres of prime Douglas-fir timberlands in northern Washington State. The local press, chambers of commerce, and the Washington State congressional delegation protested that the reserve would cause undue hardship on residents by taking away homestead and "prime" agricultural lands (the land, in fact, was not agricultural, abut[sic] heavily forested) as well as impeding the future development of the State.

181

Why is it important to talk about what was happening in Washington State?
You'll see what I'm getting at soon enough. Here's more of the article:

> After considerable pressure, Pinchot and President Roosevelt relented by, by[sic] saying that the reserve had been a "clerical" error. Soon thereafter, Senator Charles W. Fulton of Oregon, who had been implicated in the land frauds in that State, introduced an amendment to the annual agricultural appropriations bill.

I thought it was important that Roosevelt, when he got caught setting up that Forest Reserve in Washington, claimed it had been a "clerical error," withdrew the proclamation and returned the land to the State of Washington.

It's too bad he wasn't pressured into declaring the Jémez Forest Reserve a "clerical error."

Our world would have been a completely different place if that had happened. Here's the rest of the part I wanted to read:

> This amendment, the Fulton Amendment prohibited the President from creating any additional forest reserves in the six Western States of Washington Oregon, Idaho, Montana, Wyoming and Colorado; took away his power to proclaim reserves, established under the Forest Reserve (Creative) Act of 1891; and gave Congress alone the authority to establish reserves. However, before this bill was signed into law on March 4, 1907, Gifford Pinchot and the President came up with a plan.

> On the eve of the bill's signing, Chief Forester Pinchot and his assistant Arthur C. Ringland used a heavy blue pencil to draw many new forest reserves on maps. As soon as the map was finished and a proclamation written, the President signed the paper to establish another forest reserve. On March 1st and 2nd, Roosevelt established 17 new or combined forest reserves containing over 16 million acres in these six Western States. These have since been referred to as the "Midnight Reserves."

What did the Forest Service have to say about that?

Well—one thing it couldn't do was deny that President Roosevelt and Chief Forester Pinchot established all the reserves that the article mentioned because the article I was reading was from a Forest Service Newsletter. By publishing the article in a Forest Service Newsletter the government was actually blowing a whistle on itself.

The article said Roosevelt had established seventeen new or combined forest reserves containing 16,000,000 acres in the six Western States. We looked into what actually happened in those two days and the documents we found indicated that, counting other forest reserves they proclaimed outside the six Western States, they had actually converted more like 30,000,000 acres to forest reserves. Instead of seventeen new or combined reserves like the article claimed, our documents show that thirty-three reserves were actually created, combined, enlarged or modified. Of those five were new, eight were set apart from existing reserves, fifteen, including the Jémez Forest Reserve, were enlarged, and five others were modified.

Did you find any other articles about Pinchot and Roosevelt making the reserves—any other information to support what you just said? It's pretty serious, Grandpa, for you to say that the President and Chief Forester were ignoring Congress when they were making those reserves. It sounds like you're saying Roosevelt and Pinchot were intentionally converting millions of acres of private lands into public lands at the same time Congress was trying to take his power to establish forest reserves.

That's exactly what I'm saying, Hijo. I don't know of any better evidence of what I just said than what I'm going to read next—from President Roosevelt's own words—from his own memoir:

> While the Agricultural Appropriation Bill was passing through the Senate, in 1907, Senator Fulton, of Oregon, secured an amendment providing that the President could not set aside any additional National Forests in the six Northwestern States. This meant retaining some sixteen million of acres to be exploited by land grabbers and by the representatives of the great special interests, at the expense of the public interest.

But for four years the Forest Service had been gathering field notes as to what forests ought to be set aside in these States, and so was prepared to act. It was equally undesirable to veto the whole agricultural bill, and to sign it with this amendment effective. Accordingly, a plan to create the necessary National Forest in these States before the Agricultural Bill could be passed and signed was laid before me by Mr. Pinchot. I approved it. The necessary papers were immediately prepared. I signed the last proclamation a couple of days before by my signature, the bill became law; and when the friends of the special interests in the Senate got their amendment through and woke up, they discovered that sixteen million acres of timberland had been saved for the people by putting them in the National Forests before the land grabbers could get at them.

The opponents of the Forest Service turned handsprings in their wrath; and dire were their threats against the Executive; but the threats could not be carried out, and were really only a tribute to the efficiency of our action.

Have we found any information on exactly how many acres President Roosevelt placed in forest reserves during the time he was President?
Yes. We've found some information and believe it's accurate:

The forest reserves of the United States quadrupled to about 194,000,000 acres under President Roosevelt's orders, equal in area to all the states on the Atlantic coast from Maine to Virginia and the states of Vermont, Pennsylvania, and West Virginia. This is a greater area than France, Belgium, and The Netherlands combined.

Over Roosevelt's articulate objections, "An Act Making appropriations for the Department of Agriculture for the fiscal year ending June thirtieth, nineteen hundred and eight," H.R. 24815, Public Act No. 242, U.S. Congress. 59th. 2nd Session was passed on Feb. 25, 1907. Unwilling to pocket-veto the entire appropriations act, Roosevelt permitted Gifford Pinchot and his staff to identify some

16,000,000 acres of forest in Oregon, Washington, Idaho, Montana, Colorado and Wyoming which the President then designated as new national forest lands by executive order, between Congress's passage of the bill and its signing on Marth [sic] 4th by the reluctant President, who was now forbidden to create or enlarge the newly designated National Forests.

Do you have the names of the New Mexico reserves and the dates they were established?

We sure do. The Jémez was established, as we've already discussed, on October 12, 1905; the Lincoln and Portales were proclaimed on October 3, 1905; the Lincoln was enlarged on June 25, 1906; the Mount Taylor was proclaimed on October 6, 1906; the Gallinas, Magdalena, Peloncillo and San Mateo were established on November 5, 1906 and the Manzano was established on November 6, 1906.

As we said earlier, Roosevelt increased the Jémez Forest Reserve by over 223,000 acres and created the Taos Forest Reserve, all on the same day— November 7, 1906 and he created the Big Burros on February 6, 1907, and the Las Ánimas in Colorado and New Mexico on March 1, 1907.

The Jémez Reserve was enlarged in 1906?

Sure was. It was extended east toward the Río Grande Gorge and took in more land to the west.

On May 2, 1907, two months after Pinchot and Roosevelt established the "Midnight Reserves," James Wilson, the Secretary of Agriculture approved a pamphlet for publication that you're going to find interesting. Its' called, *The Use of the Forest.*

Here's some of what it says:

At first a great many of the National Forests were made without knowing exactly where the boundary lines should run. This was unfortunate; because some agricultural lands which should have been excluded were taken in, and a good deal of timber land which should have been included was left out. This could have been avoided by making examinations on the ground, but there was no money for the work, and so the boundaries had to be drawn very roughly ...

Since 1900, however, men and money have been available for field examinations and rough and inaccurate work has been done away with entirely. The old and carelessly made National Forests have been surveyed and mapped, and the President has put back into the public domain those lands which should not have been included. Now, before new Forests or additions to old ones are made, all the lands are examined on the ground.

The greatest care is used in this work. Every section of land is examined, mapped, and described, and the boundaries are drawn to exclude, as far as possible, everything which does not properly belong in a National Forest. Two very detailed maps are made. One shows just what is growing on the land, the other shows who owns or claims the land. Every bit of cultivated land is located and mapped, as well as the land which is suited to cultivation but which is not cultivated at present ...

Before any new National Forest is made it is known just why it should be made, just what effect it will have, and just where it should be located.

What do you think about that, Hijo?

All I can say, Grandpa, is whoever wrote that had no clue what Pinchot and President Roosevelt had been up to two months earlier.

Why do you say that?

Because it was the exact opposite of what they had done. Do you have any idea who wrote it?

Sure do—Gifford Pinchot.

-19-
In Trouble Again—How Stupid Was That?

You said that when Governor King granted you a pardon it left you hoping that your legal problems were over for good. Were they?

You didn't have to bring that up. But since you did it's only fair for me to talk about another serious problem I got myself into.

I was working in my shop in 1987 when a man came by and said his name was Jesus Hernandez. He said he was from Santa Fe and that he came through Canjilón quite a bit and would see my working—that he had always wondering who I was—what I was doing, so he'd decided to stop an introduce himself. We talked for a little while and he left.

A couple weeks later he stopped again.

Over the next few months he kept stopping by and I guess you could say that we became friends. One day, after he'd stopped seven or eight times he told me that he had a problem. That there was this woman in Los Alamos that he really liked but that she had a problem. He said she was hooked on cocaine and that when she would run out of cocaine she'd get desperate and sometimes she'd even beat her little children. He said he was tired of seeing the little kids all beat up and was hoping he could find her some cocaine—but that no matter how hard he looked he couldn't find any.

He asked me if I knew where he could get some and I told him I didn't. He acted like he was in a panic, that he had to find a way to get her some cocaine so she'd stop beating the kids. He said he wanted to leave some money with me and if I found some cocaine I could buy it and he'd come get it. He had me believing that if I didn't help him find some cocaine the kids were going to continue to be beaten. Like a damn fool I went around looking for cocaine for him and after a few days I found someone that was willing to sell some and I bought it with the money he had given me.

I called him and he came the next day and picked it up. As he was leaving he thanked me for helping save the children from being beaten.

A few weeks later, maybe a month, I don't remember exactly, he came back with the same story. I don't know whether you can believe your grandfather was that stupid, but over the next six or seven months I bought cocaine for that woman in Los Alamos every time Jesus would come by and tell me she was beating her children again.

Then one time he told me he knew this viejita in Santa Fe that was poor and needed fire wood to keep warm but that she didn't have much money. He asked me if I could sell her a load for $100 even though I usually sold it for a $150 or more. I could just see this little old woman that had run out of firewood trying to stay warm. I told him to pull his pickup to the woodpile and I filled it up. He handed me a $100, thanked me for helping her and drove off.

Two month later here he comes again to gave me another $300 for more cocaine and to say that the little old woman was running low on firewood— could I sell her some more? I could even see my mother, who had gone blind about fifteen years earlier, trying to keep a fire going. I told him, "sure, no problem, pull over to the pile so I can load it."

After I'd loaded the wood he handed me a $100 worth of food stamps. I asked him why he was trying to give me food stamps, that I didn't use them, and he said she was desperate for fire wood—but that all she had to pay for it was her food stamps. I felt so sorry for her that I took them.

In a few weeks, here he comes again. Said he was just stopping by to visit. While we were standing around the stove in my shop he pointed to my chain saws in the corner and since I had really helped him out he was willing to take them to Santa Fe and try to sell them for me.

I asked him what he thought I was doing with them—that my boys used them for getting firewood . Then the next time he showed up he saw some saddles and said he was going to Mexico in a couple weeks, did I want him to take them to Mexico and sell them. I told him we go to Mexico to buy saddles—not to sell them. Right there I realized he must be a cop—that I was going to be in a hell of a lot of trouble—he'd been setting me up all that time.

But you know what Hijo? He even had the güevos to come back a couple weeks later and ask if he could hide a friend's car at the back of our pasture so they could claim it had been stolen and collect insurance. I told him to get the hell off my property.

A few weeks later I was charged with about ten counts of trafficking and one count of food stamp fraud.

I called Carlos Vigil, my friend that was killed later outside the courthouse in Santa Fe. He said he couldn't handle my case—to call Mike Scarborough—see if he could represent me.

Before the case was scheduled to go to court, Mike and Robert Sena, the prosecutor, worked out an agreement. Sena—after he heard what had happened agreed that Hernandez, an under-cover sergeant with the State Police, had tricked me with his stories about children being beaten and the viejita freezing in her house.

We went to court and Mike and Robert had me plea no contest to one count of attempting to sell cocaine with all the other counts dismissed.

The judge said before he would accept the agreement he wanted the Probation and Parole Office to investigate what had happened.

The probation officer that did the investigation was in court the next time we went and he testified that the cocaine I had bought for Hernandez was exactly the same value as the amount of money he had given me. He said in all his years with Probation and Parole he had never seen a case like mine where the person charged had done nothing to make any money or keep any of the drugs—that it was clear that I hadn't kept anything for myself.

The judge accepted the agreement and entered an order that the charge we had agreed to would be dismissed it I didn't get in trouble during the next six months.

Even though the judge agreed not to enter an order that I was guilty for the next six months, Mike and Robert told him that to show the court how stupid I felt about what had happened I wanted to do something to prove it and they asked the judge if he would order me, for court cost, to deliver twenty cords of firewood, a half cord each, to forty elderly people from Río

Arriba County. Since they had both agreed for the judge to do it he went along and signed an order requiring me to deliver the firewood.

As soon as I would get a call from the county with the name of someone that needed firewood I would take them a load. Every time I would take a load I would think about how Hernandez had used the story about the viejita in Santa Fe to trick me.

A couple weeks after the hearing some of my friends started telling me that maybe I got out of the charges but I was never going to see my truck again. I told Mike what they were saying and he said he'd do what he could. Two weeks later, after paying a storage fee of $400 to the state I was driving it back to Canjilón.

May I say something, Grandpa?

Sure.

As you were telling that story I was thinking about the first time you told me about it and how you kept asking yourself how could you have been so stupid. Ever since I first heard you say that I've thought about it a lot and each time you say that what you did was stupid, it upsets me. Even though it wasn't smart, I don't think you should say it was stupid. I told my teacher about how bad I felt about what had happened and this is how he explained why you did what you did.

He said that throughout the time I've been telling him what you've been saying, the one thing that he sees that keeps coming up is how for generations our family—and the other families who lived on the grants—had to help each other just to survive.

He mentioned the story you told about how your father would feel bad when a poor family would ask if their children could crawl down the rows of your garden looking for beans, for anything they might find—just to have something to eat; how you said your father would feel so bad seeing the little children crawling along that he'd give the parents flour and cornmeal—or jerky, or one time a lamb, just so they'd have enough to eat.

He said that policeman knew exactly what to say to get you to help him. He said that many of our people would have done exactly what you did if they were faced with the problems of little children being beaten or a little old woman freezing because she didn't have any firewood. He said that it was compassion that got you in trouble, Grandpa, not stupidity.

-20-
Zía, Jémez And Santa Ana Pueblos Prevail

Read what it says at the top, Hijo.

19 Ind. Cl. Comm. 94

BEFORE THE INDIAN CLAIMS COMMISSION.

PUEBLO DE ZÍA, PUEBLO DE JÉMEZ AND PUEBLO DE SANTA ANA, Petitioners, v. THE UNITED STATES OF AMERICA, Defendant, Docket No. 137.

Now read the sentence that starts, "Upon the findings," and then paragraph two.

Upon the Findings of Fact, numbered 24 to 33 inclusive, which are this day filed herein and which are hereby made a part of this order, the Commission concludes as a matter of law.

(2) That 36,172.62 acres of petitioners 298,634 acres of Indian title lands were taken from them by defendant as of October 12, 1905, the date President Theodore Roosevelt included said 36,172.62 acres within the boundaries of the Jémez Forest Reserve by executive proclamation.

Now read the part that says: "It is Therefore Ordered ..."

IT IS THEREFORE ORDERED that the case proceed to a determination of the fair market value of the lands found herein to be taken from petitioners by the defendant as of the taking dates.

Dated at Washington, D.C. this 7th day of March, 1968.

The Indian Claims Commission found that President Roosevelt's Proclamation establishing the Jémez Forest Reserve had taken 36,172 acres from the Zía, Jémez and Santa Ana Pueblos without offering to pay for it and sixty-three years after President Roosevelt took the land the Commission was ordering the government to pay the Pueblos for it. What do you think about that?

Why should the Pueblos be paid for the 36,172 acres they lost and our people not be paid for the 800,000 acres they lost at the same time—in the same forest reserve?

According to the Treaty of Guadalupe Hidalgo, the Pueblo Indian, Spanish and Mexican people were all supposed to be treated the same, Hijo, but when Congress established the Indian Claims Commission in 1946 it ignored the treaty when it limited the law to Indian Tribes for their claims against the government. It should have been written to protect Spanish and Mexican land grant heirs too. It wasn't right that Congress passed a law protecting the rights of the Indians to make a claim for the 36,000 acres they lost and not allow the Grants to make claims for the 800,000 they lost.

The reason I'm bringing this up now is because it's time we discuss how the Court of Private Land Claims and the Supreme Court completely ignored the Treaty and took millions of acres from the Spanish and Mexican land grants.

We need to start with a paragraph from the GAO Report:

Several published studies have focused on three of the reasons noted above as core reasons why New Mexico community land grant claims were either restricted in acreage or wholly rejected. All of these reasons are reflected in decisions by the CPLC or, on appeal, [of] the U.S. Supreme Court. We found that collectively, these reasons resulted in rejection of claims for about 1.3 million acres of land in 17 different grants. As discussed below, the three reasons were: (1) restriction of confirmed grants to their individual allotments (affecting 7 grants and approximately 1.1 million acres); (2) rejection of grants because they were made by unauthorized officials (affecting 8 grants and approximately 93,000 acres); and (3) rejection of grants because the claims for them were based solely on copies of documents made by unauthorized officials (affecting 2 grants and approximately 69,000 acres)....

The GAO is saying that the courts collectively found that these reasons resulted in the rejection of claims for about 1,300,000 acres of land in seventeen different grants. But it goes on to say that the CPLC and the U.S. Supreme Court only restricted seven of the 105 confirmed community land grants to their individual allotments.

Here's a question I would like the government to answer. When it comes down to whether a grant is allowed to keep its community lands—how could seven of the grants be refused the due process and the equal protection benefits of the Constitution that the other 105 grants were provided?

What the GAO is saying is that the courts allowed ninety-eight grants to keep their community land but made seven give theirs up.

Let's look at the seven grants that were restricted—see what they had in common—what caused them to be treated different.

It doesn't take but a minute to figure out why the courts ruled the way they did—to figure out what they were interested in. The first thing we found was that eighty-six percent of the acreage, 967,175 of the 1,220,418 acres "borrowed" from the seven grants and "returned" to the public domain were from only three of the seven grants.

The next thing we see is that the three grants losing the 967,175 acres wound up with only 7,838 acres while the other four grants—that lost only 153,243 acres wound up with 8,645 acres.

Then we looked at which grants were the big losers and realized that the three grants losing the most acreage just happened to be the San Miguel del Bado, the San Joaquín del Río de Chama, which the GAO insists on referring to as the Cañon de Chama—and the La Petaca.

When we add the 967,175 acres these three grants lost to the estimated 146,000 the Juan Bautista Valdez lost because the CPLC refused to use the Cerro Blanco as the Juan Bautista west boundary, we are still left with an unanswered question. What did these four grants have in common that would cost them ninety-nine percent of their acreage? Out of 105 community grants why did the three the courts reduced and the Juan Bautista— why did these four grants lose ninety-nine percent of their land? Could it be, Hijo, that they just happened to be covered with forests? Could merchantable timber have had anything to do with it?

The GAO said:

> The issue before the courts [the Court of Private Land Claims and the U.S. Supreme Court] was whether the community or the prior sovereign—Mexico—had owned the community lands within the boundaries of a community land grant.

The question the GAO should have been investigating was—other than the over abundance of merchantable timber on the three grants the courts had reduced to their original allotments, and the Juan Bautista Valdez which had lost most of its land because the government refused to use its western boundary, what on earth could have caused the CPLC and the U.S. Supreme Court to "convert" ninety-nine percent of these four grants to the public domain forty-nine years after the signing of the Treaty of Guadalupe Hidalgo?

It's time I let you in on a little secret. We have found a ton and a half of evidence that proves why the federal government intentionally converted the four grants into public land. But before we go into that we need to talk a little more about why the CPLC—even though the grant papers said the west boundary of the Juan Bautista was Cerro Blanco—ruled that the west boundary was a little hill just to the west of Cañones.

If the west boundary of the Juan Bautista Valdez Grant was less than a mile west of Cañones like the CPLC claimed—why had hundreds of the settlers been living west of that small hill for generations—in places like Coyote, El Rito de las Encinias and Río Puerco?

Grandpa, you need to explain which El Rito and Río Puerco you're talking about.

Good idea. The El Rito I'm talking about is the one there by Coyote. Years ago it was also called El Rito de las Encinias, then El Rito, and today it's called Youngsville. And the Río Puerco I'm talking about is right next to it. I'm not talking about the El Rito that's about twelve miles east of Abiquiú or the Río Puerco that's west of Albuquerque. (Fig. 1).

During the CPLC hearing on the Juan Bautista Valdez Grant witnesses testified that the Grant extended 10 to 15 miles to the west of Cañones, "in the direction that the sun goes down." Unfortunately, the court chose to ignore the evidence.

Here's a map we need to look at. Do you see where it says Gallina Plaza—and to the right of that it says Gallina? (Fig. 8).

Yes.

And to the right of Gallina, do you see the large white area, where it says Piedra Lumbre Grant?

Yes.

Look at the bottom, south of the Piedra Lumbre Grant. Do you see where it says Juan Bautista Valdez Grant?

Yes.

Count the squares, the miles going west from the Juan Bautista Valdez to Coyote.

There are nine—nine miles between the Juan Bautista and Coyote.

Now count the miles west from Coyote to Gallina.

Counting the one that has Coyote in it there are 13—and another five going north to where it says Gallina.

So, according to the map and your count, Hijo, if the government used a small hill less than a mile west of Cañones as the west boundary, Gallina is about twenty-two miles west of where the CPLC claimed the west boundary of the Juan Bautista Grant was?

Yeah.

In order for the CPLC to claim that the west boundary of the Juan Bautista was less than a mile to the west of Cañones it had to ignore the fact that of the four settlements in the Juan Bautista Valdez Grant, three of them, Coyote, El Rito and Rio Puerco were west of the hill it was claiming was the west boundary and it had to ignore the testimony that from Cañones the grant continued another 10 to 15 miles "in the direction that the sun went down."

Look at the place you found when I first handed you the government map—Gallina Plaza. Do you see it?

Yes.

Just north of Gallina Plaza and a little to the right, to the east, between Gallina Plaza and Gallina there's a name running from the bottom of the map toward the top—what is it?

Cerro Blanco. (Fig. 8).

Now—to the right of where it says Cerro Blanco what does it say?

It says Cañón Capulín.

Turn the map over—do you see where it says the map's being sold by the U.S. Department of Interior—Bureau of Land Management—and the U.S. Geological Survey.

Yes.

Do you agree that we were able to find Cerro Blanco on this United States Department of Interior, Bureau of Land Management and U.S. Geological Survey map?

Yes.

Maybe since this map is only a few years old and wasn't available to the CPLC—maybe it's possible they didn't have a map showing Cerro Blanco. Or maybe they just didn't want to find it. On the other hand, maybe the government, the court, knew where it was but decided to act like it didn't.

When does it say the map we are looking at was prepared?

It was printed in 2004.

Where do you see that?

It's on the back when the map is folded up. It says:

2004 Magnetic declination (MN) is based on the Center of the map. Diagram is approximate.

Do you see any information on it that shows that some of the information might have been from older maps?

Well it does say: "National Geodetic Vertical Datum of 1929 was used," *whatever that means. But I think we have to do better than that, Grandpa. That was a long time after the court ruled that the west boundary was within a mile of Cañones.*

Here's an article. Read the part that's underlined.

A brief overview of the Triassic vertebrate fossils from Ghost Ranch, New Mexico…Triassic fossils were scientifically recognized in northern New Mexico just a century ago when Edward Drinker Cope, the famous paleontologist and zoologist from Philadelphia, passed through this region in 1874 on a journey from Santa Fe to Tierra Amarilla. On this trip Cope picked up a few fossil reptilian bones in the vicinity of Gallina where Upper Triassic sediments are exposed at the base of Cerro Blanco.

Skip down and read the next paragraph.

> Three areas in northern New Mexico have yielded Triassic fos-
> sils: namely the slopes at the base of Cerro Blanco (already men-
> tioned) a hogback immediately to the west of Capulin Mesa, as well
> as around the Mesa; the badlands at Ghost Ranch, and particularly
> the basal portions of the colorful cliffs which rise in spectacular
> splendor behind the ranch; ...

After we'd found Cerro Blanco on the map, we still felt like we needed to come up with more proof that Cerro Blanco existed at the time the CPLC was acting like it didn't. The information in the article about Edward Cope's trip from Santa Fe to Tierra Amarilla says the area was known as Cerro Blanco at least as early as when the CPLC was acting like it wasn't, but we still weren't satisfied. We felt we still needed to prove the government had to have known where Cerro Blanco was. We believe from what we've read that the CPLC did know where Cerro Blanco was but since the government wanted the tens of thousands of acres between the little hill west of Cañones and where Cerro Blanco actually was, it did what it did best in those days— it acted like Cerro Blanco didn't exist.

Even though the article we just read calls it Cerro Blanco maybe in 1874 the people were calling it something else.

We're way ahead of you, Hijo. We have quite a bit of evidence that Cerro Blanco was a real place. You're going to find it interesting that in order to prove the government knew about Cerro Blanco we wound up reading about a dinosaur called the *Rioarribasaurus*.

Rioarribasaurus—I can't believe someone named a dinosaur after Río Arriba County.

Read the part that's highlighted on page 192. Below where it says, *"Figure 1."*

There's a name there Grandpa, that I can't pronounce. It's spelled: C-o-e-l-o-p-h-y-s-i-s-a-n-o-m-e-n-d-u-b-i-u-m.

After that, it says:

> In 1881 David Baldwin collected fossil vertebrates for E. D.
> Cope in Río Arriba County, northwestern New Mexico, probably at
> the suggestion of Cope, who had previously collected Late Triassic

fossils in this area, including the type specimen of the aetosaur Typothorax (Cope 1875). Three of Baldwin's localities yielded fragmentary dinosaur bones that were subsequently referred to Coelophysis (Colbert 1889). Baldwin sent labels with these specimens that indicated that two localities were in Arroyo Seco which, as argued by Colbert (1889: 5-6) was probably within a few kilometers of the Whitaker quarry.

Baldwin described the locality as simply "Gallina Canyon" (Colbert 1989:5). Subsequently, Williston & Case (1912:11) claimed to have relocated the type locality of Coelophysis, north of Cerro Blanco.

While you were reading that you mentioned a map—read what it says on the map, Hijo.
Fig.1 Distribution of Triassic strata in north-central New Mexico (USA; after Dane & Bachman 1965) and the locations of the Río Gallinas, Cerro Blanco, Arroyo Seco and Ghost Ranch (Whitaker quarry). (Fig. 7).

Don't you find it odd that the 1807 grant from Spain to Juan Bautista Valdez and the other claimants identified the west boundary as a place called Cerro Blanco, Mesa Blanca and the white mesa, and yet the CPLC acted as if it couldn't find it in 1898; that witnesses testified at the hearing before the CPLC that the grant ran ten or fifteen miles in the direction that the sun goes down; that there were three—four settlements in the grant; and that the grant went to the south two to three leagues to the headwaters of the Polvadera Creek which, as it turns out just happens to be the north boundary of the Baca Location No. One? Yet the CPLC ignored all this evidence and set the west boundary less a mile west of Cañones—and the south boundary less than a league to the south of Cañones. (Figs. 6, 13).
And after all that, when the Bureau of Land Management prepared the map we're using it placed Cerro Blanco right where Edward Cope found it in 1874—more than 20 years before the CPLC acted like it couldn't find it. (Fig. 8).

As if what we've already said about Cerro Blanco and where it was isn't enough, I'm going to show you even more information that was available to the Surveyor General and the Army Corp. of Engineers in the 1870's.

It's time to introduce our family to the authors of the article on the Rioarribasaurus, Adrian P. Hunt and Spencer G. Lucas from the New Mexico Museum of Natural History. They and Andrew B. Heckert also wrote another article about Cope. Read this part:

> … On August 10, 1874, in El Rito, a local priest had shown Cope a tooth of an Eocene fossil mammal (Coryphodon) found west of Gallina. This piqued Cope's interest, so on returning to Tierra Amarilla in September; Cope totally disregarded the Wheeler expedition itinerary and broke off with a small party towards Gallina and the Eocene fossil collecting area beyond. As Simpson (1951) recounted in detail, there Cope discovered an extensive assemblage of Eocene fossil vertebrates (from strata now termed San Jose Formation), one of the most remarkable discoveries of his career. However, Cope also made a second remarkable discovery—bone fragments of a fossil reptile found in the Triassic red beds north of Gallina.

> Cope's published sketch (1875, Fig.8) of the Triassic fossil locality allowed Lucas and Hunt (1992, Fig.9) to relocate it, and it is just north of Cerro Blanco (Fig.1.25). (Fig.13).

Now look at page 27, Figure 1.25 and tell me what you think it looks like. (Fig.13).

Let's see—it's two pictures, one on top of the other. The top one looks like a copy of a photograph and the bottom one looks like—a drawing. Actually—they're the same place. Like what we were just reading, Grandpa—that Lucas and Hunt were able to locate Cerro Blanco. They took a photograph of the place shown in Cope's drawing and put it with the drawing. That's neat—we have a drawing of Cerro Blanco from 1874 and a photograph from 1992—and they look exactly alike.

We need to read a couple letters and part of a statement and then we can stop for the day.

Actually, the letters, like the pictures earlier, are on one page. The first is from George M. Wheeler, a lieutenant assigned to the United States Engineer's Office in Washington D. C., and says:

APPENDIX FF 3.— REPORT ON PALEONTOLOGY—

United States Engineer Office, Explorations and Surveys West of the 100th Meridian, Washington, D. C., October 15, 1874.

General: I have the honor to forward herewith a special report received from Prof. E. D. Cope, paleontologist to the expedition of this season, embodying some of the results of his labors in portions of New Mexico, up to 27th of September. This report contains new and valuable information relative to vertebrate fossil remains.

It's signed:

Geo. M. Wheeler,   Lieutenant of Engineers,

Below that it says:

Brig. Gen. A. A. Humphreys, Chief of Engineers—U. S. Army.

The next letter, which is the bottom half of the page I just read from, says:

Report of Prof. E. D. Cope, paleontologist. Camp on Gallinas Creek, September 27, 1874.

In accordance with your instructions to forward a report of proceedings, I beg leave to state that I returned to this camp from Tierra Amarilla on the 15th of the month, and have remained here ever since. We have been mostly employed in examining the bad lands of the Eocene of the divide between the Chama and San Juan Rivers, and in collecting the vertebrate fossils which their beds contain.

Mr. Shedd has been assisting in making collections and taking his meteorological observations at the stated times.

The health of the party continues good, and we hope to move camp to another point ere long.

Why'd you read those letters, Grandpa?

We believe they are proof that the Corp. of Engineers knew where Cerro Blanco was at least by 1874—24 years before the CPLC claimed the small hill west of Cañones was the west boundary. By using the small hill rather than Cerro Blanco the CPLC was able to reduce the Juan Bautista Valdez Grant and increase the public domain by over 146,000 acres.

There's even more proof. The boundaries of the San Joaquín del Río de Chama just north of the Juan Bautista were approved by the Surveyor General on December 12, 1872 and surveyed in 1878. The survey of the San Joaquín identified its west boundary as the Cejita Blanca at the south end and the Cuestecita Blanca at the north end. Those names are similar in meaning to the name Cerro Blanco and indicate that the San Joaquín and the Juan Bautista were supposed to have the same west boundary. (Fig. 9).

There's no way the government or the GAO can deny that the CPLC knew exactly where Cerro Blanco was—it was right where the surveyor general found the Cejita Blanca and Cuestacita Blanca in December 1872.

-21-
Hanging Out With A Bunch Of Blind Mice

Grandpa, you haven't talked much about what happened in your life after the horrible wreck that killed your sister and your nephews and nieces and after the branch fell on your legs—and after your problems with Jesús Hernandez. Would you say that you and grandma are better off today than you were twenty years ago?

Looking back it seems like we've had nothing but bad luck—but when I take a little while to think about it—it could've been a lot worse.

The worst that's happened, other than what I've already talked about, is our health has gone down.

Your grandmother still has to go to Española three times a week for dialysis. To someone that lives in a city where they have dialysis machines it wouldn't be a big deal, but when you consider she has to go 120 miles, three times a week—it takes a lot of time and money. With gas around $3.50 a gallon and a car that gets maybe fifteen miles to a gallon, that's over $350 a month just for the gas, and on top of that someone has to drive her. Getting back to when the tree fell on my legs, that was also about the time my mother went blind. But, God bless her, she managed to live like that for another fifteen or twenty years.

Most people probably wouldn't even think about it, but living here in the mountains; besides having its good points—has its bad points, too. If we lived in Española we could just stop by the dialysis center. But living here is a little rougher.

People that have never lived in the mountains—at 8,500 feet, like we do, have no way of knowing how rough it can get. But don't get me wrong, I'm just explaining—not complaining. There are a lot of people that have it a lot worse than we do. I remember watching CNN and Telemundo after the earthquake in Haiti, hearing about all the people who had died—and now the earthquake and flood in Japan. When I hear stories like that—about how those people are having to live—now that's what I call bad luck. We have it good compared to them. When I catch myself thinking about being low on firewood—or my legs are hurting, all I have to do is think about all those people in Haiti and Japan and I forget my little problems real fast.

When I get to thinking about all my friends who've died or been hurt real bad I have to say a little prayer for them—and some words for your grandmother and for her health. I guess maybe by using the bible to teach me how to read better must have worked a little, huh?

I think about Carlos Vigil a lot—how he was shot to death on his way to the courthouse. Every time I think about him I also think about Andreíta, his wife. I remember her telling me after he was killed how she had gotten a call saying he'd been shot—and about how she had run from where she was working to where he was. That when she got there she could see him on the sidewalk. Poor people—they had driven to Santa Fe together that morning never realizing that in a couple hours Carlos would be dead.

And I think about "Gorras." You knew him, Hijo. He was at the courthouse with us in Tierra Amarilla. He was killed in El Rito four years ago. I think of all my friends that have died over the past thirty years, Joe Edwards—who was killed when he wrecked his motorcycle on his 59th birthday and Charlie Hoppe—who died last year of a heart attack.

When I stop to think about how bad other people have it I realize I'm lucky really—still kicking.

You mentioned Joe Edwards and Charlie Hoppe. I don't think I've heard their names before. Who were they?

Joe was an insurance adjuster—they both were actually. I met them at Donald's cabin in the '80s—pretty soon after they started coming up here. And after a couple years Joe started bringing Jimmy Salas, one of his pool-playing buddies from Albuquerque. Jimmy and I became good friends—he still stops by a couple times a year.

One thing I'll never forget is how Joe used to love to drink rum. Sometimes he'd even have drinks as soon as he'd get up. He'd have what he liked to call the Breakfast of Champions—rum and coke and a hand full of Snickers bars. By the time we'd leave the cabin to go hunting he wouldn't be hurting at all. I'll never forget this one time we were heading toward the Canjilón Lakes and all of a sudden Joe starts yelling: "Stop! Stop—look at all those elk—Stop!"

Mike slammed on the breaks as Joe was jumping out. As soon as I saw what he was looking at I yelled for him to get back in the jeep.

What he was seeing, Hijo, was a bunch of sheep moving across the hillside.

Why would there be sheep up there at that time of the year?

The Pastores weren't required to move the sheep off the mountain until the middle of October but that year a big snowstorm had come through early and caused a lot of sheep to get lost.

I remember another time we saw some elk on the road to the lakes and Joe got out to follow them. It was snowing pretty hard and I told him that about a mile south from where we were there was a small lake—he couldn't miss it if he headed in the direction I were pointing. I told him that when he got to the lake to wait there and we'd pick him up.

Sure enough—he missed it. Well, he didn't actually miss the lake he walked right up to it, around it, and just kept going. We could tell from his tracks that he never even slowed down. By the time we found him, about five hours later, we'd worried so much about him that by the time we found him we'd drank a half a case of Bud Lite and a half-pint of Lord Calvert. We took him straight to the bar in Cebolla—your great-uncle Tony's bar—and had him replace it.

Worrying about him, Grandpa? I don't think I'm going to believe that part. Who were the best hunters?

Ernesto García was the best. When I was about 20 and he was, maybe 14, I used to take him hunting a lot. He liked hunting so much that he would walk from his house to where I lived, three or four miles—just to go hunting.

What about Joe and Charlie—Carlos—Mike? Were they good shots?

I used to tell them when we'd be leaving my house or Donald's cabin that I sure had my hands full—out there in the mountains with two lawyers and two insurance adjusters. I'd say, "I might as well be out here with four blind mice. You guys can't shoot; you can't drive in the snow; you can't build a fire when it's raining—what are you good for besides nothing and being lawyers and adjusters?"

You were just kidding— weren't you?

There you go Hijo, asking a question that—if I was forced to answer—I'd probably have to lie.

Come on–three of them are dead and Mike's helping you with your research—why can't you answer?

Because the one that's helping me's still alive.

Will you answer a question about where you would hunt when you went with them?

What are you getting at? Trying to set a trap whether we were hunting in the part of the forest that wasn't ours?

Exactly!

Most of the time we'd hunt to the east of Canjilón so I'd have to say it wasn't the land I would be free to trespass on—but it wasn't a problem because they almost always had licenses.

A few years later a whole new crop of lawyers and their friends started showing up so I had to start my training sessions all over again.

Who were they?

Tom Clark, Mike Jones and Foster—I can't remember his last name—I just remember him as Foster.

I used to get a kick out of watching those guys when they'd get here and start unloading their supplies. They'd have new rifles, camouflaged clothes—pounds and pounds of food—the works. In the beginning all you had to do to get one of them lost was take him fifty yards into the forest and turn him loose but after a year or two they got to where they knew the place and could hunt all day by themselves with no problem.

Did any of your friends ever kill an elk?

Once in a while they'd kill one—they almost always took some meat home.

Let me give you an example where Mike and Carlos didn't kill an elk but wound up with a nice set of antlers. Ernesto and I were hunting with them in an area known as Canjilón Meadows—it's a huge meadow about four miles north of the lakes—near Good Shot Dad Ridge. Mike and Carlos dropped Ernesto and me off at the east end of the meadow and drove to the far side of a spruce covered hill. Just after they were out of our sight Ernesto shot at a bull that was running through the trees. We called them on a radio and told them what had happened. They parked and started walking back toward us hoping they would either run into the elk or scare it back toward us. When they got to where we were Mike said that about ten minutes after they started walking he smelled something dead and went toward where the smell was. He said that it was a huge bull with a nice rack that had been dead a couple of days—that coyotes or a bear had already gotten to it.

He said on their way back to his truck he was going to get the rack. I told him to forget it there was no way he could find it. He started telling me how he'd been in the Air Force in the sixties and spent a lot of time flying around as a navigator—that he was going to walk right up to it. I told him I was going to follow him and see if he could find it and damn if he didn't walk right to it. Of course, the way it smelled I probably could have walked to it myself—blindfolded.

Mike and Carlos started carrying the head and antlers to where we had parked. It was stinking so bad we could hardly stand it. He and Carlos grabbed the rack and started carrying it down the hill. It wasn't long before they were complaining about how heavy it was so I told them to put it down.

I took my 30-30 and shot the antlers off the head. Just to show you how bad our luck is sometimes, Hijo—we only had one beer with us and I had put it on the ground three or four feet from where I was going to be shooting. The second time I fired the bullet kicked up a small rock that went flying through the beer can. By the time I got to it, it was empty.

You mentioned a place you called "Good Shot Dad Ridge." How'd it get that name—if you know?

That's an interesting story, Hijo. Five or ten years before Mike and Carlos found the dead bull, Carlos and his father Ernesto and three or four of us from Canjilón were hunting along a ridge when we spotted a bull in the meadow below us. There must have been eight or ten shots fired before the bull finally dropped and after it did I saw Carlos go up to his dad and say, "Good shot, Dad!"

Later that afternoon I asked Ernesto if he'd shot the bull and he kinda laughed and said he hadn't even fired a shot. After that we started calling the place "Good Shot Dad Ridge."

Did you ever find out who shot it?

Yeah. Your uncle Amarante.

What would you all do in the middle of the day—when you weren't hunting?

Sometimes we'd look for mushrooms if they were in season. Which reminds me—for years there was this woman that would come from Colorado every fall and pay me for mushrooms. I'd sell her sacks full of them and she'd take them back to Colorado to sell.

Sometimes, when Carlos was alive, we'd go up by the lakes and dig up oshá root. Some people call it Bear Root, but we always called it oshá. Carlos liked to take it to his family. It's one of the best herbs that grow around Canjilón—I've been digging it up since I was a kid. My mother used to give it to us for colds, toothaches, all kinds of sickness.

Why was it called Bear Root?

In the spring when the bears wake up one of the first thing the boars look for is oshá. They chew it to help their digestion. But the funny thing is that after they chew it all up they put it in their paws and rub it all over their bodies. I've never seen them do it, but I've even heard that they'll rub it on the sows if they can get away with it.

I need to remember that—need to tell my teacher and the class about it.

I'm glad you said you wanted to tell your teacher about it. I thought for a minute you were going to say you wanted to try it on yourself. Maybe find a girlfriend to put it on.

Come on, Grandpa. You know I wouldn't do that. I can't believe that at your age you're talking like that.

I need to finish answering about what we would do during the middle of the day, when we weren't hunting. Sometimes we'd go to Cebolla and shoot pool, drink a few beers—have some snacks. Other times if we had someone with us that hadn't been here before we'd take them to the Indian ruins at Dulce and Turkey Springs.

When I was a kid out looking for our cows I used to pass right by Dulce Spring. In those days there was pottery laying around. It didn't mean anything to me at that time and I'd just leave it there. Over the years though people must have carried it off because I never see it anymore.

It sounds like you used to spend a lot of time with your lawyer and adjuster friends. Did your friends here in Canjilón get after you for spending so much time with them?

I guess it's time to let you practice your math. Get a piece of paper I'm going to have you answer your own question. Multiply fifteen, the number of years my friends have been coming up here, times 365. Got it?

Yeah, 5,475.

Now multiple 15 times six. What does that come out to?

Come on, Grandpa. I don't need a piece of paper and a pencil to figure that out. I thought you were going to give me some complicated math problem. So far I have 5,475 and 90. What are you getting at?

Don't be impatient—tell me what part 90 is of the other number.

Finally, a real math problem. It's .016, Grandpa.

Why'd you have to get a calculator—too hard to do by hand. Now I need to ask you a question that has to do with how much time I actually spent with my friends. If they've been coming here for 15 years, once or twice a year for three days, how much of my time was I spending with them?

Okay, I see what you're getting at.

But you haven't answered my question, how much of my time was I spending with the lawyers and insurance adjusters?

You really gonna make me answer?

Sure. You asked me, why shouldn't I ask you?

I can't believe you're doing this. The answer is less than two percent of your time, Grandpa.

How much time did that leave for me to spend with my friends from Canjilón and to do everything I need to do?

Okay, you got me there—but before we stop for the day can I get you to tell one last story. The one you told me the other night about what happens when you put hair from a horse's tail in water?

I'm glad you reminded me. That's important. If you cut some hair from a horse's tail and put it in the water—after a few days they'll turn into snakes.

Why you laughing, Grandpa?

Laughing?

-22-

Presidents Harrison And Roosevelt— Governors King And Cargo

My teacher came up with some questions and asked me to see if you would answer them. The first one is, what do you and your friends think about politicians?

I can't answer for my friends, but I'll tell you what I think. We need to start with the ones from before, the ones from the 1800s—1900's. Then I'll answer about the ones when I was growing up—during the 60's.

I need to start with Presidents Polk and Harrison—and Roosevelt. Talk about what we've learned since we started our family history. As far as out grants and our ancestors are concerned those three are the ones who were our problems.

President Polk was bad because he forced Mexico to give up half of its land and sign the Treaty of Guadalupe Hidalgo which he was never going to follow. President Harrison was responsible for the Court of Private Land Claims and Forest Reserve Acts and appointing the judges and U.S. Attorney who took 30,000,000 acres of our land. His State of the Union addresses make it clear that he was against our land grants and our ancestors.

And President Roosevelt—he's the one that turned millions of acres of our grants and the Indian reservations into forest reserves without offering to pay for any of it.

But the three of them weren't alone, there were others that were bad, too. I'd say Secretary Noble, Secretary Elkins, the justices on the CPLC, the U.S. Attorney, Matt Reynolds, and Senator Albert J. Beveridge were terrible, too. And the list doesn't stop there. The Congress and the Supreme

Court didn't do us any favors either. They all, along with the GAO ignored the Treaty, international law and the Constitution when it came to the way our grants and our people have been treated.

The members of the Santa Fe Ring and Governor Manuel Armijo treated our people terrible—the Ring for stealing the land and Governor Armijo for giving thousands of acres to his friends—and for taking thousands of dollars to desert the Territory when Kearney was heading to Santa Fe. He was every bit as bad as all the others.

I'd say Governor Connelly, who asked our ancestors to join the New Mexico Volunteers and fight for the Union didn't treat our men right when he supplied them with worn out uniforms and equipment—old guns—and then, when the war was over, never really thanking them or giving them credit for helping defeat the Texans.

Other than the ones I already talked about, I saved one of the worst for last. Gifford Pinchot, the Chief of the Forest Service, was the absolutely worst one when it comes to what he got President Roosevelt to do in Río Arriba and Taos Counties—when they established the Jémez and Taos Forest Reserves. After the ones we already talked about who had helped rip the Treaty and our grants to shreds, along came Gifford Pinchot and his pal, Theodore Roosevelt and destroyed any chance our grants and our people would ever receive justice.

As for the politicians during my lifetime—the good ones—Governors King and Cargo are at the top of my list. They tried to help solve our problems. Tried to calm everyone down—went out of their way to be fair to us—tried to get everyone together to avoid the problems we had in the end.

I think Chief Joe Black of the State Police, Captain Martín Vigil and the other state police officers, the National Guard, Sheriff Benny Naranjo and his father, Emilio Naranjo all treated us as fair as they could when you consider everything that was going on.

The one person from the 1960's I still don't care for would have to be Alfonso Sánchez. Now there's a man that was absolutely up to no good. He was the worst politician we had to deal with. Even worse than the federal judges who wouldn't let us testify about our history. Of everybody that was against us during the '60's when we were trying to show the public what had happened with the land grants— Alfonso Sánchez was the worst.

There wouldn't have been any violence on June 5th, 1967, Hijo, if Sánchez hadn't had the police set up roadblocks around Coyote and arrested our people just to stop us from having a meeting.

If Alfonso Sánchez hadn't kept us from having our meeting in Coyote on June 3rd there wouldn't have been any reason for us to go to the courthouse the next Monday. I'm not saying there wouldn't have been trouble later; days, weeks, months—years later. I'm just saying that what happened at the Courthouse on June 5th wouldn't have happened. We wouldn't have had any reason to go to Tierra Amarilla—Nick Saiz and Eulogio wouldn't have been shot; Dan Rivera wouldn't have been hit over the head; Benny Naranjo wouldn't have been threatened; Pete Jaramillo and Larry Calloway wouldn't have been kidnapped—none of the damage to the courthouse would have happened. It was all because of Alfonso Sánchez' politics.

Something else I can say, now that more than forty-three years have passed, is that it's a good thing Sánchez wasn't at the courthouse that day. Even though I wouldn't have believed it at the time, he might have been seriously hurt or killed if he'd been there. I'm not saying he would have been hurt or killed at the courthouse but he would have been arrested and taken to Canjilón where we would have had a trial and he would have been found guilty and sentenced—like happened with the two Forest Rangers at the Echo Amphitheater the year before. I'm afraid now though, looking back, that he might have been hurt or killed when the police started heading for the ranch. What I'm trying to say is that when the police began showing up something might have happened. I'm just glad we didn't find him at the courthouse.

On the way to Tierra Amarilla that day I was thinking about Tijerina saying we didn't have anything to worry about if we took guns into the courthouse—that we had had guns at the Echo Amphitheater and nothing had happened.

I'm sorry Grandpa, but you already said that when you were talking about what happened at the courthouse.

We sure don't need to spend time telling the same thing over and over, do we? If you catch me doing it again, stop me right away. Don't wait until I get to the end of what I have to say.

I need to talk some more about Sánchez, about what still has me upset, about him calling us a bunch of communists. Listen to what he was saying in this article a year after we had gone to the courthouse. It starts with the title: *Alianza Set for Warfare, Sanchez Says:*

> Members of the Alianza Federal de Pueblos Libres, headquartered in Albuquerque reportedly are being trained in guerrilla warfare tactics in communist Cuba and on a ranch near Taos, District Attorney, Alfonso Sanchez told the New Mexican Tuesday.

> Sánchez also said that the Alianza, a group claiming rights to centuries-old land grants in New Mexico are importing known communists into its organization from Mexico.

He made that all up. We never had an organization in Mexico, never tried to import anyone from Mexico, let alone communists. Here's some more that he said in the article:

> "The history of Reies López Tijerina leader of the Alianza and his brothers indicates that the organization has been planning a takeover of northern New Mexico in the same manner Fidel Castro took over Cuba," Sanchez said.

> To support his contention, Sánchez cited material collected after the raid on the courthouse in Tierra Amarilla one year ago today…

> Sánchez said that it would be difficult to imagine a Communist takeover here, "but," he said, "If we gotta fight them here, we gotta."

I never heard anyone say anything about the communist party—about Cuba—about Fidel Castro—about importing communists from Mexico. Or about training in guerilla tactics on a ranch near Taos. He was making it all up, Hijo.

We believe the reason he was saying all that crap was because our trials were coming up and he was running for re-election. He wanted to scare the people who might be picked to be on the juries and to get people to vote for

him. He couldn't have believed what he was saying, he was way too smart
for that.

*I remember you telling me a few years ago about a meeting with Newt Gingrich
during the time he was the Speaker of the U.S. House of Representatives, could you
talk about that?*

Oh yeah. He's one of the ones I forgot to mention. Mike found an article mentioning what he was up to at the time he came to New Mexico. It's
too long to read the whole thing, I'll just read a few parts of it:

> The treaty mania revolves around land, votes, and regional iden-
> tity. Hispanic residents hope to use the document [the Guadalupe-
> Hidalgo Treaty Land Claims Act] to wrest from the Forest Service
> as much as 1.5 million acres that they say were granted to their
> ancestors, largely by Spain, in the 18th century.

> Republicans hope to use the land-grant issue to break a half cen-
> tury of Democratic political control of Northern New Mexico.
> Already the bill, the Guadalupe-Hidalgo Treaty Land Claims Act of
> 199[8], is creating strange bedfellows. At the Gingrich news con-
> ference, Roberto Mondragon, a longtime Democrat and member of
> the state's Green Party, gave a hearty abrazos [sic] to the Speaker
> and to the bill's sponsor, Representative Bill Redmond, this district's
> new Republican Congressman.

> Judging by the dozens of land-grant leaders who carried petitions
> to Mr. Gingrich's news conference, the bill enjoys wide support.
> Under the bill, a five-member review commission would study land
> claims and then forward a report to the President and Congress
> with recommendations for action.

*Let me see if I understand what you just said, Grandpa. Congressman Redmond
had won a special election and was running for re-election here in Northern New
Mexico and he had introduced a bill to deal with Guadalupe Hidalgo Treaty land
claims?*

Yeah.

He had a meeting in Albuquerque and Newt Gingrich, the Speaker of the House of Representatives, was there supporting Redmond?

Yep.

And Gingrich was saying that if our people supported Redmond's re-election— if they helped him get reelected—Gingrich would do what he could to pass the bill— all our people had to do was help get Redmond re-elected?

Right.

Was he re-elected?

No.

Did you ever hear from Gingrich or Redmond, again?

No! But to be fair, Gingrich did get the *Guadalupe-Hidalgo Treaty Land Claims Act of 1998* through the House of Representatives on September 10, 1978 by a vote of 223 to 187, but, even though senators Domenici and Bingaman were in the senate at the time, they never carried it through the senate—it died without a hearing. And other than that we never heard from Gingrich or Redmond again.

Is that the end of what you were going to say about politicians?

That's it.

I have a surprise for you. After I told my teacher what you had said about how bad the Forest Service has been treating our cattlemen lately he offered to do some research about grazing. After he finished the research he wrote down what he'd found and asked me to read it for you the next time we got together to show how much he appreciates what you're doing. I was going to keep it until one of our later meetings but, since we finished kinda early today, if you don't mine, I'd like to go ahead and talk about what he found.

I don't mind at all. It makes me glad to see how interested you and your teacher are about our history.

He found two articles that deal with the effect grazing has had on forest fires in the Jémez Mountains. Both articles were written by scientists after they had done tree-ring and burn studies.

Both articles were written for the Forest Service and were studies of the area where the La Mesa fire had burned in 1977. They were presented at a Forest Service conference in 1996.

Doesn't you're teacher have his years messed up, Hijo. You said the studies were requested by the Forest Service after the La Mesa fire—but then you said they weren't used until 1996. I can't believe the Forest Service—no matter how bad we claim it is—would wait nineteen years to discuss a fire that happened in 1977.

He has it correct, Grandpa. The fire was in '77 and the conference was in '96. Anyway—the first study covers 14 different sites but my teacher said we only need to discuss the information about the site with the code CPE. *That's the code for the Cerro Pedernal area, the area around Cañones where the remaining acres of our Juan Bautista Valdez Grant are located. The information he gave me starts by saying:*

The Cerro Pedernal site (CPE) also displays high frequency fire events during most of the 1600's and early 1700's, again with an obvious reduction in fire frequency after 1748 and early cessation of major fires by 1873 … Portions of the CPE area were grazed by Hispanic/Genízaro peoples since the 1720's, and the initial Spanish land grant for Cañones (immediately northeast of CPE) was provided in 1731 (Van Ness 1987). These lines of evidence suggest Hispanic grazing practices might have caused the reduction in fire frequency which is apparent after 1748 in this area … This long fire interval may be due to utilization of the CPE area for livestock husbandry by Tewa Native Americans during the unsettled years immediately before and after the 1680 Pueblo Revolt … and historic documentation of Tewa Puebloans taking refuge from the Spanish reconquest in 1696-1697…

Then it says:

There was a clear cessation in widespread fire occurrences at all sites after 1893…The end of the frequent and extensive fires coincided with the onset of the documented period of intensive livestock grazing across northern New Mexico…which reduced the continuity of herbaceous fine fuels (e.g., grasses) and hence the ability of fires to spread. Because the buildup of livestock numbers in the late 1800's was also a regional phenomenon, concurrent and similarly sharp declines in fire frequency are observed in most other southwestern fire scar…However, fire histories show earlier cessation of fires at sites with earlier periods of intense grazing…conversely fire regimes have continued little-changed well into the 20th Century at a few sites were grazing and fire suppression were limited....

Your teacher has come up with some interesting information. Since the Forest Service bought and paid for those studies and had a conference, I would've thought it would have paid attention to what the experts were saying. But it's clear from the fact the Forest Service is still cutting back on grazing that it doesn't understand that less grazing means more fires.

And Grandpa—just four years after the conference a fire near Los Alamos destroyed 47,000 acres of forest and more than 250 homes.

I know the fire you're talking about, the Cerro Grande. Be sure and tell your teacher that I appreciate what he did for us. Tell him I said he can have a copy of our history when we finish it—he's been a real help.

I will. I just remembered some more questions he wanted me to ask. Do we still have time to answer them today?

Sure, but make them short. We've been here quite a while and I'm starting to get a little tired.

He'd like to know if you were involved in burning haystacks and barns—cutting fences in the 1960's?

I wasn't involved in that. There were people that thought I was, but I never did any of that and I'll tell you why. I never blamed the people that were living here in the 60's, the Anglos, for the way our people had been treated fifty—seventy-five years earlier. Our land was taken in the late 1800's, early 1900's—not the 1950's and '60's. So, the way I felt—the way I still feel, is why should the people living here when I was growing up be blamed for something that happened before?

I knew some of the people whose barns and houses were burned. They were people like us—people trying to make a living, just trying to keep floating—like we were. I knew most of the people around here at the time and they didn't have anything to do with our ancestors losing their land.

No! I never got involved in that, and like I've already said—I'd been working in the forest for years by the time people started burning barns and cutting fences and the people who had hired me—the Anglos—had treated me like they treated their own people. Why would I want to hurt people like that—people who hadn't done anything to us.

I remember one time Mrs. Jolly, Buck Jolly's wife, asked me what we were going to do to them. Did we want their land? She was talking about all the burning that was going on and I told her I didn't have anything to do with it. The way she looked at me though—I don't think she believed me—but I was telling her the truth.

Who was doing the burning?

I wasn't there when they were doing it or when they were planning it—but sometimes I would be at places where I'd hear people talking. Sometimes when I was in my garage at night and some of my friends might start talking about what was happening—or going to happen, about cutting a fence, starting a fire. I gotta admit I did hear some of that—but I never got involved in starting fires or cutting fences.

My teacher said that from everything I've told him about our conversations you haven't said anything about the Forest Service signs that were burned near Coyote. He'd like to know if you were there—and if you weren't, what, if anything you know about it?

I wasn't there. But I knew it was going to happen.

Wait a minute, Grandpa, from what I've heard, Tijerina said he didn't know it was going to happen until his wife told him that morning that she wanted to do something for the cause and that she was going to burn a sign? How could you have known it was going to happen if he didn't know—did she tell you she was going to do it?

No. Reies told me.

But, if he didn't know it was going to happen until that morning, and you weren't there—how could he have told you about it?

I'll tell you what I know and it'll be up to you to decide when Reies heard about it.

I was working in my garage a couple days before it happened and Reies drove up. He told me that a forest sign in Coyote was going to be burned and he wanted me to be there. I told him there was no way I was going, I was already in enough trouble. He got real mad and told me I was a "chicken-shit" for not going. I told him I was sorry but I wasn't going to do anything that could get me in more trouble. So now it's up to you to figure out whether Reies knew about it before that morning.

I think you made it pretty clear, Grandpa. Only one more question. My teacher told me yesterday that after Tijerina got out of prison he started blaming the Jews for all the problems of the world and he wanted to know what you think about him saying that.

I've heard Tijerina say mean things about the Jews, too. Ever since he started talking like that I've figured he's run out of things to say. I don't like it when he starts talking about other people. So far as I know, the Jews have never done anything against our people or our grants. In fact, the only connection between our people and the Jewish people that I know about is that they had a war that started on exactly the same day that we went to the courthouse looking for Alfonso Sánchez. And that's something that has always seemed like a mystery to me. I used to think about it a lot. How could two different groups of people, half the way around the world from each other, be fighting for land that had belonged to them for generations, and the trouble start on exactly the same day.

If you remember, when I was talking about the day we went to the courthouse I mentioned that we spent the night in the forest and while we were there listening to a radio station in Los Angeles talking about a war in Israel and the revolution in New Mexico, one story after the other.

I've never understood how someone like Tijerina, that's supposed to be religious would talk bad about another race or religion. Whether you like someone or not you shouldn't blame it on their race or religion. It shouldn't have anything to do with what group they belong to. God's the one that decides what race people belong to—we don't have any say about that. Maybe there's someone I don't like, but that doesn't give me the okay to talk about their race, just because I might not like them. I don't think the race a person has anything to do with whether they are a good or a bad person. It's their personality that makes people the way they are. I can't understand why someone that used to be a preacher would say what he says. I feel sorry for him.

-23-
The United States Forest Service—Sin Ropa!

I'd like to know how the Forest Service has changed, if it has, since 1977. The reason I'm using 1977 is because you have said that for about ten years after you went to the courthouse, the Forest Service treated you more like it should have in the past. How's it been acting since 1977?

The way I see it, Hijo, the government is constantly changing the way it wants the forests to be used.

From everything I heard when I was growing up and everything I've learned since I've been on my own our problems with the Forest Service have been here for as long as there's been a Forest Service. I don't remember a single time when the Forest Service ever acted like it really gave a damn about our people. It has always been too busy kissing big companies and environmentalist to give a damn about the people that live around here. I've heard people call it "following the money;" saying the Forest Service is an expert at "following the money." Unless the government will force the Forest Service to listen to us, help us, it's never going to. You'd think the way it acts—the way it treats us—that the supervisors think the forests are their own personal property.

Listen to what a Forest Service employee was saying in this letter that was written just five years ago, less than a year after the GAO report came out.

> Over the years line officers and others have received requests for assistance [sic] someone in perfecting claims to title on National Forest System (NFS) lands. In other words, to use agency personnel time, funds, and resources to perfect someone's claim to the public's lands—NFS lands. These requests can range from small

and simple to quite complex. Either way they can involve serious legal ramifications.

Enclosed is a 1-page briefing paper—"Community Land Grant Claims & Treaty of Guadalupe Hidalgo Forest Service Actions" of March 11, 2005. It contains some background on this subject and reminders of our obligation to protect title to NFS lands.

Under "Current Status" the Briefing Paper had this to say:

Debate on this matter has intensified significantly with the release of a relatively recent General Accounting Office report ...The following key points need to be kept in mind:

The Forest Service job is to protect and manage NFS lands, and to defend US title and rights to the land–not to assist in efforts that intend to undermine US title/rights.

Forest service resources, i.e. time and funds, are not used to support the efforts of others to undermine US title/rights, regardless of how reasonable or appealing the request may be.

By saying that the Forest Service should not use its time and money to support the efforts of people regardless of how reasonable or appealing their requests might be—it's acting exactly like it was in 1905.

You said that the Forest Service always follows the money—decides issues against the needs of the local people, do you have any information that suggests what the Forest Service does when it has to decide whether to support big businesses and environmental groups or support the needs of the local communities?

Here's part of an article that seems to tell us that the Forest Service is prejudiced against local people and local interests—when it comes to making its decisions:

The preservation versus production conflict has taken over the center stage of natural resource conflict as the environmental preservation status groups have come to the political fore. Both large scale resource development interests and environmental elite groups have learned to effectively ignore the condition of the rural poor as they battle with one another over symbolic turf. Their struggle ... has only weakened the ability of agencies like the Forest Service to pursue policies of distributive justice in rural development, as they are thrown into increasing dependence on large scale economic interests to defend resource production goals.

What it boils down to is whoever has money and political power will always be allowed to use the forest. Since big business and the environmentalists have money and political power—they'll win.

When there are two or more requests to use the forest, the groups that say they want to save the environment; clear-cut a mountainside; rip up a beautiful canyon to take out a seam of coal; drill for oil and gas—they get their wish. Local cattle and sheep ranchers—firewood and latillas sellers—are always shoved to the side. When environments are interested in stopping cattle and sheep from grazing on the forests—what happens? Groups that have no interest in owning cattle are allowed to buy up grazing permits so they can stop the grazing on the forest.

One thing we'll never see will be Forest Service studies arguing against the ones your teacher used—studies that will say that reducing the number of livestock on the forests will reduce the number of wild fires. The grazing studies your teacher found—studies requested and paid for by the Forest Service, made it clear that increases in forest fires have always been during times when there was less grazing. Even though the Forest Service bought and paid for those reports that prove grazing reduces the number of forest fires and even though the number of forest fires keep increasing, the Forest Service continues to ignore the information and continues to reduce grazing. I'll bet you, Hijo, that one of these days there's going to be a fire in the Jemez Mountains that will make the Forest Service wish it had been following the advice it got from those two studies it bought and paid for. It's just a matter of time before it happens. I just hope it doesn't happen in my lifetime or yours.

My father used to tell me that when I have to learn something I need to learn it real good—because if I forget what I've learned I'll have to waste time learning it again.

Let me give you a ridiculous example of how the Forest Service spent thousands of dollars it could have used for thinning contracts or to help towns like Canjilón, but instead was wanting to impress complete strangers who'll never come here. It built a beautiful Continental Divide Trail through Trujillo Canyon from where Mesa Montosa and Mesa Yeso come together back toward Canjilón.

One day Mike and Ernesto Garcia and I were going through Trujillo Canyon and we kept seeing these little signs nailed to the trees on the north side of the road. We stopped to see what they said. You're not going to believe it, Hijo—they were signs telling us that we were on the Continental Divide Trail.

So what's wrong with that, Grandpa? I think it's nice that the Forest Service would want the tourists to know where they are.

There are three things wrong with it, Hijo. First of all, in my seventy-two years I've never seen a tourist on that road, and besides—it's not the Continental Divide. The Divide is at least 15 or 20 miles west of there—on the other side of the Chama River.

What's your other reason, Grandpa?

Think of the cost of going along mile after mile nailing signs to trees showing people where they aren't—telling them they're traveling along a trail that isn't. Thousands of dollars—hours and hours of work—for what? Why couldn't the money be spent on something useful like cell towers—microwave towers, like the one on Mogotito, so everybody who travels through here—Forest Service employees, police, hunters, hikers, bird watchers—the people that live here—could have it easier to get around, and talk to each other.

Could you talk some more about the gardens you and Grandma plant now that you're getting older?

Sure. The first thing we do in the spring is borrow a team of horses and a plow from Moisés and turn the earth upside down and we do it in the middle of May after the ground starts getting warmer.

You never will stop kidding, will you? There's no way you use a team of horses.

Did I say that? I didn't mean a team of horses—I meant a tractor. I don't know what's getting into me, I'm starting to think like I was when I was a kid.

The most important thing to know about is the seed. The seed we use are the same as the ones my father and grandfather used. I'm pretty sure the black corn seed and the squash seed I plant are the same that our family has been using for generations. After all these years some of my black corn seed seems to have become friendly with my neighbors' white and yellow corn seed. And like everything else, Hijo, once they get together they're bound to start to change. But the squash—most people who see them say they look like gourds. If they ever tasted them, I don't think they'd say that. Once they realize how good they taste.

What do you think about poaching? I know you used to trespass to get elk meat for your friends, but I'd like to know what you think about poaching.

I never believed in killing anything, other than Coyotes just to be killing something. In fact I agree that we need laws against poaching. But killing for food because you're hungry or your family is hungry—that's different. For as long as I've been living I've known people that would kill an elk or deer because they couldn't afford to buy meat. Most of them would kill a doe or a elk calf because the meat's better. But when people start killing just for the horns or the teeth—or the hide, that's wrong—a waste. Unless it's a rancher that's doing it to save his pastures, or his fences, that's different— that's necessary. I've said a lot about environmentalists and some of it has- n't been very good, but when it comes to stopping people from killing animals out of season and killing eagles, hawks, squirrels, I'm with them when it comes to laws against that. So long as it doesn't stop ranchers from protecting their land and their animals.

When it comes to borrowing firewood, latillas, vigas, to tell the truth— I've done that a lot over the years. But I almost always made sure when I did it that I was in the part of the forest that the government had taken from our ancestors.

You need to explain what latillas and vigas are, Grandpa. Fifty or a 100 years from now—if the Forest Service keeps cutting back on grazing there won't be any latillas or vigas, probably not even any firewood. The fires will have burned all the trees and our heirs won't have any idea what a forest was, much less what latillas and vigas were.

Latillas, the way I used to cut them, they were four to six inches thick and about eight feet long—and most of the ones I cut were aspen. I'd cut them in the spring, peel the bark off, and leave them outside to dry. The vigas I cut were usually a foot to a foot and a half thick and were used to support the roofs of buildings. They would be placed on top of the walls. The latillas would be placed across the vigas either straight across or at an angle depending how fancy the person building the house would want it to be. Sometimes, instead of latillas, we would use cedar, split about two inches thick and eight of ten inches wide. When we used split cedar on top of the vigas they were called "rajas." Cedar is good to use because it keeps moths away, smells good and lasts forever.

-24-
The Unlawful Conversion Of Land Grants Into Forest Reserves

I'm interested in learning more about forest reserves. Can we talk about them?
Sure.

It seems like it must have taken a lot of work for the government to come up with a plan to turn our land grants and Indian reservations into forest reserves. Do we have any information that explains how the government did it?

Every time you ask for more information, Hijo, it surprises me how interested you've become in our past. What do you think it would take to convince you that the government actually had a plan to take the land from our grants and turn it into forest reserves?

It would help if we could find out what the politicians were thinking at the time—what presidents, cabinet members—members of Congress were saying. Find out why the forests were so important to the government that it would completely ignore our Treaty and the Indian Treaties and take hundreds of thousand—millions of acres as if they didn't even belong to the grants and the reservations?

I have some statements here somewhere that Mike gave me that show what President Harrison, Secretary of the Interior John Noble and other politicians were saying about New Mexico land grants between 1889 and 1904. I think they will give our family a pretty good idea about what was going on. But before I read what they were saying I need to take a couple minutes and explain some of the connections the politicians I mentioned had with each other.

President Harrison and his Secretary of Interior, John Noble, had been college friends. When Harrison became President he named

Noble his Secretary of Interior. Some years before that Noble had been the U. S. Attorney in Missouri and while he was in that job he'd gotten to know Matt Reynolds.

Besides naming Noble Secretary of Interior, Harrison named Reynolds his U. S. Attorney for New Mexico and appointed all the judges for the Court of Private Land Claims.

Several years later he appointed Stephen B. Elkins, who'd been a law partner of T. B. Catron and a member of the Santa Fe Ring his Secretary of War.

Now that we have the names and relationships of some of the officials we'll be dealing with we can start talking about what they had to say.

On April 26, 1891 Secretary of Interior Noble was quoted in the New York Times, saying:

> The last Congress passed several measures which will affect the work of the Interior Department considerably. The land laws were very materially altered.

> The act which creates the court to settle Mexican land claims will take a great burden off the Interior Department, which has done whatever has been done in the way of adjusting these claims. The act, or something like it has long been needed, and the work of settling these cases, which involve millions of acres may now be said to be fairly begun.

What he was saying and the way he was saying it is important. He was saying that the Court of Private Land Claims was established to "adjust" the Mexican land grant claims. It's also important that he was saying that the court, by "adjusting" the claims would be taking a burden off the Interior Department. The only thing he could have meant by that was that before the Court was established it had been the duty of the Interior Department to "adjust" the claims.

Nothing—let me say that again, Hijo—nothing we have found in the Treaty gave Congress or the Interior Department the right to "adjust" the land grants.

Before I read another of Noble's statements I want to read some more of what President Harrison had said about New Mexico.

But, Grandpa—you already read what he said.

We've only read one of his statements. I need to read more of what he was saying about our land grants—about our people:

> The judges of the Court of Private Land Claims, provided for by the Act of March 3, 1891, have been appointed and the court organized. It is now possible to give early relief to communities long repressed in their development by unsettled land titles and to establish the possession and right of settlers whose lands have been rendered valueless by adverse and unfounded claims ...

Did I hear that right, Grandpa? He was saying his appointed judges were there to help Anglo settlers—that their property had become worthless because of our ancestors "unfounded claims?"

Sure did! And that's not all. Here's another paragraph from the same address:

> Your attention is called to the difficulty presented by the Secretary of the Interior as to the administration of the law of March 3, 1891, establishing a Court of Private Land Claims. The small holdings intended to be protected by the law are estimated to be more than 15,000 in number. The claimants are a most deserving class and their titles are supported by the strongest equities. The difficulty grows out of the fact that the lands have largely been surveyed according to our methods...while the holdings, many of which have been in the same family for generations, are laid out in narrow strips a few rods wide upon a stream and running back to the hills for pasturage and timber....

By claiming that there were an estimated 15,000 small holdings to be resolved the only thing he could have been referring to were 15,000 small holding claims that belonged to Anglos which were clearly not covered by the Court of Private Land Claims Act. We believe he was sending a message to the Court that he had no intention for his hand-picked judges to allow our ancestors to keep the common lands within their grants.

We need to go back and read what he was saying before the Court of Private Land Claims and Forest Reserve Acts had even become law:

>...The unsettled state of the titles to large bodies of lands in the Territories of New Mexico and Arizona has greatly retarded the development of those Territories. Provision should be made by law for the prompt trial and final adjustment before a judicial tribunal or commission, of all claims based upon Mexican grants. It is not just to an intelligent and enterprising people that their peace should be disturbed and their prosperity retarded by these old contentions.

It's hard for me to believe a President of the United States would use those words—especially in a State of the Union address.

We're not through. Read this paragraph.

>...[T]he subject of the unadjusted Spanish and Mexican land grants and the urgent necessity for providing some commission or tribunal for the trial of questions of title growing out of them were twice brought by me to the attention of Congress at the last session. Bills have been reported from the proper committees in both houses upon the subject, and I very earnestly hope that this Congress will put an end to the delay which has attended the settlement of the disputes as to the title between the settlers and the claimants under the grants. These disputes retard the prosperity and disturb the peace of large and important communities.

As if his State of the Union addresses aren't enough, here's something he said in a letter to the members of Congress.

>The entire community where these large claims exist, and indeed all of our people, are interested in an early and final settlement of them. No greater incubus can rest upon the energies of a people in the development of a new country than that resulting from unsettled land titles.

What does that word incubus mean?

I was told that the way it's used here, it means nightmare.

So what he was saying was that no worse nightmare could have fallen on the Anglo settlers during the development of New Mexico—than having to deal with Spanish and Mexican land grants?

Unfortunately!

That's all we'll be reading of Harrison's statements, but we need to read Secretary Noble's answer to a reporter's question about who should replace him as Secretary of Interior:

> Someone should be appointed who has no connection whatever with land grants in the West, unless the Administration wants to see this department of the Government attacked very bitterly on all sides....

The way we see it, John Noble, as the outgoing Secretary of Interior, should have been interested in being replaced by someone qualified to oversee the problems of the entire country not just someone who had no connections whatever with land grants in the west.

Now we can talk about the forest reserves. Here's a memorial to Congress about withdrawing forest lands from sale:

> Resolved, that we respectfully petition the Senate and House of Representative of the United States to pass an act withdrawing temporarily from sale all distinctively forest lands belonging to the Government of the United States, as recommended by the Secretaries of the Interior during the last three administrations, and providing for their protection, and authorizing the employment of the Army, if necessary, for this purpose,...

It is respectfully suggested that the true value and use of these mountain forests has never been properly considered by this Government. It has apparently never realized that mountain forest land differs from all other land in this important respect that it must, for the sake of the properly agricultural land, always remain in forest. On the contrary, it has been sold and given away like other land without any restrictions whatever upon its use in private hands, although the experience of every nation shows that the National Government alone has the power and the means for the best forest management, and that its power must be exerted even over private forest property in order to prevent disaster to the community from the actions of individuals.

While the immediate withdrawal of the public forest lands from sale and entry is absolutely essential as a first step to their preservation as forests, it will not of itself secure this end.

Temporarily some portion of the Army can be employed to guard these lands until a practical system of administration, a common sense application of scientific knowledge and the experience of other progressive nations to the needs of the place and the times can be successfully inaugurated.

Before we move on we need to understand who the government—even before Harrison became president—believed was the owner of the forests. In order to do that we need to read something President Ulysses S. Grant had said about forests.

Observations while visiting the Territories of Wyoming Utah and Colorado during the past autumn convinced me that existing laws regulating the disposition of public lands, timber, etc., and probably the mining laws themselves, are very defective and should be carefully amended, and at an early day....

The timber in most of the Territories is principally confined to the mountain regions, which are held ... in small quantities only and as mineral lands. The timber is the property of the United States, for the disposal of which there is now no adequate law.

How do you like that, Hijo, the memorial was asking the government to use the Army to protect the forests and President Grant was saying that the timber was the property of the United States—and this was happening years before President Harrison was giving his first speech.

It sure doesn't leave any doubt who the government believed owned the forests and what should be done to protect them, does it?

Now's a good time to introduce our family to Stephen Benton Elkins. Even though our ancestors may not have known who he was he certainly was no stranger to New Mexico.

Elkins and Thomas Catron had been friends long before they arrived in New Mexico—before they opened their law office in Mesilla. They'd graduated from the University of Missouri and given commencement addresses on July 4, 1860.

During the time Elkins lived in New Mexico he served in the Territorial Legislature in 1864-65; was the territorial district attorney in 1866-67 and Territorial Attorney General in 1867. He served as U.S. District Attorney from 1873 until 1877 and was a Territorial delegate to Congress in 1882.

When he left New Mexico he moved to West Virginia where he went into business with his second wife's father, Henry Davis, who was a United States Senator at the time.

Like Secretary Noble there were a number of articles written about him.

> …Kerens, Davis, and other Republican and Democratic friends of Elkins are sure that when Proctor gives up the office of Secretary of War, sufficient influence can be brought to bear upon the President to induce him to put Elkins into the Interior Department after Noble has transferred to the War Department or been given a convenient Judgeship.

Three months later his name appeared again:

> Washington Dec. 18. When the editor of the Washington Post discovered, some time ago, that "Dick" Kerens and "Steve" Elkins were here in company, and very sagely guessed that Elkins was to be pushed into the War Department by Blaine, the Post published a paragraph intimating that if Elkins was to be put in charge of public affairs, people would do well to lock their doors….

> Speculators who have found Elkins a man averse to going into anything that did not have money in it are disposed to believe that Blaine had one big job in sight when he insisted that Elkins should have employment in the Cabinet. These men go so far as to assert that Blaine has in contemplation, the acquisition of Cuba, and that

it is to be made possible through a row with Spain, to be picked in the usual diplomatic way. By drawing Spain into a rumpus that will look like a studied affront on the part of that nation toward the United States, a demand for indemnity so high that it would be refused might give the chance to pick up Cuba at our own price....

That sounds exactly like the way President Polk started the war with Mexico, Grandpa.

That's the main reason we brought it up, Hijo—to show how forty-five years after the war with Mexico and just six years before the Spanish American War people were still talking about the way President Polk had started the war with Mexico.

After Julian discussed Elkins' political history in New Mexico, he gave his personal opinion of him:

Let me inquire why Stephan B. Elkins was made Secretary of War in the last half of the Administration. His career is historic. More than a quarter of a century ago he settled in New Mexico and became a member of the Territorial Legislature. He studied the Spanish language and the character and habits of the Mexican population. President Johnson appointed him District Attorney for the Territory, which office he held three years; he was then elected a Delegate to Congress, and served two terms.

This experience amply prepared him for the brilliant ventures in real estate through which he became rich. His dealings were mainly in Spanish grants, which he bought for a small price from Mexican claimants or their grantees. The boundaries of these grants were vague and uncertain, and their definite settlement had to be determined by the surveyor general of the Territory, and largely through his influence, the survey of these grants was made to contain hundreds of thousands of acres that did not belong to them. He thus became a great land holder, for through the manipulation of committees in Congress, grants thus illegally surveyed were confirmed with their fictitious boundaries ...

He was a genius in business, and in the pursuit of his ends was singularly unshackled of a conscience. He used the surveyor general of the Territory, the Land Department in Washington and the committees of Congress as his instruments in fleecing poor settlers and robbing the government of its lands. To cheat a man out of his home is justly regarded as a crime second only to murder, and to rob the Nation of its public domain and thus abridge the opportunity of landless men to acquire homes is not only a crime against society, but a cruel mockery of the poor.

From what we've read today, Grandpa, it's becoming even clearer that the government didn't care about our people—that it was only interested in our land.

Now I'm going to read from one of the documents we mentioned when we were talking about Cerro Blanco—the one we found in the Edgar Lee Hewett file at the Fray Angélico Chávez History Library.

I'm going to start on the first page where it was describing the 1,271,732 acres it was proposing be placed in the Jémez Forest Reserve. It said:

> ... Its greatest measurement from north to south is therefore about 95 miles. The greatest measurement from east to west is 57 miles. These measurements give no conception of the area included by the boundary; since the latter is extremely irregular, being badly cut up by Spanish grants, especially in the southern part, and by grazing lands in the northern half ...

I think it's important that it said the property was badly cut up by Spanish grants, especially in the southern part. The importance of that sentence is that it doesn't even mention our Spanish Grants in the northern part. Since it doesn't say that the northern part was badly cut up by Spanish grants, it's establishing that the San Joaquín del Río de Chama, the Juan Bautista Valdez and the La Petaca grants had already been removed from the government maps by the time it was written. If the San Joaquín, Juan Bautista and La Petaca had still been on the maps the reserve would have covered 800,000 acres less than it wound up covering. (See figures 15, 16).

The document was proposing that the Forest Reserve cover all the land from south of Cochití Pueblo north and east to the Tierra Amarilla Grant and the Colorado border even though the Jémez Mountains didn't go to the Tierra Amarilla Grant or to the Colorado border. Another problem was that the reserve was including Canjilón, La Petaca, Vallecitos, El Rito, Ojo Caliente and Tres Piedras which were part of the Chama or San Juan Mountains. Here is something the document said about that:

> The largest areas seen are on the headwaters of Río de la Vaca, along the North Slope of the Jémez Divide, and in the southern part of the Chama Mountains between Canjilón Mountain and Río Vallecitos.

This sentence was saying that some of the forest proposed to be included in the Reserve was in the Chama Mountains north of the Jémez mountains. (Fig. 14).

When Roosevelt proclaimed the reserve on October 12, 1905, the land was taken, according to Roosevelt's Proclamation, because:

> … [C]onsidering the country, it will form a very valuable timber reserve, although the timber will not average more than 4,000 feet per acre for the entire area … The very best should run over 25,000 feet per acre.

The document even estimated the total amount of merchantable timber which obviously took into account that not all the land was covered with timber:

> The entire stand of merchantable timber is estimated at 2,675,000,000 feet, B.M. [Board Measure] The non-merchantable timber is estimated at 145,000,000 feet, B.M. These figures are very conservative.

By ignoring the Treaty of Guadalupe Hidalgo and the U. S. Constitution and by converting 800,000 acres of the San Joaquín, Juan BautistaValdez and La Petaca Grants to the public domain the government was not only taking the land—it was helping itself to billions of board feet of land grant timber.

On page 17 of the document it said: "stock raising is the main dependence of Mexicans and whites."

The document was identifying the Spanish and Mexican grantees and their heirs as *Mexicans*—foreigners, even though the Treaty had acknowledged that their ancestors had been citizens for over 50 years—had become citizens in 1849, one year after the signing of the Treaty.

But when it came to deciding whether our people owned the land they had been granted by Spain and Mexico decades before the United States had even arrived in New Mexico they were considered to be and treated as foreigners.

And that's not the only place in the document that our ancestors were referred to as Mexicans, as being different—as less desirable:

> The white settlers on the Río de la Vaca, [Peñas] Negras, Cebolla, San Antonio, and Bland Canyon own cattle, and as they are the most desirable settlers and since cattle are much less injurious to the range than sheep, they should be given the preference for the range near their homes …

And,

> A conflict of interests exists between white cattlemen on the Río de La Vaca, Penas Negras, Cebolla, San Antonio, and the sheep-men. Cattlemen should have an exemption area.

Referring to settlements in the area the document said:

> Bland, Perea, and Señorita, mining camps of only a few inhabitants each, are the only towns inside the line, south of the Chama. Cuba is a small Mexican village on the (western) Puerco. The old Spanish grants occupy a very large area in New
> Mexico, and two of them in particular, the Canyon de San Diego and the Baca Location, occupy a great deal of the timber lands of the Jémez Mountains. Only a few Mexicans and three or four whites live on these grants …

What I just read supports the fact that the San Joaquín, Juan Bautista Valdez and La Petaca Grants had been intentionally removed from the government maps. Otherwise Cañones, Cañon de Chama, Gallina, Coyote, El Rito de las Encinias and the other settlements in our Grants, all of which were "inside the line, south of the Chama," should have appeared on the map.

Since the San Joaquín with 472,000 acres; the Juan Bautista Valdez with approximately 147,500 acres and the La Petaca with its reduced acreage of 186,600 acres had hundreds of people living on them the government should have excluded them from the Reserve as it did the Cañón de San Diego and the Baca Location, which, as the proposal said, "had only a few Mexicans and three or four whites living on them."

One last point before we stop for the day, Hijo. If the government's feelings about our people weren't completely negative—if the government cared at all about our people, there is no way the person who wrote the document would have dared to use this sentence:

> The cattlemen favor the reserve; also the largest sheepmen in the region. The peon Mexicans are ignorant as yet, and have no ideas.

-25-
If Our Future Was Up To You, Grandpa—

Now that we're getting close to the end of our history Grandpa—can you tell me what you'd do if you had the power to end the nightmare our families have been living since the government took the land?

I don't mind saying what I think, Hijo, but who'd care what I have to say? The government—the politicians? No way! They haven't cared about our people for the last 100 years. The Court of Private Land Claims?—it didn't care. The Supreme Court?—Congress?—They didn't care.

But, Grandpa. You're not going to be saying this for the world. You're saying it for our family.

I'll give it a shot, Hijo. But first I need to ask you a question. How long would you guess it's been since everyone who cares about Northern New Mexico—the Forest Service, Departments of Agriculture and Interior, historians, politicians—church and environmental groups, cattlemen, hunters, the business people—our people—how long would you say it's been since they all got together to talk about our future?

I don't have any idea, but I believe it would be safe to say it hasn't happened in my lifetime. How long has it been?

As far as I know there's never been a meeting like that.

Between February 2, 1848 when the Treaty of Guadalupe Hidalgo was signed and today, the federal government has never had enough interest in our land grants and our people to get together with us—to listen to what we have to say. The truth is that our people have been treated as politically insignificant forty-six months out of every four years for the last 150 years. But that's going to change. One day that's all going to change.

If our future was up to me—if I had anything to do with it—the first thing I'd do would be to call everyone that has any interest in the future of this area together—everybody, whether we like each other or not—and start by trying to get to know each other. After that we could start trying to work together to make this a better place. It might take five, maybe ten Matanzas before we could get anything done, but eventually it could all come together. The fact we haven't gotten together in the past 150 years shouldn't stop us from given it a couple of shots.

If you were able to get anything you wanted for yourself, what would it be?

Now I can answer that. I wouldn't want anything for me. What we need is a future, not a past. Why, I'm older than mud—but still younger than dirt.

How can you be older than mud, but younger than dirt, Grandpa?

Come on, Hijo. You got to know the answer to that. Before you can have mud, you gotta have dirt.

Okay, you got me again.

Giving me something, anything, would be a waste of whatever you gave me. What our people need and don't have—is a future to look forward to. What we need is for our young people to start believing, to become convinced, that there is such a thing as a future. But don't take me wrong. There are people, old people, sick people, poor people, who need help, who desperately need it. There's no way I want the government to spend money on me. What our little towns could use is access to the world —and for the world to have access to us. Like I just said, our children, your children, they need to become convinced that there's such a thing as a future; that there's nothing wrong with dreaming as long as they figure out that dreaming won't work by itself. That it takes an education and hard work for their dreams to have a chance to come true.

If money was to become available from foundations, church groups, it would need to be used to build community centers, clinics, better communications. We need help with the tomorrows—not the yesterdays.

We lost a great chance to begin solving our problems back in 1968 when the Presbyterian Church offered 20,000 acres of the Piedra Lumbre Grant and the Episcopal Church was getting ready to set up some grants—when the Ford Foundation, the Catholic Church and other groups were beginning to understand that our ancestors hadn't been treated right. They were all beginning to offer to help—but for some reason it all fell apart. We came so close.

That could have been the beginning of our future.

My hope is that some day, hopefully before I die, the government and the groups that were trying to help us forty years ago will realize the devastating effect the last one hundred and fifty years have had on our people. That those groups and other groups like them will begin to do what they can to see that our young people will have the same opportunities that the more fortunate young people have always enjoyed.

One thing that would worry me though is that I wouldn't want any changes that would cause anyone to lose anything they have, their land, their jobs, just to benefit our people. It wouldn't be right to take someone else's property or jobs just to solve the problems our people have suffered.

In fact, I really think the government could save a lot of money if it returned the "use rights" to the land that the government took from our people. If the people got back some of the land and a right to "use" the parts that were originally in the grants it could give them a personal reason to help care for the land—and it might save a lot of money. And if the government would return to the right kind of grazing we probably wouldn't keep on having the terrible fires we've having.

Wow, Grandpa. That was a good answer. It'd sure be something if it all turned out the way you just said. Why, as bad as the Forest Service has treated our people, for you to come up with that answer—it just shows how much you care. I've wondered every since we started this project how it was going to come out—going to end. I feel good about the job we've done. I can't wait to tell my grandchildren what a good man their great, great grandfather was. It's awful that you won't be around to tell them the stories you've told me.

Thank you, Hijo, thank you. I'm glad we could to it—glad we've finally got it done. But before we stop I need to say that besides hoping for a good future for our people I still have two personal wishes. The most important is that your Grandmother Rose's health will get a lot better—and the other is that Officer Saiz isn't still suffering because of what I did.

-26-
Taos Blue Lake Finally Comes Home

I thought we were finished with our family story. Why'd you want to get back together?

A couple days after we finished I got to thinking about all the time you'd put into this—recalling your life and all that had happened. All the research and documents Mike put together for us so that our family can understand what our ancestors have gone through and I figured the least I could do was find something we hadn't covered and research it to show how much I appreciate what you and Mike have done.

I talked it over with my teacher several weeks ago and asked him if he had any suggestions about what I should research and talk about.

He said that if I was serious about doing the research I should read up on how the Taos Pueblo had used its patience and the Indian Claims Commission to prove the government had taken over 200,000 acres of its land when President Roosevelt set up the Taos Forest Reserve. (Fig.16).

While we were talking about how the government had taken the Pueblo's land without paying for it I remembered you saying how important it would be to show how Congress had refused to allow our people the same right to sue the government that it had given the Indians.

The book he said I should read was about how it took sixty-four years for the Pueblo to get the government to give Blue Lake back.

He said the way the Pueblo went about getting its land back is important to us and to our grants—that the book could be a kind of road map to show us a way to try and get our land back.

He said that when President Roosevelt established the Taos Forest Reserve in 1907 he'd taken most of the Pueblo's land and only left it with its original 17,000 acres that had been patented to it in 1864.

While I was reading the book I realized that, just like my teacher had said, the Taos Pueblo story is very important to our people because it supports what we've discussed before about the Commission's decision in favor of the, Zía, Jémez and Santa Ana Pueblos that had made claims for land in the Jémez Forest Reserve and that had a lot of information we can use to try to get back some of our grants.

I'm going to read some of what the book said to show how it supports what we've been saying. I'm going to start with what a man named Bert Phillips had to say during some Senate hearings. Here's part of what he said:

> In 1898, my first year at Taos, Manuel Mondragon, a member of the Pueblo now still alive, talked to me of the Indians' fear that non-Indians would move up the Río Pueblo Canyon and settle above Taos Pueblo, thus contaminating Pueblo water and taking over lands used by the Pueblo as far back as any man knows ...

Phillips testified that he'd met two men who were employees of the Bureau of Biological Survey, Vernon Bailey and C. Hart Merriam, and that they'd given Manuel Mondragon a job as a guide. Phillips said that Mondragon had become such a good assistant that he had asked him what he might do to help the Indians. Phillips, during his testimony also said:

> ...I reminded him, [Bailey] then an employee of the Bureau of Biological Survey, of the Indians' fear that they might lose this land and asked him whether it could not be made into a National Forest. Mr. Bailey was very much in favor of this idea, saying that he recognized there was Indian use as far back as was known; he told me he would take the matter up with Theodore Roosevelt personally, and that he was sure the president would share his enthusiasm for the idea of protecting this area for continued exclusive Indian use in its natural condition ...

He said that the Taos Indians were very pleased with the whole plan and continued:

> ...The process of bringing the Blue Lake area into the forest reserves began in 1903. The Secretary of Agriculture petitioned the Department of Interior ... to have the Blue Lake area and adjacent townships temporarily withdrawn from settlement ...

241

I think that's the same year that the government was setting up the Jémez and Nacimiento area.

Here's something else, Grandpa:

The first signs of trouble came in a 1909 letter from the Forest Service supervisor, Ross McMillan, to the Taos Pueblo governor. McMillian was replying to the tribe's request, made five years earlier, that at the creation of the reserve they be assured of exclusive use. McMillian tells them that their request is immaterial, since the Forest Service will protect their interests.

It is significant that McMillian did not respond to the Taos Indians' request for exclusive use. He told them only that the Forest Service would protect their grazing and irrigation rights.

He went on to say that:

Bailey and Hart Merriam told the Tribe that "the purpose of such a forest reserve including the watershed would be to protect the entire watershed for the exclusive Indian use as always in the past."

And,

… [T]hat Bailey promised personally to raise the question with Roosevelt and that, later Mr. Bailey wrote back to me from Washington telling me that the land would be so reserved, with the entire watershed for exclusive Indian use, and President Roosevelt did actually make it a National Forest.

Sorry it's taking so long, Grandpa, but I wanted to mention some more proof that the Jémez Forest Reserve wasn't the only reserve Roosevelt was establishing in New Mexico by taking land from the Pueblo Indian, Spanish and Mexican grants.

Taos Pueblo filed their claim against the United States with the same commission that the Zía, Jémez and Santa Ana Pueblos had filed their claims. On September 8, 1965 the Commission entered a unanimous decision in favor of Taos Pueblo. The opinion had a very important finding, Finding Number 19, which, like the decision in the Zía Jémez and Santa Ana case, found that the government was up to no good when it established the Jémez and Taos Forest Reserves. It said:

> 19. Based on the entire record in this case, the Commission finds that the petitioner [Taos Pueblo] has established by substantial evidence that on the 2nd of February 1848, when the Treaty of Guadalupe Hidalgo between the United States and Mexico became effective, it held aboriginal or Indian title to the land areas located in the present state of New Mexico and specifically described in Finding 3 herein; and that it continued in the exclusive possession and use of said lands without interruption until the 7th day of November, 1905, when the defendant [the United States] took said lands from petitioner without compensation and made them a part of its National Forests by the proclamation of President Theodore Roosevelt on said date. It is further found that the Pueblo grant of approximately 17,360 acres by Spain to the petitioner was not a limitation on petitioner's aboriginal title to the area involved in this proceeding.

The Indian Claims Commission found that the government had taken the land from the Pueblos without paying for it and had made it a part of the National Forest. In addition to the 36,172 acres President Roosevelt had taken from the three Pueblos and the 800,000 acres he took from our grants—he took 233,200 acres from Taos Pueblo.

How was the Pueblo able to get the land back?

After I read a little more from the Claims Commission's findings, Grandpa, I'll explain how it got Blue Lake back.

A Senate Committee subsequently reported on the entire transaction as follows:

At the time of the hearing at Taos, the Board was advised by representatives of the pueblo that no claim would be asked by the pueblo for those adverse claims within the town of Taos if the board would recommend to the Government that an area ... known as the

Blue Lake Area, was patented to the Pueblo.

Your committee believes that in this case the amount of the full appraisal in the sum of $458,520.61 should be made to the Indians in good faith, less the amount of the award heretofore made in the sum of $76,128.85, or, that the understanding at the time of the stipulation between the Indians and the Board should be carried out by either the issuances of a patent by the Government of the United States to the Pueblo of Taos for the Blue Lake area ... or the authorization by Congress of an Executive Order Reservation of the area in question by the President of the United States.

What happened to the money?

When the Pueblo refused to take the money nothing happened until 1970 when Congress passed a law finally giving back Blue Lake and the 48,000 acres around it. I think, so far as our grants are concerned, the most important part of what I just read was what the President could have done to give the land back to the Pueblo—he could have transferred the land to the Pueblo as an Executive Order Reservation so long as he had the approval of Congress.

What I'm wondering Grandpa, is—if a President could transfer land to Pueblos by an Executive Order Reservation why couldn't he transfer the land President Roosevelt took from our grants back to the grants? And why shouldn't he? What could there be, other than politics, to stop the President and Congress from using an Executive Order Grant to return the "use" rights our grants lost to the Court of Private Land Claims and the Supreme Court.

Using the way the government turned the Pueblo land into the Taos Forest Reserve backs up what we've been saying all along about how the government used the Jémez Forest Reserve to take our grants—used it to get around the Treaty.

I have one last point I'd like to bring up. We really don't know for sure whether the Government ever returned any of the other acreage it had taken from the Pueblo or paid the Pueblo for it, but these last two paragraphs might be part of the answer:

This claimant[Taos Pueblo] has processed a claim through the ICC and got an award of approximately $1,000,000. They also got the Blue Lake tract of 48,000 acres through legislative action (PL 91-550). Most recently, Taos Pueblo has gotten control of approximately 300 acres in the Bear Lake area of the Wheeler Peak Wilderness on the Carson National Forest. This last acquisition was accomplished by administrative action of the Secretary of Interior.

There have been recent, informal contacts by Taos Pueblo consultants with Carson National Forest officials concerning a claim on the Taos Canyon drainage. This case cannot be considered closed.

There you go, Hijo! That shows that the government has ways to do right by our grants—if it wants to.

Thanks for doing this research, Hijo. It means a lot to know that you were willing to find information that helps prove how different our people have been treated.

AFTERWORD

I was surprised when my Mom said you'd called and said we needed to get together again, Grandpa.

We had finished our family history and most of the political history part but there were still a couple of facts Mike felt we needed about why and how the government had taken the land before we could complete our story.

In order to feel comfortable that we had the complete story we still had two questions we needed to answer.

The first question had to do with why the Supreme Court reversed the CPLC decision that had allowed the San Miguel del Bado settlers to continue to use the land Spain said they could use.

By reversing the CPLC decision the Supreme Court left the grant with only 5,000 acres for the settlers to survive on.

What happened to the other 310,000 acres?

That's what we need to talk about. Why the Supreme Court—after Spain had given the grantees the right to use the 310,000 acres forever said they had no right to use it—that the common lands Spain had said they could use had really belonged to the United States ever since the Treaty of Guadalupe Hidalgo was signed.

Let's start with what the GAO had to say about the Supreme court decision:

> The [Supreme] court reversed the CPLC's decision, which had confirmed the entire grant for over 315,000 acres, and instead approved only about 5,000 acres in individual lots. Relying on its recent decision in the *United States v. Santa Fe* case … where the Court had concluded that under both Spanish and Mexican rule, ownership of town lands in New Mexico had remained in the sov-

ereign (Spain and then México), the *Sandoval* Court concluded that common lands within the San Miguel del Vado grant likewise had passed to the new sovereign—the United States—under the Treaty of Guadalupe Hidalgo.

We have a lot of problems with the *Sandoval* case and one is the way the GAO makes it sound like New Mexico was the only state or territory where, under both Spanish and Mexican rules of ownership, the common lands had always belonged to the government.

Another problem is why the Supreme Court chose to use the words "town lands" in the *Sandoval* case?

We believe the Supreme Court was using the San Miguel del Bado case to send a message to the Court of Private Land Claims that it would be okay to "recover" all the common lands it wanted from the remaining grants.

The Supreme Court was so interested in finding a way to turn as much of the grants as it could into public lands—so convinced that its duty was to remove the common lands from the grants —that absolutely nothing should get in its way. Here's a paragraph from the *Sandoval* case that supports what I just said:

> … [T]he general theory of the Spanish law … indicates that, even after a formal designation, the control of … outlying lands, to which a town might have been considered entitled, was in the king, as the source and fountain of title, and could be disposed of at will by him, or by his duly-authorized representative, as long as such lands were not affected by individual and private rights.

That paragraph is saying that the King could only dispose of outlying lands so long as they had not previously been affected by "individual and private rights." Those words would have stopped a fair court from going after the common land in any and every grant where Spain had granted the people right to "use" the common lands

The San Miguel del Bado Grant documents were approved November 25, 1794. Twenty-five years later, in 1819, Spain and the United States signed the Adams-Onís Treaty which established the boundary between Spain and the United States along the Sabine River—between Louisiana and Texas and along the border between California and Oregon. We couldn't find any evidence that Spain ever, between 1794 when the San Miguel del Bado was granted and 1819 when the Adams-Onís Treaty was signed or between 1819 and 1821 when Mexico won its independence, made any effort to take back the 310,000 acres the Supreme Court took from the Grant.

We couldn't find any evidence that Spain ever tried to take back the 471,000 acres from the San Joaquín del Río de Chama; the 146,000 acres from the Juan Bautista Valdez; or the 185,000 acres from the La Petaca grants—or evidence that Spain every tried to take back the "use" rights from any of its grants.

We couldn't find any evidence that Mexico, in the twenty-seven years it was the surviving party to the Adams-Onís Treaty, between 1821 and 1848, ever withdrew the settlers perpetual rights to "use" the common lands from any grant. We couldn't find any evidence that from the 1600s when Spain began granting land in New Mexico—until September 29,1894 when the Court of Private Land Claims began to take the "use rights" of the common lands from the grants that either Spain or Mexico ever made any attempt to take the "use rights" from any grantees or their descendants.

Then along comes the Supreme Court in 1897, over 250 years after Spain had started establishing grants—and forty-nine years after the signing of the Treaty of Guadalupe Hidalgo— and states, for the first time, that the United States has owned the common lands since the signing of the Treaty of Guadalupe Hidalgo. There's absolutely nothing in the Treaty that even suggests that the Supreme Court had the authority to do what it did in the *Sandoval* case—nothing the President or Congress said or did that suggested at the time the Treaty was signed that the grantees could lose their rights to use the common lands once the Treaty was signed.

If the government believed, at any time during the forty-nine years between the signing of the Treaty and the Sandoval decision that by signing the treaty it owned the common lands why did it enact the Court of Private Land Claims Act? Why hadn't congress just passed a law ordering the surveyors general to take the land?

Consider this, Hijo—the Treaty was signed in 1848 and forty-nine years later the Supreme Court claimed in the *Sandoval* case that at the time the Treaty was signed all the common land automatically became public domain.

If that's really what happened, why did the government settle all the land grant cases in California without taking their common lands? California grants would up with 75 percent of their land, remember? The government didn't convert the common lands in California's grants to public lands. California's grants couldn't possibly have wound up with 75 percent of their land if the government had claimed it had owned all of the common lands since the signing of the Treaty.

Congress confirmed seventeen Pueblo Grants in New Mexico by the 1860's. Every acre of Pueblo grant lands were owned by the Pueblo communities. How many acres of community land did the Supreme Court take from the Pueblo Grants? In fact, if you can remember, Hijo, the GAO says that as of October 2002 additional settlement payments have been made through the Pueblo Lands Board in the amount of $14,160,000 and through the Indian Claims Commission in the amount of $116, 750,000. And lets not forget that as of December 31, 2000 the Pueblos received 1,757,500 more acres than they had been granted. And how could the Indian Claims Commission have found that the Jemez and Taos Forest Reserves had taken Pueblo lands without having compensated for it if those lands, which were within the Reserves, had belonged to the United States rather than the Pueblos?

But, Grandpa, you've said you're glad the Indians were given money and land after the way they had been treated.

You're absolutely right! I said it. I meant it when I said it. And I mean it now. I'm glad they've gotten something back for the way they were treated, it's just that it's time our people—our grants—started being treated right, too.

Besides allowing California and Pueblo Grants to keep their common lands, the government allowed the Maxwell grant to keep its land; the Sangre de Cristo Grant to keep its land—and a lot of other grants that had been previously approved by the surveyors general and the Court of Private Land Claims, to keep their common lands.

Here's something else to think about. By the time the *Sandoval* decision came out the CPLC had, on September 29, 1894 mysteriously restricted the Cañón de Carnue, Cañón de Chama and the Galisteo grants to their individual allotments and restricted the La Pataca, to eleven square leagues. That raises the question whether the CPLC was aware before the *Sandoval* decision in which direction and how fast the wind was going to be blowing once the Supreme Court decided the *Sandoval* case.

Either the government knew at the time the Treaty was signed that it owned the common lands or it didn't. If it believed at the time the Treaty was signed that it owned the common lands it would have taken them from the grants in California and the Pueblos grants—and all the other grants that were lucky enough to keep common lands.

By allowing the San Miguel del Bado to keep all its common land the CPLC could not have known or believed as of April 26, 1894 that the government had received all the common lands at the time the Treaty of Guadalupe Hidalgo was signed. Since the CPLC didn't begin taking the common lands from the grants until September 29, 1894, when it restricted the Cañón de Carnue, Cañón de Chama and the Town of Galisteo grants to their "individual allotments," something had to have occurred in the five months between the San Miguel del Bado decision on April 26, 1894 and the September, 1894 decisions to alert the CPLC that in the future all common lands were going to belong to the government.

What's very important, Hijo, is what President Harrison's handpicked CPLC justices were thinking during these times.

Don't tell me we finally have information that helps us figure out what the judges on the CPLC were thinking?

Okay—I won't.

Just what does, "okay—I won't," mean, Grandpa?

It means that as long as you ask me not to tell you something—I won't. Besides, if I was to tell you, all it would do, Hijo, would be to, like Governor Bruce King used to say—open a box of Pandoras.

The 1904 CPLC Annual Report that I was quoting from a moment ago, helps us a little. It shows that the seven community grants in Table 23 of the GAO Report were claiming to be entitled to 1,136,903 acres yet the Court reduced them to 16,485 acres—reduced them to less than two percent of the land they had been awarded. By reducing them the Supreme Court and the CPLC were able to "return" 1,120,400 acres to the government. And that just happened to made them available for withdrawal under the Forest Reserve Act.

Even though we were fortunate to find a lot of important statements from Presidents, cabinet secretaries and senators—and others—we weren't going to give up until we found something that explained why the government, all of a sudden started claiming that all the common lands had belonged to the government since the signing of the Treaty. We believed it might help if we could find some statement from one or more of the Court of Private Land Claims judges— convinced that somewhere there might be some statement that could possibly turn out to be more important than all the information we had previously found.

The reason he believed something a judge might say could be more important than anything President Harrison had said was because, even though he had appointed the judges to the CPLC, he never had the personal power, the judges had, to control the outcome of the cases.

If we could find such a statement or statements, they might answer a lot of the questions the GAO refused to answer; might provide an answer to whether racial prejudice had contributed to shortcomings in the land grant adjudication process; might answer whether the United States had fulfilled its obligation under the treaty as a matter of international law.

The statement we were hoping to find had actually been available for over 100 years as a permanent part of the 1904 Annual meeting of the New Mexico Bar Association. As it turned out the answer we were looking for had been in an article that was cited on a number of occasions. Just never cited in the context we were interested in. The article had even appeared in the Denver Post in 1903 under the title: *The Only Court of its Kind in the World*, and had been written by Wilbur F. Stone, one of the justices on the Court of Private Land Claims.

We have yet to locate the original Denver Post article but found that it had been reproduced in Governor Miguel Otero's 1903 New Mexico Annual Report to the Department of Interior. The reproduction of the article was interesting—but not as interesting as what we were able to find next.

The 1903 Denver Post article had clearly been written for the public while the information we found important appears to have been written for a very select audience: the New Mexico Bar Association.

Before we read from the article we need to read what the Bar Association Secretary had to say about Justice Stone and his article:

Hon. Wilbur F. Stone, Associate Justice of the Court of Private Land Claims has prepared a brief history of that court and its work which he furnished at my request, and I consider it of such importance to our Territory and Bar that I present the same here, and would ask that it be incorporated in our printed minutes. This court will cease to exist in June next, and this will be the only account of its organization and services of which I know outside of its records which will be transferred to Washington on the termination of the Court. The great good this court has accomplished in settling our land titles is not generally known or appreciated, and to preserve even this brief account of its existence is I think germane to the objects of this Association.

Justice Stone's article describes what the Court of Private Land Claims was really like, but it certainly wasn't what one would expect of a judge who had already served for twelve years on *The Only Court of its Kind in the World*.

Before we read the final sentence though we need to read some of his other statements to get an understanding of the man we are dealing with:

[M]any private acts were passed by Congress to confirm and quiet title to some of these grants, but this was a very unsatisfactory mode since it was wholly unjudicial, ex-parte and in some instances unjust, acting less by the laws properly applicable than the influences of favor and prejudice... confirming those grants which ought not to have been done and leaving unconfirmed those which ought to have been done.

The claimants and possessors [grantees and their heirs] of lands under such titles were constantly harassed by refusal of new settlers to recognize their claims.

Even the local land offices of the government did much to encourage these abuses. Not through ignorance ... but from disregard of grant rights and lust for fees.

He went on to say that:

The whole number of cases filed in the court for confirmation of title to land grants was 301.

Number of acres embraced in these [the CPLC] claims: 36,000,000;

Number of these grants confirmed: 87

Number of acres in the confirmed grants: 3,000,000

Number of acres restored to the public domain: 33,000,000.

And to make it clear that:

The land of all grants finally rejected reverts to the public domain of the United States, subject to disposal under the public land laws of the government.

Our immediate response upon seeing the words "restored," "rejected" and "reverts" caused us to recall the *Sandoval* decision. Why would an Associate, Justice who had been on the Court for twelve years, be using words such as restored, rejected and reverts? His use of these words became even more questionable when, in looking into his background we found that he was fluent in four languages: French, German, Spanish and English; had been a member of the Colorado Supreme Court; and had a considerable reputation as a writer.

Justice Stone also said:

For years a common impression has prevailed that many of the Mexican land grants were wholly illegal, forged and fraudulent, and that the court, upon investigation would so find. On the contrary, it was found that such cases were extremely rare.

and,

A number of grants have had their boundaries stretched and areas marvelously expanded. But this has been done mostly by Yankee and English purchasers and not by the original Mexican owners.

Then there was a twist:

> For more than a quarter of a century New Mexico and Arizona
> land titles were burdened with the incubus of uncertainty. The
> investment of capital, the development of mines and vast tracts of
> land, immigration and growth of cities, towns and industries were
> all retarded.

There's that "nightmare" word again, grandpa. And that other word I remember, "retarded." It's weird to me how these words keep being repeated.

Justice Stone made a number of other questionable comments in the article but it was his final sentence that puts everything President Harrison, Interior Secretary Nobel, Senator Beveridge, Gifford Pinchot, President Theodore Roosevelt, the Court of Private Land Claims, the United States Supreme Court said and everything the GAO refused to say, in perspective:

> In addition to the benefits mentioned, the reversion to the pub-
> lic domain of the general government of more than 30,000,000
> acres of land comes the [sic]like new cession of country to the
> United States—a region illimitable in the undeveloped wealth of its
> coal, metals, agriculture and health—giving climate.

I can't believe my ears, Grandpa. I could kinda understand it if you had read about someone that got caught stealing a cow saying it was because his family was hungry. But for a judge, who had been on the Court for over twelve years, to admit that the court took 30,000,000 acres because it was valuable—that's something else. Just think—if he hadn't admitted what they did--we might never have known why the court acted the way it did.

NOTES

CHAPTER TWO

CHAPTER THREE

CHAPTER FOUR

36   IN HIS 1894 REPORT TO THE ATTORNEY GENERAL: Mark
      Schiller, La Jicarita News, November, 2005; Attorney General of the
      United States, Report of the United States Attorney for the CPLC,
      Attorney General's Annual Report, No. 3318, H. Exec. Doc. No. 7, at
      3–4, (3d sess. 1894).

37   THE AMOUNT OF LAND SAVED: Mark Schiller, La Jicarita News,
      November 2005; Attorney General of the United States, Report of the
      United States Attorney for the CPLC, Attorney General's Annual
      Report, No. 3318, H. Exec. Doc. No. 7, at 3–4, (3d. sess. 1894).

37   THE CELEBRATED COCHITÍ CASES: Mark Schiller, La Jicarita
      News, November 2005; Attorney General of the United States, Report
      of the United States Attorney for the CPLC, Attorney General's Annual
      Report, No. 3318, H. Exec. Doc. No. 7, at 3–4, (3d sess. 1894).

40   THE REGION'S VIEW ON THE RECENTLY: Robert Cordts,
      Regional Title Claims Specialist USDA, Forest Service BRIEFING
      PAPER. Northern New Mexico-Southwest Region, June 15, 2004.

40   ESPECIALLY WHEN HIS BRIEFING PAPER INDICATES:
      Robert Cordts, BRIEFING PAPER.

40   YOU SHOULD BE RECEIVING SHORTLY: June 7, 2004 Letter
      from Senators Domenici and Bingaman to Wayne Thornton,
      Albuquerque Regional Office of the U. S. Forest Service.

42   THANK YOU FOR YOUR JUNE 7, 2004 UPDATE ON THE
      RECENT FINAL REPORT BY THE GENERAL ACCOUNTING
      OFFICE: Letter, Harv Forsgren to Congressman Udall, July
      8, 2004.

45   KIT CARSON AND HIS VOLUNTEERS COULDN'T: Jacqueline
      Dorgon Meketap, Ed. Legacy of Honor: The Life of Rafael Chacon,
      page 175. Albuquerque, University of New Mexico Press, 1986; Hamp-
      ton Sides, Blood and Thunder, The Epic Story of Kit Carson and the
      Conquest of the American West, p. 362, New York, Anchor Books, 2006.

47   BY MANY THE PEOPLE ARE LOOKED UPON: 1892 New Mexico
      Annual Report to the Secretary of the Interior: Character of the Popula-
      tion, Washington D. C., Government Printing Office.

CHAPTER SIX

CHAPTER EIGHT

CHAPTER TEN

113   THE GOVERNMENT GAVE THE PUEBLOS $130,000,000: GAO
        Report at Tables 28 and 29, pp. 158-159.

114   THE GAO HAS ADMITTED THAT THE GOVERNMENT
        HAS A DUTY: GAO Report, Chapter 4, pp. 146-147.

114   APPENDIX VII, SEC. 12: GAO Report, Appendix, SEC. 12:
        GAO Report, Appendix VII only contains excerpts from the 1891
        Act Establishing the Court of Private Land Claims, pp. 184 188.
        The Act in its entirety may be found at: FIFTY-FIRST CONGRESS,
        Sess. II. Chapters 538, 539, pp.854-862.

115   STARTING AT THE BOTTOM of PAGE 859: GAO Report, Appen-
        dix VII only contains excerpts from the 1891 Act Establishing the Court
        of Private Land Claims, pp. 184 –188. The Act in its entirety may be
        found at: FIFTY-FIRST CONGRESS, Sess. II. Chapters 538, 539,
        pp.854-862.

116   IT SHALL BE LAWFUL FOR AND THE DUTY: GAO Report,
        Appendix VII, Section 8, fourth paragraph, p. 185.

118   IF IN ANY SUCH CASE, A TITLE SO CLAIMED TO BE PER-
        FECT: GAO Report, Appendix VII, Section 8, second paragraph, p. 185.

120   THAT'S $2,950,000 MORE THAN THE "SUBSTITUTE" JUDGE:
        Navajo Times, Cobell Settlement Headed to Obama, December 2, 2010.

120   A TREATY IS VOID IF ITS CONCLUSION HAS BEEN PRO-
        CURED BY THREAT: Vienna Convention on the Laws, Article 52,
        signed May 23, 1969.

122   THE SPANISH AND MEXICAN RESIDENTS OF NEW MEXICO
        AND ARIZONA: Howard Roberts Lamar, The Far Southwest, 1846-
        1912: a territorial history, New Haven, Yale University Press, p. 13. See
        also: Charles Edgar Maddox: The Statehood Policy of Albert J. Bev-
        eridge, 1901-1911, 1938 Master's Thesis, University of New Mexico;
        Randall and Donald: The Civil War and Reconstruction, (U.S. Census,
        1860, Population, pp. 598-599).New York, W. W. Norton & Co., 2001.

124   WHEN IN THE EARLY FALL OF 1902, HIS COMMITTEE
        TOOK UP: Howard Roberts Lamar, The Far Southwest, 1846-
        1912: a territorial history, New Haven, Yale University Press, p. 491.

124   IT APPEARS THAT BEVERAGE'S REAL REASONS WERE:
        Howard Roberts Lamar, The Far Southwest, 1846-1912: a territorial
        history, New Haven, Yale University Press, p. 427.

124   SENATOR BEVERIDGE IS PREPARING AN EXHAUSTIVE
        REPORT: New York Times, The Statehood Fight, December 6, 1902.

125   THOSE WHO SHALL PREFER TO REMAIN IN THE SAID
        TERRITORIES:, Treaty of Guadalupe Hidalgo, Article VIII.

125   SENATOR ALBERT BEVERIDGE GAVE THIS SPEECH ON
        THE SENATE FLOOR. Microsoft Encarta 2006 [CD] (Redmond,
        WA: Micro soft Corporation, 2005).

126   THE OPPOSITION TELLS US THAT WE OUGHT NOT TO
        GOVERN: Sen. Albert Beveridge, March of The Flag Speech, Senate
        floor, 1898.

127   BEVERIDGE WAS NOT TO BE DEFEATED: Howard Roberts
        Lamar, The Far Southwest, 1846-1912: a territorial history, New Haven,
        Yale University Press, p. 428.

127   FOUR YEARS AFTER BEVERIDGE HID: Howard Roberts Lamar,
        The Far Southwest,1846-1912:a territorial history, New Haven, Yale
        University Press, p. 493.

CHAPTER FIFTEEN

134   EVEN LARRY CALLOWAY, AN ASSOCIATED PRESS
        REPORTER: See, Coverage Distorted, Reporter Says, Río Grande Sun,
        (Salza Supplement) The Courthouse Raid: Twenty Years Later: Lieu,
        Jocelyn, ed. Ben Neary, May 28, 1987, p. C11.

140   THERE WERE TWO ANGLOS AND A SPANISH GUY: Juan was
        not aware of the way the meeting was set up. For an accurate account of
        the meeting, see: Peter Nabokov, Tijerina and the Courthouse Raid
        Albuquerque, University of New Mexico Press, 1969, Chapter 11: Jour-
        ney to the Hideout, pp. 129-140.

144   I DO NOT THINK SHOTS FIRED IN ANGER AT T. A: Albu-
        querque Journal, Calloway, Larry, JUNE 5, 1967: The Courthouse Raid
        Recalled 40 Years Later, June 5, 2007.

144   VALDEZ COVERED HIM WITH A .44-CAL. PISTOL AND
DEMANDED: Article: Wounded Officer Went for Gun, Río Grande
Sun, (Salza Supplement) The Courthouse Raid: Twenty Years Later:
Lieu, Jocelyn, ed. Ben Neary, May 28, 1987, p. C10.

144   JUAN VALDEZ HAD A WEAPON ON ME: Landon, Susan,
Courthouse Raid Remains Vivid Memory, Albuquerque Journal, p.
A10, June 5, 1987.

CHAPTER SIXTEEN

166   THE RUINS REFERRED TO IN THIS BULLETIN ARE DIS-
TRIBUTED: Edgar L. Hewett, Antiquities of The Jémez Plateau, New
Mexico, Washington D.C., Government Printing Office, 1906; Intro-
ductory Note, p. 9.

168   THERE WAS NO NATIONAL FOREST IN THE AREA IN 1906:
Edgar L. Hewett, Antiquities of The Jémez Plateau, New Mexico,
Washington D.C., Government Printing Office, 1906; Introductory
Note, p. 9.

168   THE ONLY SECTION That had anything to do: Only one section of
the Forest Reserve Act, Section 24, had anything to do with forest
reserves. (Section 24 of the General Land Law Revision Act of 1891, also
known as the Creative Act; 26 Stat. 1103;16 U.S.C. §§ 471, repealed
1976 by P. L. 94-579.

168   THE PRESIDENT OF THE UNITED STATES MAY, FROM TIME
TO TIME: Section 24 of an Omnibus bill passed on March 3, 1891 and
which has been referred to as the Forest Reserve Act.

169   THE COURT OF PRIVATE LAND CLAIMS ACT: The Court of Private Land Claims Act; (Fifty-First Congress, Sess. II, Ch. 539 1891, p.
855) was enacted March 3, 1891 and became a tool of the United States
Government to remove 30,000,000 acres from legitimate Spanish and
Mexican Grants between March, 1891 and June, 1904.

169   THE COMMISSIONER OF THE GENERAL LAND OFFICE
(GLO) ORDERED: For further research into what was to happen to
land grants within the area being converted into forest reserves, The
Forest Reserves of New Mexico by I. B. Hanna, Superintendant of For-

est Reserves in New Mexico and Arizona, as reprinted in: The Annual Report of the Governor of New Mexico to the Secretary of Interior, September15, 1903, p. 473.

CHAPTER SEVENTEEN

176   STATE REP. NICK SALAZAR, THEN A RÍO ARRIBA COUNTY COMMISSIONER: Article: Officials Disagree on Raid's Impact, Río Grande Sun, (Salza Supplement), The Courthouse Raid: Twenty Years Later, Jocelyn Lieu, ed. Ben Neary, May 28, 1987, p. 14.

CHAPTER EIGHTEEN

177   I'LL START WITH SOME OF THE GRANTS THAT WERE PATENTED BY CONGRESS: GAO-04-059, p. 73. DON FERNANDO DE TAOS: GAO-04-059, p. 113. The following note appears below Table 23: In the CPLC's 1897 Annual Report, the Don Fernando de Taos land grant was listed with an estimated claimed acreage of 38,400 acres, an estimated approved acreage of 1,000 acres, and an estimated rejected acreage of 37,400 acres. The grant was confirmed by the CPLC on October 5, 1897. The acreage figures presented in table 23 are from the CPLC's 1904 Annual Report. This note establishes the length the GAO was willing to go to put the best spin on the actions of the CPLC that it possibly could. The actual difference between acreage claimed and acreage awarded was 36,000 acres not 71.76 acres: the CPLC removed 35,928.24 more acres of the Don Fernando de Taos Grant than the GAO was willing to admit.

178   LAST MONDAY MY TEACHER BROUGHT A NEWSPAPER TO CLASS: Albuquerque Journal, At Rest, At Last, Sunday, January 4, 2009, Section B.

178   WON'T SPEND A DIME FIXING UP: Dabovich, Melanie, Buffalo Soldiers To Be Buried, Albuquerque Journal, July 29, 2009, pp. B1, B4.

179   EXCEPTING FROM THE FORCE AND EFFECT OF THIS PROCLAMATION: Proclamation 316 -Setting Apart as a Public Reservation Certain Lands in the Territory of New Mexico, January 11, 1892.

180   LISTEN TO HOW THAT PART OF ROOSEVELT'S JÉMEZ
       PROCLAMATION READ: Proclamation 603 Establishment of Jémez
       Forest Reserve, New Mexico, October 12, 1905.

180   THAT THE SAID RESERVE HAS BEEN ESTABLISHED AND
       SET APART: New Mexico Legislature Joint Memorial II; Acts of the
       Legislative Assembly of the Territory of New Mexico, approved Febru-
       ary 4, 1905, states clearly how the New Mexico Territorial Legislature
       viewed the establishment of the Jémez Forest Reserve eight months
       before President Roosevelt proclaimed it on October 12, 1905.

181   IN JANUARY 1907, THERE WAS CONSIDERABLE OPPOSI-
       TION: Gerald W. Williams, New Forest Reserves USDA, Forest Ser-
       vice—Pacific Southwest Newslog, 2004, (an employee magazine in
       publication since1914). The author later included the article in: The
       Forest Service: Fighting for Public Lands, Understanding our Govern-
       ment, Westport, Greenwood Press, 2007.

182   AFTER CONSIDERABLE PRESSURE PINCHOT AND PRESI-
       DENT ROOSEVELT RELENTED: Gerald W. Williams, New Forest
       Reserves, USDA, Forest Service—Pacific Southwest Newslog 2004.

182   THIS AMENDMENT, THE FULTON AMENDMENT PROHIB-
       ITED: Gerald W. Williams, New Forest Reserves, USDA, Forest Ser-
       vice—Pacific Southwest Newslog 2004.

183   INSTEAD OF SEVENTEEN NEW OR COMBINED RESERVES
       THE DOCUMENTS: Theodore Roosevelt Proclamations, 707
       through 740.

183   WHILE THE AGRICULTURAL APPROPRIATION BILL WAS
       PASSING THROUGH: Theodore Roosevelt: Theodore Roosevelt An
       Autobiography, New York, The Macmillan Company, 1913, p. 440.

184   THE FOREST RESERVES OF THE UNITED STATES QUADRU-
       PLED: Theodore Roosevelt Association, Conservationist Theodore
       Roosevelt org/life/conNatlForests.htm.

185   DO YOU HAVE THE NAMES OF THE NEW MEXICO
       RESERVES: United States Statutes at Large, Volume 34, Part 3, pp.
       110-111.

185 AT FIRST A GREAT MANY OF THE NATIONAL FORESTS
WERE MADE: Gifford Pinchot, The Use of the National Forests,
United States Forest Service, GPO, (Call No. SD426.A5 1907a), 1907,
p. 8.

CHAPTER TWENTY

192 PRESIDENT ROOSEVELT'S PROCLAMATION ESTABLISHING
THE JÉMEZ FOREST RESERVE HAD TAKEN 36,172 ACRES:
The Indian Claims Commission Act, 605 Stat. 1060, 25 USC 70a,
August, 1946, was established to hear claims of Indian tribes against the
United States for, among other reasons seeking compensation for land
taken without payment of compensation.

195 HERE'S A MAP WE NEED TO LOOK AT: BLM Edition-2004 Surface Management Status- New Mexico-Abiquiú, Printed by the United
States Department of Interior-Bureau of Land Management.

196 HERE'S AN ARTICLE, READ THE PART: Colbert, Edwin, The Triassic Paleontology of Ghost Ranch, New Mexico, presented at a conference at Ghost Ranch. 1974.

197 RIOARRIBASAURUS—I CAN'T BELIEVE SOMEONE NAMED A
DINOSAUR: Article; Adrian P. Hunt and Spencer G. Lucas, New Mex-
ico Museum of National History, Rioarribasaurus, New Name for a Late
Triassic Dinosaur from New Mexico, p. 192.

199 THEY ALSO WROTE: Lucas, Spencer G., Adrian P. Hunt and Andrew
B. Heckert, E. D. Cope and the First Discovery of Triassic Vertebrate
Fossils in the American West, (written for the New Mexico Geological
Society's Fifty-sixth Annual Field Conference, September 21-24, 2005),
Eds. Lucas, Spencer G., Kate E. Ziegler, Virgil W. Lueth and Donald E.
Owen, p. 26.

199 LOOK AT PAGE 27, FIGURE 1.25, TELL ME WHAT YOU
THINK: Figure 1.25 is duplicated at our Figure 14. 199WE NEED TO
READ A COUPLE MORE LETTERS AND PART OF A STATE-
MENT: The letters were found in The Annual Report upon the Geo-
graphical Explorations West of the 100th Meridian [Wheeler Survey],
Appendix FF 3, Annual Report Chief of Engineers for 1875, p. 115.

CHAPTER TWENTY-TWO

212 ALIANZA SET FOR WARFARE, SANCHEZ SAYS: The New Mexican, Jack Stamm, Alianza Set for Welfare, Sanchez Says, June 5, 1968.

213 THE TREATY MANIA REVOLVES AROUND LAND, VOTES, AND REGIONAL IDENTITY: New York Times, James Brooke: Hot Issue in Northern New Mexico: Fine Print of an 1848 Treaty, February 19, 1998.

213 GUADALUPE-HIDALGO TREATY LAND CLAIMS ACT OF 1998: The title of bill introduced in the House of Representatives by Congressman Bill Redman passed the House on September 10, 1978 and died in the Senate without any activity.

214 HE FOUND TWO ARTICLES THAT DEAL WITH GRAZING AND FIRES IN THE JÉMEZ MOUNTAINS: Touchan, Ramzi, Craig D. Allen, Thomas W. Swetman, Fire History and Climatic Patterns in Ponderosa Pine and Mixed-Conifer Forests of the Jémez Mountains, Northern New Mexico, presented at the Symposium on the La Mesa fire, Funding provided by the USDA National Park Service and USDA Forest Service,1996; and, Touchan, Ramzi, Thomas Swetman, Henri D. Grissino-Mayer, Effects of Livestock Grazing on Pre-Settlement Fire Regimes in New Mexico Funding provided by the USDA National Park Service and USDA Forest Service, 1995.

215 THE CERRO PEDERNAL SITE (CPE) ALSO DISPLAYS HIGH FREQUENCY FIRE: Touchan, Ramzi, Craig D. Allen, Thomas W. Swetman, Fire History and Climatic Patterns in Ponderosa Pine and Mixed-Conifer Forests of the Jémez Mountains, Northern New Mexico, p. 42.

215 THERE WAS A CLEAR CESSATION IN WIDESPREAD FIRE CESSATION: Ibid.

CHAPTER TWENTY-THREE

219 OVER THE YEARS LINE OFFICERS AND OTHERS HAVE RECEIVED REQUESTS FOR ASSISTANCE [sic]: The letter, dated March 26, 2005, was sent with a March, 2005 Briefing Paper to the For-

est Supervisor(s) of the Carson National Forest, Cibola National Forest and the Santa Fe National Forest; Subject: Land Claims & Forest Service Actions—Treaty of Guadalupe Hidalgo. It was signed: H. Wayne Thornton, Director, Lands and Minerals and had the March 2005 Briefing Paper as an "Enclosure;" copies were sent to: District Rangers-NMex & AZ, Forest Supervisors-NMex & AZ, Dir. Of Range Mgt-R3, Dir. Of Lands-WO, Mary Ann Joca-OGC, Jim Snow-OGC, Dir. Of PAO-R3. The last paragraph of the letter states: The enclosed briefing paper provides a clear framework for our actions in the management and protection of NFS lands.343

CHAPTER TWENTY-FOUR

CHAPTER TWENTY-SIX

cate it is from the Paul J. Bernal Papers, New Mexico State Archives, Expandable 3, Folder 26a, November 23, 1903).

242 THE FIRST SIGNS OF TROUBLE CAME IN 1909: R. C. Gordon-McCutchan, The Taos Indians and the Battle for Blue Lake, Santa Fe, Red Crane Books, 1991, P. 14.

243 BASED ON THE ENTIRE RECORD IN THIS CASE: The United States of American, 15 Ind. Cl. Comm. 666, Finding No. 19.

243 AT THE TIME OF THE HEARING AT TAOS, THE BOARD: Pueblo of Taos v. The United States of American, 15 Ind. Cl. Comm. 666, Findings No. 22-23. We also found this information at Oklahoma State University, referencing Senate, Rep. 25, pt. 2, 72nd Cong, 1st Session, p. 685.

243 THIS CLAIMANT [TAOS PUEBLO] HAS PROCESSED A CLAIM THROUGH THE ICC AND GOT APPROXIMATELY $1,000,000: April 5, 2005 Letter from H. Wayne Thornton, Direct-or of Lands and Minerals at the Regional Office in Albuquerque to Ms. Susan E. Lott, a senior analyst at the GAO that had a page attached with the title: "1. Taos Pueblo." ICC Docket No. 357-A, Indian Title Claims Status Report-Region 3, p. 5.

AFTERWORD

246 THE [SUPREME] COURT REVERSED THE CPLC'S DECISION: GAO Report at p. 115.

249 CONGRESS CONFIRMED SEVENTEEN PUEBLO GRANTS IN NEW MEXICO: GAO Report, p. 157.

249 SETTLEMENT PAYMENTS HAVE BEEN MADE THROUGH THE PUEBLO LANDS BOARD: GAO Report, pp. 158-159.

250 THE 1904 CPLC ANNUAL REPORT OFFERS SOME HELP: GAO Report, p. 113.

251 THE ONLY COURT OF ITS KIND IN THE WORLD: Denver Post, The Only Court of Its Kind in the World,1903, Stone, Wilbur F., also published in New Mexico's1903 Annual Report to the Department of Interior. pp.378-386.

252   WHAT THE BAR ASSOCIATION SECRETARY SAID ABOUT JUSTICE STONE: New Mexico Bar Association Annual Report, 1904.

252   THE CLAIMANTS AND POSSESSORS : New Mexico Bar Association Annual Report, 1904.

253   THE WHOLE NUMBER OF CASES FILED IN THE COURT: New Mexico Bar Association Annual Report, 1904.

253   THE LAND OF ALL GRANTS FINALLY REJECTED REVERTS TO THE PUBLIC DOMAIN: New Mexico Bar Association Annual Report, 1904.

253   FOR YEARS A COMMON IMPRESSION HAS PREVAILED THAT MANY OF THE MEXICAN GRANTS: New Mexico Bar Association Annual Report, 1904.

253   A NUMBER OF GRANTS HAVE HAD THEIR BOUNDARIES STRETCHED: New Mexico Bar Association Annual Report, 1904.

254   NEW MEXICO AND ARIZONA LAND TITLES WERE BURDENED WITH THE INCUBUS OF UNCERTAINTY: New Mexico Bar Association Annual Report, 1904, p. 26.

254   THE REVERSION TO THE PUBLIC DOMAIN OF THE GENERAL GOVERNMENT OF MORE THAN 30,000,000 ACRES COMES LIKE A NEW CESSION: New Mexico Bar Association Annual Report, 1904, P. 26.

BIBLIOGRAPHY

BOOKS

Anderson, George B. *The History of New Mexico: Its Resources and People, Volume II*. Seattle: Pacific States Publishing Co., 1907.

Blawis, Patricia Bell. *Tijerina and the Land Grants: Mexican Americans in Struggle for their Heritage*. New York: International Publishers, 1971.

Bryan, Howard. *Wildest of the Wild West*. Santa Fe: Clear Light Publications, 1991.

Bullock, Alice. *Living Legends of the Santa Fe Country*. Denver: Green Mountain Press, 1970.

Burke, James T. Rev. *This Miserable Kingdom: The Story of the Spanish Presence in New Mexico and the Southwest from the Beginning of Time until the 18th Century*. Albuquerque: Our Lady of Fatima Church, 1994.

Busto, Rudy V. *King Tiger: The Religious Vision of Reies Lopez Tijerina*. Albuquerque: University of New Mexico Press, 2005.

Chávez, Fray Angélico. *But Time and Change: The Story of Padre Martinez of Taos, 1793-1867*. Santa Fe: Sunstone Press, 1981.

Davis, W. W. H. *El Gringo: New Mexico and Her People*. Lincoln: University of Nebraska Press, 1982.

Debuys, William, *Enchantment and Exploration, the life and Hard Times of a New Mexico Mountain Range*, Albuquerque: University of New Mexico Press, 1985.

Dodge, Bertha S. *The Road West: Saga of the 35th Parallel*. Albuquerque: University of New Mexico Press, 1980.

Duffus, Robert Luther. *The Santa Fe Trail*. New York: Tudor Publishing Co., 1930.

Dunbar- Ortiz, Rosanne. *Roots of Resistance: Land Tenure in New Mexico, 1680-1980*. Los Angeles:Chicano Studies Research Center Publications and American Indian Studies Center, University of California, Los Angeles, 1980.

Ellis, Richard N. *New Mexico Past and Present: A Historical Reader.* Albuquerque: University of New Mexico Press, 1971.

Fergusson, Harvey. *Río Grande: The Classic Portrait of the Río Grande Valley of New Mexico.* New York: William Morrow and Company, 1967.

Fugate, Francis L. and Roberta B. *Roadside History of New Mexico.* Missoula: Mountain Press Publishing Company, 1989.

Gordon-McCutchan, R. C. *The Taos Indians and the Battle for Blue Lake;* Forward by Frank Waters. Santa Fe: Red Crane Books, 1991.

Gutiérrez, Jose Angel. Ed. Tr. *They Called Me "King Tiger": My Struggle for the Land and Our Rights.* Forward by Henry A. J. Ramos. Houston: Arte Público Press, 2000.

Hillerman, Tony. *The Great Taos Bank Robbery: And Other True Stories of the Southwest.* Albuquerque: University of New Mexico Press, 1973.

Horgan, Paul. *Great River: The Río Grande in North American History.* Hanover: Wesleyan University Press, 1984.

———. *The Centuries of Santa Fe.* New York: E. P. Dutton & Company, 1956.

Ise, John. *The United States Forest Policy.* New Haven: Yale University Press, 1920.

Jenkinson, Michael. *Tijerina, Land Grant Conflict in New Mexico.* Albuquerque: Paisano Press, 1968.

Jenkins, Myra Ellen and Albert H. Schroeder. *A Brief History of New Mexico.* Albuquerque: University of New Mexico Press, 1974.

Lamar, Howard Roberts. *The Far Southwest, 1846-1912: A Territorial History.* New York: W.W. Norton &Company (the Norton library), 1970.

Lavender, David. *Bent's Fort.* Garden City: Doubleday, 1954.

McHenry, J. Patrick. *A Short History of Mexico.* Garden City: Dolphin Books/Doubleday & Company 1962.

Meketa, Jacqueline Dorgon, Ed. *Legacy of Honor: The Life of Rafael Chacon, A Nineteenth Century American.* Albuquerque: University of New Mexico Press, 1986.

Nobokov, Peter. *Tijerina and the Courthouse Raid.* Albuquerque: University of New Mexico Press, 1969.

Pettitt, Roland. *Los Alamos Before the Dawn.* Los Alamos: Pajarito Publications, *1972.*

Rothman, Hal K. *On Rims and Ridges: The Los Alamos Area Since 1880.* Lincoln:
University of Nebraska Press, 1992.

Sálas M, Rubén. *The Santa Fe Ring: Land Grant History in American New Mexico,* Albuquerque: Cosmic House, 2008.

Simmons, Mark. *The Last Conquistador: Juan de Oñate and the Settlement of the Far Southwest.* Norman: University of Oklahoma Press, 1991.

———. *New Mexico Mavericks: Stories from a Fabled Past,* Santa Fe: Sunstone Press, 2005.

Sides, Hampton. *Blood and Thunder, The Epic Story of Kit Carson and the Conquest of the American West,* New York: Anchor Books, 2006.

Takaki, Ronald. *A different Mirror: A History of Multicultural America.* New York: Back Bay Books, Little, Brown and Company, 1994 (2008 edition).

Trujillo, Frank R. "Skitt." *Don "Fernando" De Taos: And the Lost Common Lands.* Albuquerque, Commercial Printing, Inc., 2002.

Van Ness, John R., Christine Van Ness, eds. *Spanish & Mexican Land Grants in New Mexico and Colorado.* Manhattan, Ks., Sunflower University Press, 1980.

STATE OF THE UNION ADDRESSES*

Grant, Ulysses S., Dec. 7, 1875, www.presidency.ucsb.edu/ws/index.php?pid=29516

Harrison, Benjamin, Dec. 3, 1889, www.presidency.ucsb.edu/ws/index.php?pid=29530;

———.Dec. 1, 1890, www.presidency.ucsb.edu/ws/index.php?pid=29531;

———.Dec.1, 1891, www.presidency.ucsb.edu/ws/index.php?pid=29532;

———.Dec. 6, 1892, www.presidency.ucsb.edu/ws/index.php?pid=29533.

Taylor, Zachary, December 4, 1849, www.presidency.ucsb.edu/ws/index.php?pid=29490.

Washington, George, Dec. 7, 1796, www.presidency.ucsb.edu/ws/index. php?pid=29438.

*(From the American Presidency Project, research by Gerhard Peters, University of California, Santa Barbara: www.presidency.ucsb.edu/sou.php).

MAPS

Archaeological Map-Jémez Plateau-New Mexico-Forest Service U.S. Dept. of Agriculture, 1906 (also containing a title in the upper left-hand corner stating: Bureau of American Ethnology, Bulletin 32, Plate XX).

Pajarito Plateau and Vicinity-New Mexico, Drawn by G. W. Lindenberg, 1906. This can be found in GPO Pamphlet: *Antiquities of the Jémez Plateau, at Plate XVII, Hewett, Edgar L., 1906.*

Jémez Forest Reserve. U.S. Dept. of Agriculture, 1906; U.S. Statutes at Large, Vol. 34, Part 3, pp. 3182-3183 and pp. 3260-3261

Taos Forest Reserve, New Mexico, Forest Service. U.S. Dept. of Agriculture, 1906; U.S. Statutes at Large, Vol. 34, Part 3, pp. 3262-3263.

T27N-R4E Plat, Plat of portion of San Joaquín Land Grant. General Land Office-U.S. Dept. of Interior, February 8, 1884. (Altered to include the name: Jémez Forest Reserve).

T27N-R4E Plat, Plat of portion of San Joaquín Land Grant. U.S. Surveyor General's Office, Dec. 4, 1918.

T26N-R5E Plat, Plat of Canjilón Area, Río Arriba County. General Land Office, U.S. Dept. of Interior, May 1, 1883. (Altered to include the name: Jémez Forest Reserve).

T27N-R/s 7-9E, Plat of La Petaca Land Grant. U.S. Surveyor General's Office, 1878.

T28N-R8E Plat, Plat of La Petaca Land Grant. U.S. Surveyor General, Plat of the La Petaca Grant. U.S. Surveyor General's Office, April 8, 1902.

Plat of San Joaquín Grant showing approval of the grant at 472,736.98 acres on Dec. 17, 1872. Surveyor General's Office, Sept. 7, 1878.

Plat of San Joaquín Grant showing grant reduced by the Court of Private Land Claims from 472,736.98 acres to 1, 422.62 acres. Surveyor General's Office, dated Sept. 20-30, 1901.

Plat of Juan Bautista Valdez Grant, (which originally contained approximately 147,515 acres), showing the grant as reduced by the Court of Private Land Claims to 1,468.57 acres. Surveyor General's office, dated September 14, 1899.

Plat of the Polvedera Grant, (which was not reduced in size) 35,761.14 acres. Surveyor General's Office, Surveyed Aug. 11-17, 1897.

Plat of the Piedra Lumbre Grant containing 48,336.13 acres. Surveyor General's Office, Jun. 19, 1877.

Plat of the Piedra Lumbre Grant containing 49,747.89 acres, (an increase of 1,411.76 acres). Surveyor General's Office, surveyed Nov. 14-28, 1897.

Topographical Map-New Mexico-Abiquiú 2004-United States Department of the Interior, Bureau of Land Management.

Rand &McNally 1897 Map, reproduced by the New Mexico Humanities Council, showing some of the land grants in Río Arriba County, New Mexico, including the San Joaquín Grant as approved in 1872.

U.S. Land Acquisition from Mexico, 1845-1853; Government Accountability Office (GAO) electronic version of Report: GAO-04-59, Figure 4, page 25.

Generalized Depiction of U.S. Expansion; Government Accountability Office (GAO) printed version of Report: GAO-04-59, Figure 3, page 23.

PERIODICALS

Colbert, Edwin. The Triassic Paleontology of Ghost Ranch, New Mexico. New Mexico Geol. Soc. Guidebook, 25th Field Conf., Ghost Ranch (Central-Northern N.M.), 1974.

DeBuys, William. Fractions of Justice: A Legal and Social History of the Las Trampas Land Grant, New Mexico. Albuquerque: University of New Mexico Press, (January, 1981).

Harrison, Birge. *Española and Its Environs*, First Published by Harper's New Monthly Magazine, Vol. LXX, No. CCCCXX, (May, 1885); Later Reprinted by Las Trampas Press, (1966).

Heckert, Andrew, Spencer Lucas, Robert Sullivan, Adrian Hunt. *Rioarribasaurus, a New Name for a Late Triassic Dinosaur from New Mexico (USA).*Volume 70, numbers 1-2, Berlin. Palaontologische Zeitschrift,

Lucas, Spencer G., Robert M. Sullivan, Andrew Heckert and Adrian Hunt. *E. D. Cope and the First Discovery of Triassic Vertebrate Fossils in the American West.*

Meinig, D. W. *Southwest: Three Peoples in Geological Change 1600-1970.* Oxford: Oxford University Press, 1971.

Springer Berlin/Heidelberg, (March, 1996).

Raish, Carol, Environmentalism, the Forest Service, and the Hispano Communities of Northern New Mexico, Society & National Resources, 13:489-508. 2000.

Torrez, Robert J., *El Bornes: La Tierra Amarilla and T. D. Burns.* New Mexico Historical Review, Vol. 56: 2. Albuquerque, University of New Mexico Press, April, 1981.

Touchan, Ramzi, Craig D. Allen, Thomas W. Swetman. *Fire History and Climatic Patterns in Ponderosa Pine and Mixed-Conifer Forests of the Jémez Mountains, Northern New Mexico.* Presented at the Symposium on the La Mesa Fire; Funding was provided by the USDA National Park Service and USDA Forest Service, (1996).

Touchan, Ramzi, Thomas Swetman, Henri D. Grissino-Mayer. *Effects of Livestock Grazing on Pre-Settlement Fire Regimes in New Mexico.* Funding was provided by the USDA National Park Service and USDA Forest Service, (1995).

Williams, Gerald W. *New Forest Reserves,* USDA Forest Service-Pacific, Southwest Newslog, (September, 2004).

NEWSPAPER ARTICLES

Armijo, Patrick. *Old Fights Create a New Alliance: Land-Grant Heirs Back Redmond.* Albuquerque Journal, September 13, 1998.

Calloway, Larry. *The Courthouse Raid Recalled 40 Years Late*, Albuquerque Journal, June 5, 2007.

———. *The Courthouse Raid 25 Years Later: Skeletons of the Past Live With Her*, Albuquerque Journal, June 5, 1992, A1, A5.

Dabovich, Melanie. *Buffalo Soldiers to be Buried*, Albuquerque Journal, July 19, 2009.

Kraul, Chris. *Mexicans on U.S. Death Row Denied Rights, Court Says*. Los Angeles Times, April 1, 2004.

Landon, Susan. *Courthouse Raid Remains Vivid Memory*. Albuquerque Journal, June 5, 1987.

Lieu, Jocelyn, ed. Ben Neary. *The Courthouse Raid: Twenty Years Later.* Española, Twenty-eight page Supplement to the Río Grande Sun, May 28, 1987.

Schiller, Mark. Matthew G. Reynolds and the Adjudication of Spanish and Mexican Land Claims. Chimisal: La Jicarita News, November., 2005.

Thompson, Fritz. *The Courthouse Raid 25 Years Later: Rebel's Achievements Unclear.* Albuquerque Journal, June 5, 1992, A1, A3.

Brooke, James: *Hot Issue in Northern New Mexico: Fine Print of an 1848 Treaty*, New York Times, February 19, 1998.

GOVERNMENT PRINTING OFFICE AND GOVERNMENT ACCOUNTABILITY OFFICE DOCUMENTS

Hanna, I. B. *The Forest Reserves of New Mexico*. Report Of The Governor Of New Mexico to the U.S. Department of the Interior, 1893.

Hewett, Edgar L. *Antiquities of the Jémez Plateau, New Mexico.*1906.

Pinchot, Gifford. *The Use of the National Forests.* U. S. Department of Agriculture, Forest   Service, 1907.

Prince, Bradford. *Report Of The Governor Of New Mexico* to the U.S. *Department* of the *Interior.* 1892.

Powell, John Wesley. *Report on the Lands of the Arid Region of the United States.*

Treaty of Guadalupe Hidalgo: Findings and Possible Options Regarding Longstanding Community Land Grant Claims in New Mexico.GAO-04-59 June 4, 2004.

CORRESPONDENCE

C. A. Merker, Forest Supervisor, Carson National Forest to Amarante Valdez, March 20, 1937.

W. L. Graves, Forest Supervisor, Carson National Forest to Amarante Valdez, July 26, 1954.

H. Wayne Thornton, Director, Land and Minerals to Forest Supervisors, May 26, 2005.

Robert Cordts, Regional Lands Claims Specialist, "Briefing Paper," June 15, 2004.

Harv Forsgren, Regional Forester to Honorable Tom Udall, July 8, 2004.

CASES

Rio Arriba Land and Cattle Company vs. United States, 167 U.S. 298, decided May 24, 1897.

United States vs. Sandoval, 167 U.S. 278, decided May 24, 1897.

STATUTES

Court of Private Land Claims Act, 26 Stat,854, (Mar. 3, 1891); (Only Section 24 of the Act pertains to the CPLC).

Forest Reserve Act (Mar. 3, 1891); 26 Stat. 1095, (Dec.3, 1891).

Homestead Act, 26 Stat. 1095, (May 20, 1862).

Indian Claims Commission, 60 Stat. 1049, (1946).

Indian Lands Claims Act, 43 Stat. 253, (June 2, 1924).

Surveyor General Statute-California, 9 Stat. at Large 631, (March 3, 1851).

Surveyor General Statute-New Mexico Territory; 10 Stat. 308,309, (July 22, 2854).

Surveyor General Statute –Oregon Territory; Donation Land Claim Act of 1850, 9 Stat. 496, (September 27, 1850).

THESIS

Maddox, Charles Edgar. *The Statehood Policy of Albert J. Beveridge, 1901-1911*. Master's Thesis, University of New Mexico, 1938, page 42.

INDEX

CPSIA information can be obtained at www.ICGtesting.com
Printed in the USA
LVOW062003151211

259658LV00002B/2/P